D0712909

DATE DUE

AG 8 97			
NO 7 97			
MY 7 98			

DEMCO 38-296

*Spirits, Blood,
and Drums*

SPIRITS, BLOOD,
and DRUMS

The Orisha Religion in Trinidad

James T. Houk

Temple University Press

Philadelphia

Temple University Press, Philadelphia 19122
Copyright © 1995 by Temple University. All rights reserved
Published 1995
Printed in the United States of America

☉ The paper used in this book meets the requirements of the American National
Standard for Information Sciences — Permanence of Paper for Printed Library
Materials, ANSI Z39.48-1984

Text design by Gore Studio, Inc.

Library of Congress Cataloging-in-Publication Data
Houk, James T., 1955–
    Spirits, blood, and drums : the Orisha religion in Trinidad /
James T. Houk.
        p. cm.
    Includes bibliographical references and index.
    ISBN 1-56639-349-3 (cloth : alk. paper). — ISBN 1-56639-350-7
(pbk. : alk. paper)
    1. Blacks — Trinidad and Tobago — Religion. 2. Trinidad and Tobago —
Religion.   3. Houk, James T., 1955–   . I. Title.
BL2566.T7H68   1995
299'.6'0972983 — dc20   94-46666

The poem that opens Chapter Eleven is used by permission of Carver Milton Scobie.
Copyright © 1965 by Carver Milton Scobie.
The prayers on pp. 159–61 are from a collection compiled by the Orisa Youths Cultural
Organization. Used by permission.

For Aldwin Scott,
1938–1994

Contents

PART IV

Tables and Illustrations

TABLES

FIGURES

ix

PHOTOGRAPHS

Preface

After doing preliminary literature research for my first visit to Trinidad in the summer of 1985, I felt confident that I had a fairly good grasp of the beliefs and practices of the Orisha religion in Trinidad. My research topic was spirit possession; my focus was the possessing agents and the belief system of which they were a part. The first handful of shrines I visited seemed to be typical of those described in the literature: there were flags planted for African gods, and statuettes and iconography of Catholic saints in the *chapelle* (a small, enclosed sanctuary). Then I met Aldwin Scott. His shrine contains the typical flags and "stools" (small shrines) for the *orisha* and saints, but it also displays flags and paraphernalia for Hindu deities (one of whom, I was told, was "on the African side"), an African "power" (not technically one of the *orisha*, which are primarily spirits derived from the religion of the Nigerian Yoruba), and personal spirits. His compound also holds a Spiritual Baptist church. I soon realized that this religion was much more complex than I had thought — and more complexity was to come.

During the last week of my first visit I interviewed Elder Jeffrey Biddeau at his shrine in northeastern Trinidad. When Jeffrey had to leave on business, he allowed me to remain behind and take photographs. As I walked around the compound, I found a small room attached to the back of his house (but not part of the family's living quarters) full of religious paraphernalia that I could not identify. When I asked Jeffrey's wife, Lydia, about the room, she advised me to wait and talk to Jeffrey about it. Later, when I did so, he introduced me to the Kabbalah, a European-derived, esoteric, and diabolical belief system.[1] The room was the focal point of Elder Biddeau's Kabbalistic worship.

By the time I left Trinidad after my first visit, my perception of the Orisha religion had changed dramatically. I saw that worshipers had combined the religious elements of not just two but five traditions — African, Catholic, Hindu, Protestant, and Kabbalah — to form an "Afro-American religious complex," a network of religious activities. When I returned to the States, I decided to conduct a thorough and extended examination of the Orisha religion.

Orisha is an old, established form of worship in Nigeria and its environs, which has been transplanted to the New World. As a religion, it stands on its own to meet the needs of its devotees. Some worshipers in Trinidad, the Orisha "purists," minimize the integration of extraneous elements so common to New World African-derived religions, proclaiming with pride that this African religion is as sophisticated and complex as any other. Borrowing is nevertheless a primary and important characteristic. That is why, although my primary topic is the Orisha religion, I sometimes use the terms "Afro-American religious complex" and "Orisha religious system." The Orisha religion is not technically a syncretism of all five religious traditions mentioned above; in fact, worshipers have syncretized only Catholic and, in a small number of cases, Hindu elements with the original Nigerian Yoruba beliefs and practices. Protestantism (here in the form of the Spiritual Baptist religion), the Kabbalah, and Hinduism are, for the most part, practiced side by side in a pluralistic fashion with the Orisha religion. It is significant, however, that the same individuals, most of whom are African, practice more than one and, in some cases, all of these various forms of religious worship.

The Orisha religion, arguably the most purely African cultural practice left on the island, is the one common thread that binds together all the worshipers of the Afro-American religious complex. A large majority of those who affiliate in some way with that complex participate in Orisha activities. I chose the Orisha religion as the focus of my inquiry because all the various aspects of the more general Afro-American religious complex, whether ideological, ritualistic, or demographic, are found in it. My primary objective was to explore the dynamics of this eclectic religion, to examine the form and structure of the interrelationship of the five traditions it encompasses.

I visited the Republic of Trinidad and Tobago four times between 1985 and 1992. In 1985 I made many of my initial contacts and formed several friendships. I returned to Trinidad in October 1988 and remained for one year. My final two visits took place during the summers of 1990 and 1992.

The research samples I refer to in the text were generally opportunistic, but I took special care to avoid obvious biases. I collected many of my data during weekly visits to Orisha feasts around the island. Given the large number of shrines on the island and a feast season usually limited to some thirty-five weeks, there was often more than one feast being held at the same time; I sometimes attended as many as four in the same week. The fact that each feast drew large numbers of worshipers for a continuous four-day period allowed me to conduct a number of interviews and to distribute questionnaires. I also recorded detailed information regarding the age of the shrine, the person in charge of it (the "shrine head"), the physical layout, and the spirits and powers enshrined there.

I attended various Spiritual Baptist ceremonies and Kabbalah banquets as well. In fact, I was able to observe all the basic rites and ceremonies of the Orisha religion, the Spiritual Baptist religion, and the Kabbalah, with the exception of the Kabbalah initiation. I was also present at a number of Hindu ceremonies, including prayers in both personal and public temples, Sunday services of the Kali-Mai sect, and public weddings.

Many of my interviews were conducted with individuals who did not want their identity disclosed. Others, especially those with whom I worked closely for an extended period of time, are identified with their permission. In discussing conflicts, spiritual warfare, and unusual goings-on at ceremonies, I do not provide the names of the individuals involved unless I was given permission to do so.

Some explanation of terminology may be helpful. I have chosen to drop the term "Shango cult," traditionally used to identify what I refer to as the "Orisha religion," because the worshipers themselves find it distasteful and disparaging. First, Shango is merely one (albeit an important one) of many *orisha*. Second, identifying the group as a cult implies that its system of beliefs and practices has not yet attained the stature of a full-blown religion. All the *orisha* worshipers I spoke with approved of this change in terminology. Consequently, when referring to the religion itself, I use the proper noun or proper adjective form, Orisha; when referring to the gods of the religion, I use *orisha* in italic lowercase letters. Similarly, I use "Spiritual Baptist" to refer to that religion and "Spiritual Baptists" to refer to its worshipers.

My use of "Afro-American" to describe or identify cultural practices that are at least somewhat African in derivation and form may strike some readers as anachronistic, given the current popularity of and general support for the term "African American" (see Houk 1993b). The latter, however, is not an appropriate ethnic or racial designation outside the United States and, perhaps, Canada. As far as I know, the peoples of Brazil and the Caribbean, the core area of African-derived culture in the New World, do not use the term. Trinidadians refer to dark-complexioned people of African derivation as "Africans," and I continue that usage here.

It is certainly the right of dark-complexioned people of African descent in the United States to call themselves "African Americans" (a linguistic analogue to "Italian Americans," "Japanese Americans," "Mexican Americans," and so on), and indeed, in that context I do consistently use that term. But I believe there is still a place for the culturally descriptive "Afro-American." The term has a long and rich legacy in cultural anthropology, where it has been used to identify events, practices, attitudes, beliefs, and material culture that are African-derived to some degree, with no regard to the phenotypes of those in question. Thus, peoples of European and Asian extraction can (and do) embrace or practice some form of Afro-American culture; for example, thousands of relatively light-complexioned people are, like me, initiates and devotees of New World African-derived religions. On this model, I use the term "Afro-American" to identify cultural behavior or practices found anywhere in the New World that are at least somewhat African-derived.

This work comprises four parts. Part I (Chapters One, Two, and Three) provides background information to familiarize the reader with the history, religion, and peoples of Trinidad and with the research project itself. Part II (Chapters Four through Seven) concerns the five religious traditions that make up the Afro-American religious complex. Part III (Chapters Eight through Eleven) provides ethnographic information on Orisha rites and ceremonies, the Orisha pantheon, and the social organization of the religion. Part IV (Chapters Twelve through Fifteen) is explanatory and interpretive, addressing those processes that have combined to transform the religion through time.

Acknowledgments

This work is the culmination of graduate research begun in 1985 at Louisiana State University and guided by Miles Richardson, Jay Edwards, and Jill Brody. Later, in the doctoral program of the Department of Anthropology at Tulane University, I continued my research under the watchful, concerned, and enthusiastic eyes of Victoria Bricker, Munro Edmonson, William Jankowiak, and William Balée. Completion of the work would not have been possible without the generous funding provided by a Fulbright Fixed Sum Grant.

This project has of course benefited greatly from the support and assistance of many of the fine people of Trinidad — among them, Leon, Mano, Wells and his wife, Molly Ahye, Carli and Denise, Sam, Fitsy, Ralph, Shorty, Garcia, Trevor, Michael Corridon, Berty, Hollis, Cuthbert and Mother Alvarez, Mother Fleming, Mother Doris, Mother Jean Bob, Mother Whittaker, Mother Ulla, Mother Marjorie (deceased), Mother Elaine, Mother Millie, Mervyn Williams, Mother Gretel (the *iya olorisha*), and Clarence Ford (the *baba olorisha*). I thank them all, and others too numerous to list, for their friendship and cooperation.

During my four visits to Trinidad a core group of close friends graciously offered their assistance and companionship at the many feasts and ceremonies around the island. Special thanks go to Edmond David (Gock), Joseph Henderson, Charlo, Po, Tacoma, Shaka, Michael, Jason, Dexter, and Panco.

I want to acknowledge also the assistance of Henry White. This Orisha priest and Kabbalah practitioner par excellence opened his shrine to me and shared hours of enthusiastic conversation about the beliefs and practices of the Afro-American religious complex in Trinidad.

Jeffrey and Lydia Biddeau have been close friends since my first visit to the island. Elder Biddeau has abundant knowledge of the Orisha religion, Yoruba traditions, and the Kabbalah, and my work benefited greatly from his assistance.

Aaron Jones and his wife, Rhonda, graciously offered their assistance at various stages of my research. Because Aaron is an accomplished drummer, Orisha priest, and Kabbalah medium, his contribution was invaluable. Our professional relationship aside, however, it is our friendship that I value most.

Finally, it is impossible to express enough gratitude to two special people who offered their assistance not only to me but to many in need, often without compensation. Aldwin and Joan Scott opened their home to me and spent countless hours discussing the religions and peoples of Trinidad. Their specific contributions to this work are too numerous to catalogue, but both my professional life and my spiritual understanding benefited from their knowledge and experience as prominent figures in the Orisha and Spiritual Baptist religions in Trinidad.

Unfortunately, Leader Aldwin J. Scott of Basta Hall Village, Trinidad and Tobago, erstwhile politician and statesman, orator, priest, and sublime worker of the religious arts, died on September 19, 1994. I regret that he was not able to see the finished product that he contributed to so greatly; I would like to think that he would be pleased with the result. *Mo juba*, Aldwin Scott, *mo juba*.

Part I

ONE

Orisha Experiences

Seventy to eighty people crammed themselves into a small church in Barataria in northwest Trinidad on a warm and muggy June night, and another fifty or so stood outside peering in the doors and windows. Almost everyone was African, although a few East Indians could be seen scattered here and there in the crowd. Also in attendance was a white foreigner doing his damndest to conduct himself in a manner befitting an anthropologist. The crowd engulfed and carried me as it swayed back and forth to the spiritual rhythms of an ancient religion. The clapping, singing, joy, and enthusiasm were contagious, and I could hardly restrain myself from joining in. It was a little after 1:00 A.M., and the singing and drumming had brought down a few of the *orisha*[1] (primarily African-derived gods and spirits, although the term could technically refer to any ancestor) on the heads of some of the worshipers. Those so possessed, mere adumbrations of their usual selves, ran around the church embracing startled onlookers. Using a small cassette recorder and pen and paper, I had surreptitiously managed to preserve many of the sights and sounds around me, and I was beginning to feel comfortable in these somewhat bizarre surroundings.

Sitting sideways with my back against the right wall of the church near a window, I had a good view of the activities. I was struck particularly by a young, attractive, and well-dressed woman sitting in the row behind mine. Like a debutante at a cockfight, she seemed to be indulging her curiosity, showing just enough poise and civility to hide her natural inclination toward condescension and making an obvious effort at "distancing" herself from the activities around her.

The individuals on whom the *orisha* manifest themselves will often move from person to person, rubbing their faces, legs, or arms with olive oil. Such contact is considered to be a general gesture of good will

3

toward the worshiper, although sometimes the intent may be to heal a specific part of the body or to assuage pain. I have always dreaded these attentions, since they leave one uncomfortably wet and unctuous; nevertheless, I take my medicine politely out of respect for the *orisha*. The young woman behind me, however, did her best to avoid the touch of possessed worshipers as they made their rounds. When she was unable to avoid contact, she would quickly wipe off the oil, fix her hair, and adjust her dress.

I was soon distracted from her prim behavior by the possession of another worshiper, a woman about fifty years of age whose chaotic behavior seemed more in the style of Spiritual Baptist than Orisha possessions. (This particular Orisha ceremony was being held in a Spiritual Baptist church, which partially accounts for the Baptist form of some of the possessions; see Chapter Four.) For the first couple of hours, all the possessions had been fairly routine, or about as routine as such events could be. Suddenly, I heard a bloodcurdling scream and turned just in time to see the demure woman behind me spring out of her seat into the center aisle of the church. She began to writhe on the floor like a snake in the throes of death, tearing at her clothes, her eyes as big as silver dollars. She ripped the front of her dress, exposing herself for a few seconds before the female worshipers at her side could tend to her. She continued to scream and groan and roll around on the floor for what was only five to ten minutes but seemed like an eternity to me, as I stretched time in my attempt to incorporate this incredible experience into my personal belief system. No matter how I tried, however, I could not reconcile the scholarly or "scientific" explanations of ritual dissociation with what I was witnessing. Certain aspects of spirit possession are, perhaps, simply ineffable and must be personally experienced before they can be grasped.

The *orisha* eventually "settled" on the young woman's head, and she began the ritualistic dance of Osain (or Osanyin), the man of the bush whose domain is the healing herbs, roots, and leaves of the forest. Other *orisha* would come and go throughout the night, but the episode involving the young woman remained in my memory.

The stocky "slayer" walked past me in a very businesslike manner holding the cutlass he would use to dispatch the various animals to be offered to the *orisha*. Worshipers were parading goats and chickens inside the *palais* (a covered but open-sided rectangular structure) where drums were being beaten and songs sung for the *orisha* who would receive the sacrificial offerings on this night. The presence of the tightly packed crowd, the strong odor of the goats, and the nearly deafening sound of drums, clapping, and singing combined to make me feel light-headed and ebullient.

First one, then two *orisha* mounted their "horses" (the term used for those of whom the spirits take possession) as the sacrificial animals were ritualistically cleansed in an herbal bath. It was as if the spirits had come to see that the worshipers were carrying out the work of the gods to their satisfaction. The procession moved to the shrine of Papa Ogun (the Yoruba god of war and metal), where a goat was readied for the sacrifice. Tethered on a four-foot rope, the animal was allowed to wander a bit until it moved into a position to the slayer's liking; then he swung the cutlass and took off its head with one powerful stroke. The carcass was held in such a way as to direct the flow of blood from the stub of the neck onto Ogun's shrine. The slayer placed the goat's head, eyes and ears still twitching, on a white plate, which was paraded around the shrine atop a worshiper's head. An *orisha* (probably Ogun) suddenly seized a woman standing near Ogun's shrine and threw her down in the blood and remains of the dead animal. She screamed and fought as if caught by an invisible web. Finally, she stood and danced the mythology that had been danced a million times before, her face wearing an expression that seemed to be devoid of humanity, her clothes dripping with the blood of earth, offered to a spirit of heaven.

I arrived at the shrine compound to find that the man in charge was still "down the road." The woman of the house, in typical "Trini" fashion, fixed me a plate of food and a cool glass of juice. After an hour or so of waiting I was getting restless, so I began to poke around the compound on my own; the woman did not seem to mind. I first walked up to the *perogun* (an open-air, three-sided structure inside which a number of *orisha* are enshrined) to see the small shrines ("stools") and the colorful flags that marked them. Arranged around the bases of the flagstaffs were hollowed-out turtle shells, goat horns, feathers from a variety of fowl, candles, goblets of water, rum bottles, olive oil, and various other items. This area was obviously a focal point of worship. A number of Hindu flags and paraphernalia were located just past the *perogun*. Although I had been in Trinidad only a few weeks, I could easily identify the symbols and materials of Hinduism, since they are found all over the island, but I was puzzled at their presence in an African shrine.

Behind the house where the shrine head and his wife lived was a church. Inside, there were pews and an altar on which were laid Bibles, rosaries, and hymnals. At first glance it looked like a hundred churches I had seen in the States. As I walked around inside, however, I noticed paraphernalia and symbols that seemed out of place for a Christian church. For example, there were mysterious chalk drawings in the four corners and on the left and right walls; a large doubleheaded axe — the traditional symbol for Shango, the Yoruba god of fire, thunder, and lightning — was propped up against a shepherd's crook in the front right corner behind the altar; turtle shells like those found outside in the *perogun* were lying on the ground to the left of the altar; and posters of Hindu deities joined the lithographs of saints adorning the walls on all sides.

Outside, toward the back of the compound, I stumbled upon a separate one-room structure full of ornate paraphernalia and surrounded by esoteric "seals" on the walls and floor. I had done some reading on the magical arts of the Middle Ages, and much of what I saw before me seemed to be drawn from that tradition. The whole area had a sort of diabolical flavor, as if dedicated to something spiritually powerful yet potentially harmful.

I left the mysterious little room, said goodbye to the woman (her husband had not returned), and made my way back to my quarters. My haphazard tour of the shrine compound had left me confused. I considered myself reasonably well read in the African-derived religions of the New World, especially those of Trinidad, but I was not prepared for the religious complexity that I had just observed. There seemed to be at least five religious traditions present in some form in the compound. The religions of Old World and New, of good and evil, of Europeans, Africans, and East Indians had been somehow blended to form what had to be one of the world's most complex religions.

During my first visit to Trinidad in the summer of 1985 I observed a number of "textbook" possessions, in which dissociation commenced rather unceremoniously and the "horses" danced out the ritualized routines associated with the more prominent *orisha*. On the basis of these experiences, it was easy for me to attribute the religious claims of the insiders to their metaphysical and generally transcendent biases. Soon, however, my own biases were seriously challenged. In some of the wilder and seemingly uncontrollable possessions I witnessed, the worshipers appeared to leave behind their own complex of attitudes, phobias, and emotions to become someone (or something?) entirely different. In some instances their physical motions transcended the everyday repertoire of human behavior. The highly animated and apparently genuine behavior of the possessed worshipers I observed cast doubt on many of the standard biochemical, psychological, and sociopolitical explanations of spirit possession. In short, the reality far surpassed the various explanations of possession with which I was familiar. The range of my personal experiences and the resulting ideology I had developed over time had not sufficiently prepared me for such an intense expression of culture-specific ideology.

According to George Devereux's notion of "countertransference" (1967, 41–46), when an individual comes into contact with an event or activity that falls outside the range of experiences constituting his or her personal consciousness (the realm of the Freudian ego), anxiety results. The traumatic event serves to trigger repressed notions and desires. The resultant anxiety level can be low when an individual encounters an event that falls just outside the boundaries of what he or she considers acceptable cultural behavior, or it can be high if the event activates deeply repressed experiences. In my case, a belief system that I had never considered to be anything more than mythology and cultural metaphor was confirming itself before my eyes. My materialistic ideology was being challenged empirically — a most serious challenge, given the nature of my personal convictions.

I had always looked at possession as a ritually sanctioned mechanism whereby individuals may express hidden desires, draw attention to themselves for whatever reason, or climb the socioreligious ladder by claiming to be a receptacle for the gods; my mind-set was admittedly positivistic and materialistic. Even though I had always championed sensitivity to the beliefs of others, I had never considered that spirit possession could substantiate religious claims regarding gods, spirits, and demons. But the intensity of the behavior and the dramatic and radical personality shifts I was observing seemed, disconcertingly, to confirm the reality of the possession; the behavior was quite obviously not feigned. And now, ten years later, after witnessing hundreds of ritual possessions, I find the occurrence as enigmatic as ever. Though I am still inclined to invoke Occam's razor to explain paranormal phenomena by first exhausting known or natural mechanisms, my experiences in Trinidad have caused me to be more respectful of the sentiments of the worshipers themselves.

The people of Trinidad are generally hospitable and gregarious; virtually everywhere I went I was greeted with a plate of food or a drink of rum or juice. But, not surprisingly, the *orisha* worshipers were suspicious of me and my work, at least initially. Their religion suffered during colonial times from repressive laws that prohibited the practice of Afro-American religion; today, many members of an unsympathetic public, both African and Indian, consider *orisha* worship to be demonic or primitive. Eventually, however, as I became a fixture at feasts and various other ceremonies, I established contacts and made friends all over the island.

During my first visit the Smith family, who lived in the southern part of the island, was kind enough to provide me with lodging. Because I was having trouble establishing contacts in the Orisha religion, Mrs. Smith took me to meet an old friend, Aldwin Scott, who was one of the island's most prominent Orisha *mongba* (priests) and Spiritual Baptist leaders.[2] Even before she had finished the introduction, however, Leader Scott, as he is popularly known, launched into a harangue against "arrogant" anthropologists and a particular French scholar who had come to Trinidad to disparage and belittle the "Shango cult."[3] Both Mrs. Smith and I were ill at ease and embarrassed, and eventually she left me alone with him, as I had asked her to do before we arrived.

When Leader Scott finally let me get a few words in, I apologized for showing up without an appointment, explained that I knew nothing of the Frenchman or any other researchers, and asked for a few minutes of his time. Much to my relief, once the topic came around to his religion, he and his wife, Mother Joan, invited me inside to continue our discussion. This was the most auspicious meeting I had during my early fieldwork, for this renowned Orisha priest and Spiritual Baptist leader and his wife became close friends and patient sources of much of the information I collected in Trinidad during my four stays.

Another friend is Jeffrey Biddeau, whom I met at a feast in Claxton

Bay, on the west coast of the island, in June 1985. Elder Biddeau is very knowledgeable in the affairs of the Orisha religion and is regarded as one of its ranking elders in Trinidad. He is also strong-minded and has an immense amount of personal pride, finding it difficult to compromise. The religion has no written liturgy, no official priesthood, and a variable complex of beliefs and practices drawn from a number of traditions. Many of its heads and elders exploit that eclecticism to their advantage and are willing to change or compromise their personal ideology to accommodate any number of sentiments. Elder Biddeau, however, was initiated into the Orisha priesthood in Nigeria and practices one of the purest forms of *orisha* worship on the island. He insists on the correctness of his own tenets and demands the respect due him as a ranking elder.

Our relationship deteriorated during my year-long stay in 1988–89. During his feast in September 1989, annoyed with his negative assessment of my behavior in the *palais*, I walked out of his compound, an action that I have regretted ever since. During my last visit to Trinidad in the summer of 1992, however, I traveled out to visit Elder Biddeau, and we settled our differences. I am happy to say that he is assisting in my research again, and we remain friends.

It is not uncommon for anthropologists in the field to develop close friendships with their contacts, as I did with Aaron Jones and his wife Rhonda. Over a five-year period I watched Aaron move from a small Port of Spain tenement to a full-blown Orisha compound. He is now an accomplished priest with a number of followers.

I first met Aaron in Woodford Square in Port of Spain on November 29, 1988, where he was one of the major disputants in an informal public debate. The nature of the working and personal relationship that Aaron and I gradually developed was greatly influenced by that first meeting. Discussions at the "University of Woodford Square," as it is called, are taken seriously; participants include some of the most famous Trini scholars and personalities—for example, historian and former prime minister Eric Williams. Although the debates are informal, they are guided by a number of unspoken rules for both the audience and the speakers. The two primary disputants and, at times, a moderator carry on their discussion in the "court," surrounded by a small crowd. Only the two debaters are allowed to speak; if they begin to talk over each other, the moderator will attempt to restore order. Participation from persons outside the "court" is discouraged, and any such comments — however relevant — are usually shouted down by others. Also, participants must never strike or physically threaten a fellow debater, must not use foul or abusive language, and must avoid ad hominem tactics. In sum, debaters must generally conduct themselves in a dignified manner. On one occasion, when a disputant farted loudly and seemingly without embarrassment, although the audience responded with laughter and caustic remarks, one listener chastised him for showing so little respect for the "court."

The form and structure of public disputation in Woodford Square is, in many ways, a microcosm of public encounters in Trinidad. Trinis usually avoid public displays of anger; they are generally stoic and reticent even when taken advantage of. For example, one hot morning I waited in a long line for about an hour for a bus out of Port of Spain. Some of those in the line were traveling with small children, and many were carrying bags and boxes of goods purchased in town. The press of the crowd and the heat made the queue uncomfortable, and when the bus finally pulled into the loading gate, a number of people from the end of the line pushed forward to board. Although many of the passengers at the front of the line were understandably annoyed, and a few were cursing under their breath, no one complained or confronted those breaking the queue. I, on the other hand, was angry at having lost my seat on the bus, and I let the guilty parties know it. Much to my chagrin, the only verbal support I got from the other passengers came from one elderly gentleman who excused my behavior by saying that I was a foreigner and that the people of Europe and America, being "more civilized," were not accustomed to such unruliness.

Experiences like this one help explain the form and structure of the Woodford Square discussions. Any Trini who is willing to argue publicly for a particular point of view is taking a risk; ordinarily, only vagrants, the inebriated, or the otherwise socially marginal would transgress the important social rule that frowns on doing so. Heated discussions and confrontation, including those in Woodford Square, constitute a violation of the norm. But in Woodford Square the "violators" are protected by a code of behavior that permits free and lively discussion in which they can assert themselves with impunity. The highly structured and rule-governed form of these debates allow the individual to vent his anger (the disputants are almost exclusively male) or state his opinions, whatever they may be, on a variety of topics without fear of social disapprobation.

At any rate, one morning I arrived at the square to find a somewhat overbearing and distinguished-looking man engaged in a debate with a feisty Rastafarian—Aaron. The central topic was the existence and nature of God. Both were making good points (not really hard to do, considering the indeterminate nature of the subject matter), but Aaron's opponent seemed to be gaining favor with the audience for reasons that had more to do with his style and delivery, I suspect, than with the substance of what he was saying. I had already decided that I did not like the arrogant philosopher's condescending tone and his attempt to bully Aaron and the audience into agreeing with him, so at one point I could not resist the temptation to jump into the fray. Being a Woodford Square neophyte and having little knowledge of proper debate decorum, I was immediately shouted down by those around me. Aaron, however, seemed to respect the fact that I had been willing to violate important behavioral norms to make what he thought was a good point. In fact, I eventually worked my way into the "court" and was able to hold my own against the imperious philosopher, much to Aaron's delight.

It took me a while to convince Aaron of my sincerity and my desire to learn about the Orisha religion, but he eventually agreed to work with me. His assistance was especially helpful in my search for shrine houses throughout Trinidad, a large island by Caribbean standards.

Relationships with most of my contacts began simply as an exchange of money, goods, or services for information and assistance. Eventually, however, as I became more involved in the religion, the line separating me and my contacts became blurred. My interest in Orisha and my eagerness to participate in the various rituals and ceremonies no doubt facilitated my assimilation into the group. One particular instance comes to mind.

In November 1988 I attended a feast in the sparsely populated northeastern part of the island near the town of Sangre Grande. The shrine head had only recently moved there from the extreme southwest, and this fact, as well as the area's meager population, probably contributed to the small turnout of about ten worshipers. Normally, a small attendance is not a problem as long as there is someone to direct the feast, three people to play the drums (one of whom can be the person directing the feast), and enough others to support the singing and praying and to handle such chores as sacrificing, preparing, and cooking animals, tending to visitors, and cleaning worship areas. On this particular night, Michael Corridan, a young *mongba*, directed the feast and played the *bemba*, the lead or middle-range drum; and a male member of the shrine played the *congo*, the lower-range or "bass" drum. But no one could be found to play the upper-range drum, the *oumalay* (three drummers are not absolutely necessary, but such an arrangement is deeply traditional and customary). A few of the worshipers tried, but they were unable to effect the quick and steady rhythm that the Orisha songs call for. During the first "intermission" (everyone takes a break from time to time, since a typical feast night lasts from 10:00 P.M. to about 6:00 A.M.), as Michael continued to play his drum, I picked up the *oumalay* and began to play along with him. His response was favorable, and he asked me to play the rest of the night. I gradually became quite proficient with the small drum, and Michael, Aaron, and I became a team of sorts as the primary drummers at two ceremonies before I left in 1989.

———————

It was undergoing initiation, perhaps more than any other action on my part, that led to my eventual acceptance by the group. Elder Biddeau encouraged me to affiliate formally with the Orisha religion early in 1988. I was against the idea initially; I felt that my agnosticism would prevent me from according the ceremony the dignity that it deserved. In time, however, as I became more active in the daily affairs of the religion and as my circle of friends continued to grow, I got used to the idea. Finally I sat down with Leader Scott and Mother Joan and told them of my apprehensions; they already knew about my skepticism, but they were also aware that I had a great deal of respect for them and the Orisha religion, and advised me to go through with the ceremony. After further discussions with Elder Biddeau and Henry White, a close friend and accomplished *mongba* and Kabbalah practitioner with whom I was working at the time, I agreed.

My particular initiation was to involve both the baptismal ceremony of the Spiritual Baptist religion and the head washing and incising of the Orisha religion. It was important to me that Leader Scott, Elder Biddeau, and Henry all be involved in one way or another. We decided that Leader Scott would direct the water baptism at his shrine, and Elder Biddeau would conduct the head washing and incising at his shrine, with Henry assisting in both locations. Unfortunately, some time before my initiation, while attending Elder Biddeau's Kabbalah banquet, Henry conducted himself in a way that Elder Biddeau found inappropriate, and the two had a temporary parting of ways. As a result, Henry decided not to assist at my head washing and incising rites, and as it turned out, a prior engagement prevented his attendance at my baptism as well.

The baptism began on Saturday evening, May 27, 1989, and lasted about ten hours. The ceremony consisted of two basic parts: praying, singing, and praising in the church; and immersion in the sea. I was "banded" during the first part. ("Banding" involves wrapping the entire head with various colored cloths upon which special "seals" or religious symbols have been drawn. This procedure generally renders the initiate totally blind, but depending on who does the banding and how securely the cloths are fastened, the difference between light and dark may be perceptible.) The ceremony began at 8:00 P.M. By 3:00 A.M. or so I was exhausted and irritable, mostly from lack of sleep but also from other factors: I was made to kneel on the dirt floor while the others were praying, and from time to time I was spun around. (This is done to facilitate possession or to induce an altered state of consciousness.) Also, during the entire ceremony inside the church, I was encouraged to move my arms and, when not kneeling, my legs as if marching. (This movement is considered to be symbolic of the initiate's march toward a higher state of spiritual enlightenment.)

Sometime around 4:00 A.M. I had what could loosely be called visions. These were more like daydreaming and imaginal thought (à la the "mind's eye") than hallucinations; nevertheless, I was greatly impressed by the intensity of the experience. Although I am not at liberty to divulge the content of my visions, given the sacred context in which they occurred, their underlying theme involved my drawing closer to the other worshipers spiritually as well as on the level of everyday life. I was immersed in the sea later that morning and then returned to the church, where the ceremony was brought to a close. A final brief ritual that concluded the baptismal rites took place on the following Wednesday.

The second part of my initiation, the head washing and incising, occurred one week later. These rites were more trying and difficult for several reasons. Before they took place I underwent two and a half days of semi-fasting (I was given only crackers, tea, and rice) and semi-

isolation (Elder Biddeau would stop by from time to time to instruct
me on various aspects of the religion), beginning the night of Sunday,
June 4, 1989. I spent most of this time lying on the dirt floor in the
chapelle (generally a small enclosed sanctuary, although Elder Biddeau's
chapelle was much larger than the norm). Since my head was banded,
my only visual sensation was a small amount of light during the day-
time hours. Early in the morning of the third day, Wednesday, my
banding cloths were removed, prayers were said, drums were beaten,
and songs were sung for Ogun, my patron *orisha*. A cock was sacrificed
over my head to Ogun at about 7:00 A.M.

My head was washed and incised a few hours later. The incising of
the top of the head and the forehead is, perhaps, the most significant
initiation rite. Using a razor blade, Elder Biddeau made small incisions,
into which he then rubbed various oils and herbs. The washing and
incising signify the "seating of the head" for a particular *orisha*, in my
case Ogun. I could now, at least theoretically, be possessed by Ogun.
Although one need not necessarily go through the initiation ceremony
in order to be possessed, anyone who wants to be a *hounsis* (a formal
"horse" or medium) for a particular *orisha* is expected to undergo the
washing and incising rites.

I had another "vision" that morning, this one much stronger. One
of my close friends, Carli Rawlins, possessed by Ogun at the time,
instructed me to drink a medicinal liquid from Shakpana's calabash
(Photo 1). I could not determine its exact ingredients, but they seemed
to include rum and various legumes. (The concoction is purported to
be medicinally potent and is administered as a cure for a number of
maladies.) By this time, I was exhausted from lack of rest and nauseated
after ingesting olive oil, rum, raw obi seeds (obtained from the kola
tree), and other things, and I really did not want to drink from the
calabash. Nonetheless, I took it. As I peered down into the murky and
malodorous liquid, I had an amazing and frightening vision (which,
again, I cannot disclose) which seemed as real as the ground beneath
my bare feet. A few hours later, after the ceremony was brought to a
close, I discussed my vision with the others who were present. All
denied observing what I had seen, but the worshipers did not doubt my
sincerity or deny the veracity of my claims. Such "spiritual seeing,"
they explained, was a personal and unique occurrence experienced by
an individual in an elevated state of spirituality. Apparently what had
seemed so real, so empirical from my point of view, had actually taken

place not on the plane of physical reality but rather on some other plane. In other words, the event actually did occur, but its nature was highly existential or individual-specific.

Although I cannot discuss the details of my experience, I can say that the vision was highly specific in Orisha terms; that is, the content was symbolically significant in the context of worship in the Afro-American religious complex in Trinidad. The occurrence of such a vision was startling enough, but even more astonishing, at least in my mind, was the fact that the "language" or cultural syntax, so to speak, was not my own. During this exercise in cultural assimilation I had glimpsed ever so briefly the spiritual world of my contacts. My initiation into the Orisha religion served to bridge not only the social gap between my world and theirs but the conceptual gap as well. More important, the whole experience legitimized, in my eyes, the religious life of my contacts; their movements, activities, and attitudes suddenly became imbued with a substance and an honesty that I had ignored or overlooked.

As a cultural anthropologist, I had always been fascinated by indigenous and culture-specific accounts of gods, demons, shamanistic forays into the spirit world, "voodoo death," spirit possession, and the like. But try as I might, I could not overcome my gut feeling that these phenomena were nothing more than exotic and curious bits of local lore. I was comfortable with a scientistic mind-set that sought validation and substantiation of claims and theories — whether religious, social, scientific, or whatever — by means of demographic data, analyses of social structure, historical documentation, environmental factors, and so on. Before my experience with the calabash, I had never considered factoring ostensibly subjective and personal data into the mix, but I do now.

I think it important to point out that my work remains empirically sound and adheres to the highest standards of sober, informed, and responsible social science research; I have by no means jumped headlong into the abyss of postmodernistic nihilism. In fact, I still believe that claims and theories can be sufficiently evaluated by assessing their "fit" to local demographic, historical, and environmental parameters. Now, however, I am willing to expand my list of relevant parameters to include factors that are important to the insiders themselves: for example, the status of their relationship with their gods, and existential concerns such as religious doubt and apprehension regarding the afterlife.

As a discipline, cultural anthropology's foremost contribution to scholarship has been its apparent success in translating local knowledge and behavior into a form that is palatable to a wider audience. Bolstered by my encounter with the calabash, I have ventured into pockets of Trinidadian culture I once viewed as being too esoteric or personal to deal with, thus greatly enlarging the purview of my research. Whether or not I have successfully translated the Afro-American religious culture of Trinidad into more general, culture-universal terms, I can say with some confidence that my broader and more intimate understanding of the religious life of my contacts has greatly decreased the cultural gap that separated us and, not surprisingly, has made my work more meaningful to the Spiritual Baptists and *orisha* worshipers themselves.

Just before I left Trinidad in September 1989, Aaron described to me the physical appearance of various *orisha* and Kabbalah entities (spirits). He explained that he had seen these gods and spirits at different religious functions around the island and that they appeared to him to be as real as anyone else there. In light of my own experiences, rather than simply listening politely to his descriptions as I might have done at one time, I took copious notes and asked him to go on. Such data are acutely subjective, it is true, but the information was related to me by a source I consider reliable and is on some level a genuine part of Trini religious life.

The subjective nature of visions and the like is particularly problematic to anthropology, a discipline that generally focuses on "culture" and "society," two concepts that imply collectivity, sharing, and some degree of conformity. An in-depth discussion of this problem would take us far beyond the scope of this book, since my primary intent here is to focus on the Orisha experience from a variety of perspectives. Nevertheless, I had to address the issue at least in a functional and pragmatic way before I could formulate a research methodology.

TWO

Religion, Postmodernism, and Methodology

Perhaps the most problematic and troubling theoretical issue in sociocultural anthropology today is the postmodernist controversy and its ramifications for theory, fieldwork technique, and ethnographic writing. One problem is the lack of a clear statement regarding just what postmodernism is. A few works — such as George Marcus and Michael Fischer's *Anthropology as Cultural Critique* (1986) and James Clifford and George Marcus's *Writing Culture* (1986) — are generally recognized for their postmodernist critique of traditional ethnography, but, as Ernest Gellner (1992, 23) writes, we have "no 39 postmodernist articles of faith, no postmodernist Manifesto."

Still, we need to formulate at least a working description of postmodernism as it manifests itself in sociocultural anthropology. At the foundation of postmodernism is the relativistic idea that "truth" is not simply a function of reason but can be, and often is, affected by mythology, morality, religion, and other social or cultural constraints or factors. Particularly germane here is Michel Foucault's notion that knowledge or "truth" is intimately associated with the power dynamics of culture and society. Postmodernism, however, at least in its extreme form, goes beyond basic cultural relativity to a more drastic and, in my opinion, less tenable position. Postmodernists generally argue that objective facts and independent social structures and models are largely the products of Western hubris regarding the assumed superiority of scientific rationalism. In the place of empiricism and positivism they speak of "multivocality," "polyphony," and the decentralization of cultural authority.

Although it seems unnecessary to eschew Cartesian rationalism and scientism altogether, postmodernism's challenge to the assumptions of modernism and traditional ethnography is an important one. Post-

17

modernists have rightfully sought to elevate the discourse of the "native" (or the "Other," or those considered culturally marginal) to the level of serious consideration. The postmodernist movement is thus a logical concomitant to multiculturalism and its assault on the biases of Eurocentrism. Postmodernism cannot be dismissed, à la Steven Sangren (1988, 414), as merely a seditious power play intended to dethrone traditional ethnography in order to secure a niche for itself in academe.

But the admittedly existential and subjective biases of postmodernism and its philosophical counterpart, nihilism, must be tempered with a desire to translate the culture-specific notions of the Other into terms that are intelligible to a culturally heterogeneous audience. One response to extremist postmodernism is Gellner's "rationalist fundamentalism," the notion that a rational and culturally transcendent standard does exist and can be utilized to evaluate human behavior in a critical and objective manner:

It is a position which, like that of the religious fundamentalists, is firmly committed to the denial of relativism. It is committed to the view that there *is* external, objective, culture-transcending knowledge: there *is* indeed "knowledge beyond culture." All knowledge must indeed be articulated in some idiom, but there are idioms capable of formulating questions in a way such that answers are no longer dictated by the internal characteristics of the idiom of the culture carrying it but, on the contrary, by an independent reality. The ability of cognition to reach beyond the bounds of any one cultural cocoon, and attain forms of knowledge valid for *all* — and, incidentally, an understanding of nature leading to an exceedingly powerful technology — constitutes *the* central fact about our shared social conditions. (Gellner 1992, 75; original emphasis)

The pessimistic assumptions of postmodernism notwithstanding, countless ethnographic accounts do succeed, at least in part, in explaining the Other and making culture-specific lifeways at least somewhat comprehensible to a wider audience. There is obviously some common ground on some level; I would guess that material and biological needs and contingencies, the dynamics and nature of which are shared cross-culturally, are significant here.

There are strong points to be made by the postmodernists, on the one hand, and the rational fundamentalists, on the other. We cannot overlook the richness and the significance of belief and ideology on a personal level, but we must not forget that the task of the social scientist is to interpret and explain in a way that can be broadly appreciated and grasped. We must begin with the often ambiguous because multivocal nature of insider behavior and ideology. We must assume that in his or her own view the insider is behaving and thinking rationally and reasonably. We should also (humbly) recognize that we outsiders can never fully understand the culture and society in question and, thus, that our explanations and interpretations are only imperfect facsimiles; this is, perhaps, the best we will ever be able to do. It is still better, however, than either succumbing to a nihilistic fatalism engendered by a belief that we can never understand the Other or arrogantly assuming that our own epistemology sets the standard for rationality by which local epistemologies may be judged.

The most fruitful approach will not arbitrarily designate this or that datum, however subjective it may seem, as irrelevant. Yet the researcher must be continually aware of the material, ecological, social, and biological constraints of cultural behavior; these should serve as an evaluative baseline for interpreting and explaining data (defined here in the broadest sense) cross-culturally:

We are particularly concerned to discover what the people under study believe to be the functional relationships among the entities that they think are part of their environment, and what they take to be "signs," indicating changes in these entities or relationships, which demand action on their part; but *the important question concerning the cognized model* [roughly, the natives' point of view], *since it serves as a guide to action, is not the extent to which it conforms to "reality"* (i.e., is identical with or isomorphic with the operational model [roughly, the anthropologists' point of view]), *but the extent to which it elicits behavior that is appropriate to the material situation of the actors, and it is against this functional and adaptive criterion that we may assess it.* Maring [Papua New Guinea tribesmen] notions of disease etiology are certainly inaccurate, but the slaughter and consumption of pigs during illness is just as effective when undertaken to strengthen or mollify spirits as it would be if it were specifically undertaken to alleviate stress symptoms. (Rappaport 1967, 239; original emphasis)

As an illustration of how this explanatory strategy might be applied, consider the puzzling problem involving the determination of feast dates in the Orisha religion. There are more than 150 Orisha shrines in Trinidad, and virtually every one holds an annual *ebo*, or week-long celebratory feast. The traditional feast season runs from the first Tuesday after Easter to Advent: that is, thirty-two to thirty-six weeks, depending on the date of Easter Sunday. The dates of the sixty feasts that I charted revealed fairly even distribution throughout this season. There is no written tradition and there appear to be no strict guidelines that worshipers must follow; nonetheless, there must be some method at work to achieve such a smooth distribution. According to the worshipers, the Orisha feast dates are determined primarily on the basis of Catholic feast dates of those saints that have been syncretized with particular African *orisha*. Since only about ten *orisha*-saint pairings are generally recognized around the island, however, if all the feasts were in fact dated to fall on these Catholic saints' days, one would expect to find peaks of feast activity, preceded and followed by periods of relative inactivity. But this is not what the data show.

After charting the movement of particular worshipers from week to week, I noticed that many of those who travel the feast circuit on a weekly basis are generally unemployed or underemployed, and some have no permanent place of residence. These transient worshipers serve as cooks, drummers, or song leaders or in some other capacity during the week of the feast. They are given room and board, and, depending on the extent of their involvement, some are even paid. Since the feasts are sponsored by the more well-to-do worshipers, what happens is, in effect, a redistribution of funds and goods among the many members of the religion. It should also be pointed out that in the last decade or so some shrine heads have begun to hold their feasts outside the traditional Easter-to-Advent period, a practice that has served to spread the distribution of feast dates further and to make support available virtually year-round for the more indigent and transient worshipers.

In short, the existing pattern of feast dates, worked out over a long period of time, results in a feast calendar that makes possible the redistribution of wealth among the many members of the religion. Redistribution of this sort is obviously beneficial to the transient worshipers. The system also benefits the shrine heads, however. For one thing, since the number of feasts on a particular date is kept to a minimum, each shrine's feast attracts large numbers of worshipers, and the ability to attract worshipers is one important criterion upon which the prestige of a shrine head is based. Moreover, this system practically guarantees the presence of the large support staff that is necessary for a successful feast. In fact, I found cases in which new shrine heads planned their feasts to fall before or after other nearby feasts in order not to split the existing pool of worshipers.

A few of my contacts reluctantly admitted that other criteria were occasionally used to determine feast dates — for example, the phases of the moon or seasonal change. It may be that adding these to the original determinant, the Catholic calendar of saints' days, allowed for the relatively even distribution of feasts throughout the season. In any case, this line of questioning revealed the greater importance of Catholicism at an earlier time, a fact that was also confirmed by a positive correlation of shrine age and the presence of Catholic elements.

In my analysis of the determination of feast dates, I have assumed the existence of objective, empirical facts: namely, the feast calendar and at least one of its apparent functions, redistribution of wealth. While I am aware of the problems that have been raised by postmodernists regarding such "facts," the feast calendar and redistribution are certainly included in that category of information described by Gellner (1992, 54) as "knowledge beyond culture." On the other hand, I am aware that the Orisha religious system as it is practiced and conceived of by the worshipers is meaningful, rational, and reasonable at least to them. But if we totally submerge ourselves in the pool of Orisha ideology, how can we, as outsiders, expect to make sense of it? The Orisha religion is based on an oral tradition and comprises a number of built-in mechanisms that induce change and variation through time. In other words, many different styles of worship exist within it. If we assume the validity of Gellner's "rationalist fundamentalism," however, the basic principle upon which traditionalist ethnography and scientific inquiry are founded, we can explain and interpret in a way that is understandable and intelligible to a wider audience.

Any culture should be allowed to speak for itself. In Trinidad it is voices of the culture, after all, that reveal the early significance of Catholicism and the additional criteria of feast-date determination that allow the worshipers to work out the existing feast calendar. There are other "voices," however, that "speak" as well — for example, empirical data and objective facts — and we do a great disservice to sociocultural anthropology and the general study of human behavior if we ignore them.

Religion is particularly amenable to the approach discussed here, involving as it does symbols, mythology, and metaphysics on the one hand, and an activity sphere embedded in the material dimensions of everyday life on the other. Particularly important is the degree to which the insider's meaning-oriented model and the outsider's cause-oriented model differ; this will often be an indication of the built-in flexibility of cultural systems — that is, rules for breaking rules — and implicitly held notions that clash to some degree with cultural ideals. Both points are illustrated in the case of the feast calendar.

The compromise I am arguing for is justified if for no other reason than that it will prevent us from embracing or applying the more egregious notions of either postmodernism or scientism. The dangers of extremist relativism are ethnocentrism, racism, and nationalism. The primary problem with unyielding empiricism is the tendency to bracket the insiders' or natives' point of view because of its assumed irrational nature. Let us consider both cases in turn.

Cultural relativism is a generally defensible view in the social sciences which encourages the ethnographer to take seriously the comments, ideas, and attitudes of his or her contacts. It is further argued that these culture-specific notions can be best understood if they are interpreted or explained in the context of the culture in question. The cultural relativistic approach has been a fruitful one for sociocultural anthropology, since it has encouraged the fieldworker to avoid assumptions regarding the supposed superiority of his or her own culture. The emphasis on "the natives' point of view" has resulted in culturally rich ethnographies that have brought us closer to understanding the lifeways of the Other. Those sympathetic to the cultural relativist approach have developed various paradigms, methodologies, and approaches — for example, ethnoscience, humanistic anthropology, symbolic anthropology, and interpretive anthropology — which have served to temper the absolutist tones of cultural materialism.

We must be careful, however, not to give credence to the more exclusivist notions of particular groups that wish to assert themselves politically, economically, or otherwise at the expense of other groups. After all, the sublime and generally honorable intentions of postmodernism notwithstanding, we will occasionally encounter culture-specific notions that are damaging at worst, discriminatory and disparaging at best, when directed at other groups. It is not uncommon for a particular ethnic group, for example, to champion its own heritage, abilities, phenotype, and even intelligence in an attempt to gain some sort of political or social advantage over another group. So social scientists, especially those of an extremist relativist or postmodernist persuasion, should avoid championing the natives' point of view in terms giving the impression that certain racist or nationalist notions are true or accurate in any sort of absolute sense.

On the other hand, the deprecation of "insider knowledge" has its own pitfalls. Primary among them is the temptation to interpret or explain in terms that are comfortable to the outsider but are, in all probability, alien to the culture in question. In fact, as examples from the ethnographic literature show, we would do well to recognize the relevance of the natives' point of view to the interpretation of sociocultural behavior. Rappaport (1967), for example, tells of the Tsembaga of New Guinea, who build their huts above 3,500 feet in order to avoid the attacks of fever-inducing spirits that live below that altitude. The epidemiologist argues that the Tsembaga are simply unaware of the disease-carrying capacity of low-altitude anopheline mosquitoes, but this explanation, though it can be called superior in a strictly etiological sense, tells us little about the behavior of the Tsembaga. In other words, the Tsembaga avoid low altitudes not because they fear the mosquitoes but rather because they fear the spirits. Thus, both the outsider's empirical notions (the operational model) and the native's point of view (the cognized model) have a certain (but each in its own way) limited utility:

> This is not to say, of course, that the cognized model is merely a less adequate representation of reality than the operational model. The operational model is an observer's description of selected aspects of the material world. It has a purpose only for the anthropologist. As far as the actors are concerned it has no function. Indeed, it does not exist. The cognized model, while it must be understood by those who entertain it to be a representation of the material and nonmaterial world, has a function for the actors: it guides their action. (Rappaport 1967, 238–39)

In a somewhat similar case, the Murngin of Australia claim that people can be killed by sorcery. There are, in fact, several recorded cases of so-called "voodoo deaths" in which unfortunate individuals ostensibly succumbed to the workings of the local sorcerer. An extensive anthropological literature (see, e.g., Cannon 1942; Eastwell 1982; Lex 1974; and Warner 1958) points to psychosocial and physiological factors that may account for these deaths; Harry Eastwell, for example, attributes "voodoo death" in Australia to dehydration brought on by the confiscation of fluids that is part of the complex of sociocultural behavior attending death by sorcery. But, again, the Murngin ultimately fear the sorcerer and his putative power, and this is what drives their behavior.

In sum, we must avoid the temptation to indulge either our own world view or that of others. Both the operational and the cognized points of view are "correct" in their own way. Wherever our sympathies lie in regard to the postmodernist issue, sober and responsible evaluation must continue to be an integral part of the science of human behavior. I argued earlier that evaluation of sociocultural behavior should be done within the framework of Gellner's "rationalist fundamentalism." In the ethnographic examples discussed above and similar cases, such evaluation would involve assessing the relative fit of both insider and outsider explanations to the material, ecological, sociocultural, and biological parameters of the local environment.

I have attempted to guide my research into Afro-American religion in Trinidad by this sort of program, to apply empirical, quantitative, and demographic explanatory strategies that facilitate transposing the "slippery" subject of religion into terms more readily grasped by a wider audience. At the same time, I do not wish to gloss over religion's ineffable, subjective, and existential aspects. My method here is to balance the material and tangible features of religion with culturally meaningful aspects by including the verbatim comments of my contacts on a variety of subjects. The end result of such a research strategy will, I hope, be morphologically similar to the topic of inquiry.

THREE

The Setting

Trinidad lies at the southernmost tip of the Lesser Antilles and is only eleven kilometers (about seven miles) from the northern coast of Venezuela at its closest point (*Annual Statistical Digest* 1988, 1). In fact, Venezuela is often visible from the west coast of the island if viewing conditions are good. Geologically, Trinidad lies on the South American continental shelf and is actually an extension of the South American mainland.

There are three mountainous or hilly ranges on the island, the northern, central, and southern ranges. The northern range, running roughly east to west across the entire island, is the most prominent, with elevations reaching up to 940 meters, or 3,084 feet (*Annual Statistical Digest* 1988, 1). It acts as a sort of barrier between the areas to the south, which are more densely populated, and the sparsely populated north shore, which is relatively underdeveloped — although Maracas Bay is a popular tourist attraction with its white sandy beaches and crystal clear blue-green water surrounded by picturesque mountains. The central and southern ranges, which also run roughly east to west, are considerably less extensive both in area and in elevation. Between them are flatlands, small hills, and rolling plains.

Although Trinidad is relatively large for a Caribbean island (in fact, the second largest, after Jamaica, in what was formerly known as the British West Indies), it has an area of only about 4,800 square kilometers and is approximately 80 kilometers (50 miles) from north to south and 50 kilometers (31 miles) from east to west across the narrow "waist." That is, it is slightly smaller than the state of Delaware. Nevertheless, travel between extreme points can sometimes take an entire day. Good roads run east and south out of Port of Spain, the capital, which is located in northwestern Trinidad (see Figure 1 for the location

25

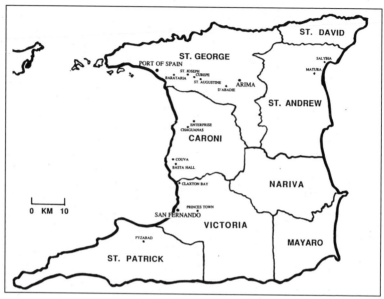

FIGURE 1. *Trinidad.*

of towns, villages, and the eight counties of Trinidad), but these dwindle into substandard roadways before reaching either the eastern or the southern coast. The worn and damaged roads on the rest of the island make traveling difficult.

The problem is not so much the engineering and technology, since Trinidad has a rather impressive industrial infrastructure and a large number of engineers and technicians for its size, but rather the lack of funds to finance repair and upkeep. The public transportation system is extensive and cheap but not always efficient, so I soon realized that I would have to hire, rent, or buy a car if I planned to cover the various religious activities around the island. I eventually purchased a dilapidated Toyota that served me well enough during my year-long stay.

When traveling in Trinidad, one does well to keep an umbrella handy, especially from May to December, the traditional rainy season. The climate is distinctly tropical, with little annual variation in temperature and virtually continuous tradewinds. Temperatures generally range between 22 and 32 degrees Celsius (about 72 to 90 degrees Fahrenheit), the coolest occurring during the dry season, which runs roughly from January to May (*Annual Statistical Digest* 1988, 5). Few private residences have air conditioning, but most houses are built to take advantage of the almost constant winds.

One would expect the natural beauty, fertile soil, and strategic geographical location of Trinidad to have attracted the attention of early inhabitants. And indeed a thriving indigenous population consisting primarily of Ienian Arawaks (relatively peaceful agricultural and fishing people) and Caribs (a more hostile group) did settle on the island perhaps as much as 15,000 years ago: the Arawaks in the southern and southeastern part; the Caribs in the north and northwest, with additional settlements on the northern and eastern coasts (Brereton 1981, 1; Black et al. 1976, 37). The Caribs appeared, however, to prefer Tobago, Trinidad's smaller sister island. The aboriginal population of Trinidad at the time Christopher Columbus arrived is estimated at 20,000 to 30,000 (Newson 1976, 76).

Columbus spotted Trinidad on his third voyage to the Americas in 1498, when, after sighting three peaks in the small southern range, he apparently named the island for the Holy Trinity (Carmichael 1961, 12). His brief stay allowed the Spanish to get a foothold there, but they failed in their attempt to displace the indigenous Amerindians and to develop and settle the island as they had hoped. Columbus's arrival did, however, usher in a period of gradually increasing ethnic complexity, with various groups jockeying for power at one time or another.

During the following century the native Trinidadians strongly resisted attempts by the Spanish Crown to bring the island under control. Not until 1592 did the Spanish finally establish their first permanent settlement, St. Joseph, in northwestern Trinidad approximately ten kilometers (six miles) east of present-day Port of Spain (Brereton 1981, 1). For the next two centuries, despite a few brief periods of moderate prosperity and agricultural success, this colony fared little better than the Spanish had during their first century. A profitable tobacco industry developed during the early seventeenth century, but its success was short-lived, thanks to competition from English colonies in North America and the Spanish Crown's insistence on enforcing the "exclusion," a mercantile strategy that restricted trade only to ships sailing under the Spanish flag (Williams 1964, 10). In the early part of the eighteenth century a flourishing cacao bean industry produced a profitable and high-quality crop, but it too eventually failed. The colony did not again develop an agricultural crop with a production level sufficient for international trade until the end of the eighteenth century, when the important sugar cane industry developed; it is still flourishing today.

The uncertain economic base, basic indifference and neglect on the part of the Spanish Crown, an uninterested Spanish population with little desire to settle in Trinidad, and recalcitrant indigenous inhabitants all combined to keep the European population of the island meager until the end of the eighteenth century. Just after the fall of the cacao crop in 1725, for example, there were only 162 non-Amerindian adult males on the island (Brereton 1981, 4), but by 1765 the total had climbed to about 1,200, with approximately an equal number of Amerindians (Harricharan 1981, 26).

A decline in the number of aboriginal people accompanied the steady growth of the European population during the colonial period. By 1797 only 1,082 of the 20,000–30,000 Amerindians remained (Newson 1976, 190). Their eradication by European swords, guns, and diseases occurred everywhere in the New World; in the case of Trinidad, disease and malnutrition were apparently the primary culprits (Newson 1976, 170). Toward the end of the eighteenth century, Europeans hired Amerindians, their original lifeways long destroyed, to work on rural estates that covered what had once been aboriginal lands (Newson 1976, 232). Thereafter, the indigenous peoples gradually integrated themselves into the general population. The few remaining Amerindians live today in north-central Trinidad near Arima.

In the latter half of the eighteenth century Spain decided that Trinidad had become more of a burden than an asset. Consequently, during the revitalization program of the Spanish Empire under Charles III (1759–88), the Crown finally opened the island to foreign settlement. Thus began the next major stage of Trinidadian history, when it would finally nurture a significant Creole population that, with the aid first of African and then of East Indian and Chinese labor forces, would produce a cash crop sufficient to support further growth and development of the colony.

In 1776, as part of its revitalization program, the Crown put into effect a new settlement policy that allowed the immigration and subsequent settlement of Catholic Europeans from the rest of the Caribbean (Brereton 1981, 11). Promises of substantial land grants and a friendly, pro-Catholic government first attracted the French Catholics of nearby British and chiefly Protestant Grenada. The French planters and their slaves arrived in increasingly large numbers during the latter part of the eighteenth century. The year 1783 ushered in a period of rapid development that would forever change the face of Trinidad. That year marked the beginning of African slave labor on the island, which lasted until 1834. After full emancipation of the African slaves occurred in 1838, East Indians and Chinese arrived in the 1840s and 1850s to fill the consequent labor shortage in the productive sugar industry.

In the meantime, yet another European power was making its presence known. Toward the end of the eighteenth century the powerful and extensive British Empire could no longer overlook the growing economic and strategic importance of Trinidad. In 1797, Admiral Sir Ralph Abercromby led British forces against an outmanned and outgunned Spanish force and took the island with hardly a fight (Williams 1964, 49). The Treaty of Amiens in 1802 formally ceded Trinidad to Britain (Black et al. 1976, 45), which ruled until 1962, when the twin-island nation of Trinidad and Tobago achieved independence.

The British did not begin to assert themselves socially and culturally until approximately forty years after gaining control. The period of Anglicization that began in the 1840s, however, eventually became a serious threat to French Creole cultural hegemony. Tensions between British Protestants and French Creole Catholics were assuaged toward the end of the nineteenth century, when the British government recognized the Anglican and Catholic churches as state equals and disbursed financial aid to both in an equitable fashion. By that time, however, French Creole culture had already begun to wane, since school curricula were being Anglicized and English was quickly becoming the language of instruction. By the turn of the century, most of those of French Creole ancestry no longer spoke French (Brereton 1981, 122).

There are few historical accounts of the early development of the non-European residents of Trinidad during the colonial period, for

tensions between the French and English sections became so absorbing to the white elite that they seemed to ignore altogether the non-white majority. The white society was curiously isolated from the wider island milieu. It seemed possible to ignore the existence of non-whites except as domestics and labourers. When upper-class Trinidadians spoke of "our heterogeneous society," as they often did, they were thinking of the national divisions in white society: English, French, Spanish, German, Italian. (Brereton 1981, 121)

TABLE 1
Ethnic Populations of Trinidad

Ethnic Group	Number	% of Total
Indian	428,539	42.17
African	393,896	38.76
Mixed	170,859	16.81
White	9,780	0.96
Chinese	5,528	0.54
Syrian/Lebanese	931	0.09
Not Stated	3,982	0.39
Other	2,724	0.27

Source: *Annual Statistical Digest* (1988, 14); my calculations.

The situation has changed little today. Virtually all the whites (about 1 percent of the total population) have sequestered themselves both culturally and geographically, primarily in sections north and west of Port of Spain. Whites generally do not participate in the island's cultural activities. During the course of my work in the many Orisha shrines and Spiritual Baptist churches, for example, I observed only two Trini whites in attendance.

The majority nonwhite population was making its presence felt by the end of the nineteenth century. Africans and East Indians, especially, had already begun to develop cultural and social institutions that would eventually become salient and integral parts of the sociocultural fabric of Trinidad. The twentieth century was to belong to the domestic servants and fieldhands, who eventually led the march toward independence from British rule, while the white Creoles became minor players in the island's history. Trinidad has given the world the renowned writer V. S. Naipaul, the noted Marxist scholar C.L.R. James, and the historian and statesman Eric Williams. It is the birthplace of calypso and the steel band and annually stages one of the largest pre-Lenten carnivals in the world.

The presence of so many different peoples, none of whom constitute a clear majority, is rare in the world and is especially unusual in the Caribbean, where the dominant demographic group on most islands is of African origin. The 1980 census figures show a total Trinidadian population of 1,016,239, of whom 80.93 percent are African and Indian (in roughly equal proportions). The number of persons in each

TABLE 2
African and Indian Populations of Western Trinidad

County	African		Indian	
	No.	*%*	*No.*	*%*
St. George	226,308	50.24	104,777	23.26
Victoria	65,362	29.66	126,450	57.37
Caroni	27,998	19.94	99,539	70.90
St. Patrick	46,712	37.70	61,855	49.92

Source: Annual Statistical Digest (1988, 14); my calculations.

ethnic group and its percentage of the total population of Trinidad are given in Table 1. The significant percentage in the "mixed" category is an indication of the general tolerance for miscegenation.

Population density is highest in the western part of the island, where the counties of St. George, Caroni, Victoria, and St. Patrick account for approximately 92 percent of the total. This is the result of settlement patterns during the early period of Spanish missionary activity and the later colonial period, when sugar plantations were concentrated in this area. The numbers and percentages of the two major ethnic groups in these counties are shown in Table 2. Africans tend to predominate in the north (St. George County); Indians predominate in the south (Victoria, Caroni, and St. Patrick Counties) as a result of their becoming the primary labor force in the cane fields there after emancipation in 1838.

A tendency toward racial or ethnic tolerance is evident in many different spheres of social interaction. For example, when Trinidad achieved its independence in 1962, two primary political parties existed: the Democratic Labor Party (DLP); and the People's National Movement (PNM), led during most of its existence by Eric Williams, historian, Oxford-educated scholar, and prime minister of Trinidad from 1956 until his death in 1981. During the early period of independence, the predominantly African PNM and the European/Indian DLP pursued a policy of political segregation along ethnic lines. The present-day political climate, however, reflects a trend toward the racial or ethnic integration of political parties. The leader of the PNM, Prime Minister Patrick Manning, and the leader of one of the major opposition parties, the National Alliance for Reconstruction (NAR), A.N.R. Robinson, are both African, but neither party can be said to be dominated by the interests of a particular ethnic group. The third major political party, the United National Congress (UNC), is headed by an Indian, Basdeo Panday. (The DLP is no longer in existence.) While it is true that some UNC officials have spoken of "Indian alienation" from the society at large and raised other racially charged topics, my impression is that the general public, both African and Indian, find "race talk" distasteful and somewhat anachronistic.

Nonetheless, many signs of racial or ethnic prejudice and segregation do still exist, vestiges of a sociocultural dynamic that was formed in the nineteenth century, when Indians established rural and agricultural settlement patterns and Africans migrated to urban areas. The Indians, consequently, became associated primarily with agricultural work, and the Africans with civil service occupations. The agricultural label proved to be something of a burden to the Indians, who found it difficult to break away from the pattern and move into occupations of higher status. As late as the 1960s, only 11 percent of civil service employees and less than 3 percent of the police force were Indian (Black et al. 1976, 92). This imbalance has since improved considerably, however, with Indians now entering the civil service ranks in increasing numbers.

Although both Indians and Africans live throughout Trinidad, the distribution of ethnic groups greatly influences the cultural flavors of the north and south. In Port of Spain to the north, the major urban area in St. George County, Africans dominate the markets, stores, churches, and parks. Numerous shops trade in the crafts, oils, clothes, hats, and so on associated with the Rastafarian or, more generally, African lifestyle. The impromptu gatherings of debaters, musicians, vendors, and worshipers in Woodford Square are almost exclusively African. The predominantly African Spiritual Baptists hold outdoor worship services in "town" (the Trini term for Port of Spain) almost every day, singing and praying in the parks and squares. African street vendors hawk their Jamaican-style reggae and rap cassette tapes, salted and fresh (unsalted) peanuts, cigarettes, candy, newspapers, leather sandals (crafted by Rastafarians), and clothing.

If one travels approximately twenty-five kilometers south, however, down the Uriah Butler Highway to Chaguanas, one is surrounded by Indians and the Indian life-style. Here in the heart of Caroni County,

Indian sidewalk vendors hawk their "doubles," two small flat pieces of fried bread wrapped around *channa* (chickpeas) and peppers in a curry-based sauce. One of the most successful Hindu temples in Trinidad is located just south of Chaguanas in Edinburgh. Indians dominate the stores, markets, and sidewalks. Only a few shops catering to the Rastafarian life-style can be found, and peanut vendors, who tend to be almost exclusively African, are virtually nonexistent here.

A general trend toward Westernization has left its mark on the sociocultural fabric of Trinidad, but many traditional elements remain, especially in the Indian communities. According to Morton Klass (1961, 3), as late as the 1950s, rural Indian village life reflected a strong sentiment toward things Indian, including "village exogamy, caste endogamy, Hinduism, and 'Hawaiian Cousin' kinship terminology." The village he studied was "a highly integrated, cohesive community, . . . structurally [East] Indian rather than West Indian." During the nineteenth century, the British government gave Indians the opportunity to purchase land, a policy, according to Klass, that greatly facilitated the retention of traditional values and customs; he adds, however, that the Old World Indian caste system was less prevalent in Trinidad (Klass 1961, 22, 56). For example, occupation is not caste-linked, as it is in India (Niehoff and Niehoff 1960, 90–91), a fact that has perhaps eased the assimilation of Indians into Trinidadian social life.

This assimilation has gradually become more noticeable. The number of Hindi speakers seems to be declining, since the language is no longer a standard part of Indian enculturation. Traditional or arranged marriages are not as common as they once were. Indians are beginning to make their mark on the calypso music industry, and Western rock-and-roll has become popular among young Indians.

Nevertheless, although the social distance separating Africans and Indians in Trinidad has decreased, it is still evident. According to both groups, for example, when visiting soccer and cricket teams from India or Guyana play the Trinidadian teams, Trini Indians cheer for the visitors. Vera Rubin (1962) argued that Indians tend to support their community first because it is their own, while Africans support the nation as a whole because they consider it to be a "Negro nation." An important factor here is the historical context of African "immigration" as compared with Indian immigration. Since most Africans came to Trinidad as slaves, their traumatic relocation to the New World severely disrupted their traditional life-styles. The Indians, on the other hand, came as voluntary indentured laborers, and changes in their traditional life-styles were no more than what would be expected in any unforced, migratory movement. While African "survivals" are still evident in Trinidad (see, e.g., Elder 1988), the Orisha religion being perhaps the most obvious example, traditional African culture has not been nearly as salient and pervasive as traditional Indian culture.

The tendency of Indians to put Indian culture before Trini culture and that of Africans to think in terms of nation rather than community are also evident in the island's religious life. The Hindu religion is ethnically endogamous; the Afro-American religions are not, as reflected by the salient presence of Indians in both the Spiritual Baptist and Orisha religions.

Ethnic relations between European-derived Creoles and Africans in Trinidad, and the Caribbean as a whole, are largely predicated on correlations involving skin color and socioeconomic status. According to Michael Lieber (1981, 13), the fundamental dichotomy in the realm of values, attitudes, and sociocultural institutions in the Caribbean can be attributed to the perceived separation between European Creoles and Africans. The interaction between Europeans and Africans, though an important aspect of Caribbean sociocultural development, has had little impact on Afro-American religions in Trinidad in recent years, a fact that can no doubt be attributed to the virtual absence of whites in Afro-American religion and in the broader cultural affairs of the island.

Especially in regard to African-Indian relations, then, Trinidad represents something akin to what E. K. Francis (1976, 383) calls a "demotic society," an ethnically heterogeneous and complex society that is ultimately linked to a centralized political organization. Deep-rooted traditional sentiment and general geographical segregation in Trinidad — trademarks of a peaceful and culturally pluralistic society, according to Chester Hunt and Lewis Walker (1974, 7) — act to temper any tendency toward assimilation and integration.

Eclectic Trinidadian culture is being modified by off-island influences, however. American football and basketball are gaining in popularity. CNN (the Atlanta-based Cable News Network) is broadcast every day and, during the weekends, all night as well. Television programming is dominated by American soap operas, dramas, game shows, and situation comedies. The Latin American influence of nearby South America has also left its mark on Trinidadian culture in the form of a Christmas music custom known as *parang*. Finally, as a

Caribbean island, Trinidad has adopted some cultural traits that can best be described as West Indian — illustrated, for example, by Rastafarianism from Jamaica.

As a developing nation, the Republic of Trinidad and Tobago is somewhat anomalous in that it has been healthy financially, in large part thanks to the refining of oil drawn from local reserves. In fact, it was lending money to its neighbors as recently as the 1960s. Trinidad has recently undergone an economic downturn, however. The island had never developed a tourist industry to match those found in many other Caribbean islands, and attempts are now being made to diversify the economy along these lines. Still, the per capita income of Trinidad and Tobago, $3,070 US, is among the highest in the area; Barbados, at $5,250 US has the highest (*World Factbook* 1990, 312, 27). The existence of satellite television, the availability of American television programming and movies, and a booming video rental business have all been made possible, no doubt, by a relatively healthy economy.

The influence of all the varied elements of Trini culture is especially noteworthy in the religious life of Trinidad, which includes Catholicism, Hinduism, Islam, Anglicanism, Protestantism (Pentecostals, Seventh Day Adventists, Jehovah's Witnesses, Presbyterians, Methodists, Baptists, and Moravians), Christian Scientists, and Afro-American (Spiritual Baptist and Orisha) religions (see Table 3). Trinidadians may

TABLE 3
Religious Affiliations and Membership Totals

Religion	Number	Percentage
Roman Catholic	343,963	33.85
Hindu	262,740	25.85
Anglican	141,289	13.90
Muslim	63,227	6.22
Presbyterian	40,226	3.96
Pentecostal	34,257	3.37
Baptist	24,390	2.40
Adventist	22,069	2.17
Methodist	11,164	1.10
Jehovah Witness	7,732	0.76
Other	55,680	5.48
None	9,502	0.93

Source: Annual Statistical Digest (1988, 15); my calculations.

share a general way of life, but when it comes to religion there is a distinct parting of ways: the Hindus have their temples, the Moslems their mosques, the Catholics and Protestants their churches, and the *orisha* worshipers their shrines. So although Trinis carry out their daily affairs in the context of a highly complex but integrated sociocultural system, in the religious sphere segregation (in regard to beliefs and affiliation) and a rigidly defined pluralism are the norm.

The one glaring exception to the general rule of religious segregation is the Afro-American religious complex. An unwitting visitor venturing into an Orisha compound for the first time, for example, is confronted with a dizzying array of symbols and paraphernalia. Some compounds have an almost surrealistic appearance, with their juxtaposing and sometimes outright blending of Christian, African, Hindu, and Kabbalistic components. It is not uncommon to see symbols and paraphernalia from all these traditions inside one small structure that serves alternatively as an Orisha *chapelle*, a Spiritual Baptist church, and even, on rare occasions, a Kabbalah room.

The same confusing degree of eclecticism is evident in the beliefs and practices of the entire Afro-American religious complex in Trinidad. Those who are affiliated with all or part of this complex participate in a form of worship that is highly multicultural, comprising elements drawn from a number of traditions. The complex can be broken down analytically into three basic components — the Spiritual Baptist religion, the Orisha religion, and the Kabbalah — but in reality the situation is much more complicated.

The Spiritual Baptist religion comprises what we can call "orthodox" and "nonorthodox" groups. Orthodox worship is highly "Protestantized"; nonorthodox worship is somewhat Africanized. The two forms do not constitute a dichotomy, however, but rather fall somewhere on a continuum according to the degree to which they contain Protestant or African elements.

The Orisha religion is African-derived but includes in its worship complex the beliefs, rituals, and material culture not only of Yoruba *orisha* worship but also of Catholicism and, to some extent, Protestantism and Hinduism. Well over 50 percent of *orisha* worshipers are also Spiritual Baptists and participate in the activities of both religions on a regular basis.

The Kabbalah is an esoteric and sophisticated religious system based on the beliefs and practices of various arcane philosophies

brought to Trinidad by Spanish, French, or, possibly, English colonizers. (Though the Kabbalah is Jewish in origin, with roots in the Old
World, the term refers here to a derivative form resulting from a
unique pattern of development on this island.) Most Kabbalah practitioners (again, well over 50 percent) are also either Spiritual Baptists or
orisha worshipers or both. The picture is further complicated by the
fact that some of those who affiliate with the Afro-American religious
complex also practice Catholicism. In a questionnaire sample of forty-
two *orisha* worshipers, for example, ten said that they participated in
the activities of the Catholic Church as well.

The Spiritual Baptist and Orisha religions have been involved in a
reciprocal exchange of religious elements for years, an exchange that
has given rise to the nonorthodox Spiritual Baptists. Most of the orthodox Spiritual Baptist churches, by contrast, have resisted the influence
of the highly Africanized Orisha religion. The Kabbalah has remained
far more distinct as a religious system; there has been very little exchange of beliefs and practices between it and the Spiritual Baptist and
Orisha religions, even though they may be practiced side by side.

The Orisha religion, by far the most eclectic and syncretic of the
three, began as a transplanted West African (Yoruba) religion and
through time gradually took on Catholic, Protestant, and Hindu elements, in that order. Its complexity and eclecticism can be attributed,
at least in part, to colonial activity in Trinidad. The Spanish, French,
and English all made their influence felt here at one time or another,
bringing with them Catholicism, Anglicanism, Protestantism (in its
many forms), and probably the Kabbalah as well. Their enslavement of
peoples from western and west-central Africa brought a number of
African religious traditions to the island, most important among them
the Ewe/Fon, and the Kongolese; their post-emancipation encourage-
ment of African migration from Sierra Leone and Saint Helena resulted in a significant Yoruba cultural influence among plantation
workers; and their enticement of East Indians to work as indentured
servants brought Hinduism and Islam. The Orisha religion was originally dominated by lower-class Africans, and they still constitute a
large segment of the membership; however, *orisha* worshipers now
include business executives, military officers, university students, government workers from ministers on down, and others drawn from the
middle and upper classes.

Because of its complexity and the fact that some *orisha* worshipers are also Spiritual Baptists and Kabbalah practitioners, the Orisha religion can help us understand something about aspects of Afro-American religious worship in Trinidad in general. Traditionally, religion has been viewed as a harmonious blend of beliefs and rituals, combining to form a coherent whole. Many scholars conceive of religion as a smoothly functioning system of worship and devotion that individuals can depend on to give direction and stability to their lives. This is not necessarily the case with Orisha. Like any other religion, of course, it guides and enriches the lives of its practitioners, but the nature of this guidance and enrichment varies considerably through time and from shrine to shrine. There is no written liturgy or even a generally agreed-upon oral liturgy. There is no generally recognized governing body, although the organization called Opa Orisha (Shango) may eventually achieve such status (see Chapter Nine). And there is no standard process by which one becomes a member. There is, in short, no particular form of worship that is considered standard or proper by the group as a whole. Some Orisha *mongba* and *iya* (an *iya*, the female counterpart to a *mongba*, is a priestess who directs the rites and ceremonies of the religion) choose to recite Christian prayers before calling down the *orisha* at the annual feasts; some do not. Some *mongba* and *iya* are active Spiritual Baptists and may even direct Spiritual Baptist services; others choose not to affiliate with that tradition. Hindu flags and paraphernalia are displayed prominently at some Orisha shrines and not at all at others. Some *orisha* worshipers believe that the Kabbalah augments and complements Orisha beliefs and practices; others consider it diabolical or even satanic.

Orisha, then, is not a religious system in the strict sense of the term but an amorphous collection of individuals linked by a shared tendency to tolerate many forms of religious worship. The resulting configuration of beliefs and practices is often the source of confusion and conflict, as the following example illustrates.

On April 15, 1989, a well-known shrine head conducted a pilgrimage to the sea on the east coast, near Salybia, where he offered a burnt sheep to Shango. Although the ceremony attracted a large number of worshipers, many *mongba*, *iya*, and other worshipers chose, on theological grounds, not to attend. They objected primarily to the burning of the offering and secondarily to the location by the sea. Even though an *orisha* may on rare occasions manifest itself during an annual feast and order the burning of an animal slain in his or her name, these believers felt that a burnt offering is usually made for personal reasons, often with malicious intentions, and some attributed such motives to persons involved in this incident. And because Shango is not a water power, they felt that the seaside location was not appropriate. Moreover, the oral liturgy in this case deviated greatly from even the most generally acceptable range of liturgical patterns. This pilgrimage generated a lot of gossip and discussion. Some criticized it categorically — one *mongba*, for example, called the ceremony blasphemous — but the offering confused many rank-and-file members. To complicate popular attitudes toward the event further, the shrine head who conducted it died shortly after the ceremony, and those who objected to the pilgrimage viewed his death as confirming their objections.

Confusing rites and practices like this one are common, much to the chagrin of the worshipers. Even though the range of acceptable devotional patterns is broad, certain individuals step outside this range and operate in ways that are sometimes unique. Admissible behavior ranges from forms of worship that are thought effective by some worshipers to those that are considered a waste of time; none of these, however, are considered heretical or blasphemous. Actual behavior includes these forms and more, including behavior that some *orisha* worshipers consider improper or even heretical.

Of course, every religion has its "black sheep," its heretical factions. But Orisha is unusual in this respect. A significant proportion of *orisha* worshipers participate in Kabbalah ceremonies (of a sample of forty-two, eighteen said that they had attended a Kabbalah banquet during the previous year); others consider such practices anathema. Well over half of *orisha* worshipers believe that the Yoruba *orisha* and the Catholic saints are two sides of the same coin, so to speak; many others see no relationship whatever between them. Physical settings differ from shrine to shrine; the *orisha* (or *orisha*/saints) that are prominently displayed at one shrine may not appear at all at another. The significance of this variation is reflected in the fact that although Trinidad is a small enough island to allow the *orisha* worshiper to visit a number of different shrines (there are more than 150), I have sometimes seen worshipers who were entering a particular shrine for the first time unable to identify some of the *orisha* displayed there.

An underlying factor at work here further encourages variability. Orisha practitioners greatly respect the ability to manipulate a variety of religious symbols and practices; virtually all the ranking shrine heads

TABLE 4
Historical Events Significant to the Orisha Religion

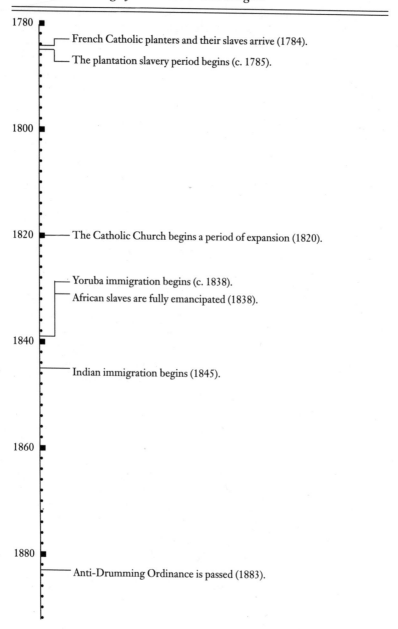

1780

— French Catholic planters and their slaves arrive (1784).

— The plantation slavery period begins (c. 1785).

1800

1820 —— The Catholic Church begins a period of expansion (1820).

— Yoruba immigration begins (c. 1838).
— African slaves are fully emancipated (1838).

1840

— Indian immigration begins (1845).

1860

1880

— Anti-Drumming Ordinance is passed (1883).

TABLE 4
Continued

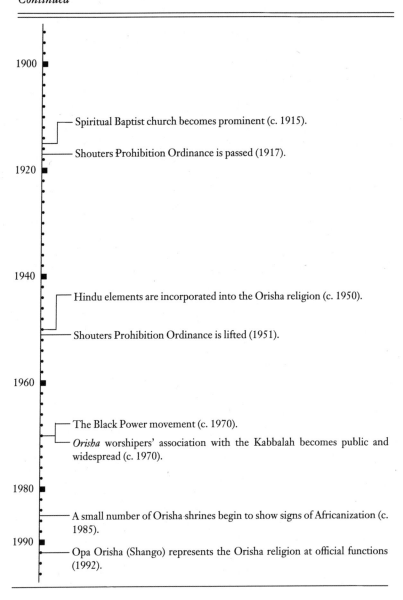

1900

Spiritual Baptist church becomes prominent (c. 1915).

Shouters Prohibition Ordinance is passed (1917).

1920

1940

Hindu elements are incorporated into the Orisha religion (c. 1950).

Shouters Prohibition Ordinance is lifted (1951).

1960

The Black Power movement (c. 1970).

Orisha worshipers' association with the Kabbalah becomes public and widespread (c. 1970).

1980

A small number of Orisha shrines begin to show signs of Africanization (c. 1985).

1990

Opa Orisha (Shango) represents the Orisha religion at official functions (1992).

have considerable expertise in this regard. Thus, although the number of *mongba* and *iya* is small, their idiosyncratic influence on the form and development of the religion is disproportionately large.

Because religious ideology on the level of the individual is constantly challenged, the potential for change or at least adjustment is always there. *Orisha* worship is truly an existential enterprise, since the individual actively engages in a constant struggle to merge her or his personal ideology with a perceived group ideology. Worship is an exercise in "becoming" in the Hegelian sense of the term; it is a dialectic pushed to extremes. Regardless of whether the discussion involves the basic tenets of the religion or specific ritual details, there seem to be as many opinions and ideas as there are worshipers. Still, there is a religion here, a group one can refer to as *orisha* worshipers. The tenuous web constructed by the worshipers may be showing signs of wear and tear in certain areas, but it is a web nonetheless.

What is striking about Orisha is that the being/nothingness/becoming dialectic, rather than simply being the driving force behind the construction of social reality, has taken over the whole process; it is not only change or potential for change that disrupts the day-to-day existence of *orisha* worshipers but the rate at which change is occurring. For example, the incorporation of elements of Hinduism and the increased involvement in the ceremonies of the Kabbalah has taken place within only the last thirty or so years. (A summary of significant events affecting the historical development of the Orisha religion is illustrated in the form of a timeline in Table 4.)

The Afro-American religious complex in Trinidad has had ample opportunity to draw on a number of other religious traditions in this culturally rich island. A tendency toward eclecticism, one of the defining characteristics of the religions of sub-Saharan Africa, has been carried over to their New World counterparts: for example, Umbanda, Candomblé, Santería, and Vodoun, as well as Orisha. A religious system cannot expand indefinitely, however. If it did, the collection of beliefs and practices would undoubtedly become so diffuse as to be incomprehensible to the majority of its worshipers. This level of confusion may not be far off for the Orisha religion.

But reactive or tempering nativistic mechanisms and processes have arisen to counteract this expansion — specifically, a renewed emphasis on African "roots," which has most recently involved a tendency among a handful of shrine heads to expurgate the Christian and Hindu elements from *orisha* worship and to return to a liturgy that is exclusively Yoruba (the Kabbalah, which is supplemental to *orisha* worship, does not directly affect it). This Africanization process, an important transformative mechanism of religious practice and ideology in the Orisha religion (see Chapters Nine and Thirteen), differs from shrine to shrine and takes many different forms, but it essentially involves the ascendancy of African elements at the expense of other, "extraneous" elements.

Viewed with a wide-angle lens, then, the Orisha religion presents a picture of tension, both on the everyday level of worshiper interaction and on the more conceptual level of the religious system itself, where basic components are involved in a lively dynamic that is the religion's life force.

Part II

FOUR

African Roots of the
Orisha Religion

The *Orisha religion in Trinidad,* like the other African-derived
religions of the New World, originated during the colonial
period when European colonizers brought in millions of Africans
to work on sugar, cotton, and tobacco plantations. From the mid-
fifteenth century, when the Portuguese began to colonize certain eastern Atlantic islands (the Azores, Cape Verde, the Madeiras), until 1888,
when Brazil abolished slavery, the slave trade greatly affected virtually
the entire Western Hemisphere, both socially and culturally.

The colonial economies were based on a variety of crops, including
cacao, cotton, tobacco, and sugar. It was sugar, however, that would
have the biggest impact on the New World colonial ventures:

The association of sugar cane, the slavery of transported Africans and the
large agricultural estates commonly called "plantations" is both intimate and
ancient — so much so that we need to be reminded how much that association
is an artifact of particular historical circumstances. Sugar cane has numerous
intrinsic characteristics — above all, that it must be ground as soon as it is cut,
to maximize its yield of sugar — but nothing says it must be grown only on
plantations, or only by slaves. Yet its importance in the expansion of European
agro-industry in this hemisphere so set the terms of its production that the
triadic image — plantations, sugar cane and African slaves — has come to
epitomize whole centuries of post-Columbian, Caribbean experience. (Mintz
1974, ix; cited in Knight 1983, 219)

The social and cultural transformation of virtually an entire hemisphere could be accomplished only with an incredible amount of human energy. The many estimates of the total number of Africans
shipped to the New World during the slave period range from Philip
Curtin's (1975, 107–8) estimate of 9.42 million to Paul Lovejoy's
(1983, 19) 11.7 million and Noel Deerr's (1949–50, 284) 11.77 million.

These figures, however, do not take into account the thousands of Africans who perished during the Middle Passage. Those mortality rates ranged from 26.6 per thousand per month for the British trade from Africa to Jamaica during the period 1791–98, to a high of 96.0 per thousand per month for the Dutch trade from Angola to the Caribbean during the period 1680–1749 (Cohn 1985, 689). The British slave trade of 1761–1807 loaded 1,529,180 slaves and landed 1,422,807; thus, 106,373, or nearly 7 percent, perished during the passage (Anstey 1975, 12).

The causes of death during both loading and passage included gastrointestinal disorders (such as dysentery), fevers (malignant, pleuritic, bilious, yellow), respiratory illnesses, scurvy, accidents, suicides, and insurrections (Steckel and Jensen 1986, 59–62).

Slaves were taken from various points in Africa and Madagascar (see Franco 1979, 93), but most scholars agree that the majority were from west-central Africa (in the area of present-day Zaire and Angola) and West Africa, that sub-Saharan region extending roughly from Senegal to Cameroon. In fact, a majority of the slaves shipped across the Atlantic until the latter part of the seventeenth century were from west-central Africa, and even later that area continued to account for a large share (Lovejoy 1983, 52).

During the critical period of the development of Afro-American culture in the New World, the eighteenth and first half of the nineteenth centuries, west-central Africa and the coastal areas of the Bight of Benin (extending roughly from eastern Ghana to western Nigeria) and the Bight of Biafra (from central Nigeria to western Cameroon) accounted for over 75 percent of the total number of Africans shipped to the Americas (Lovejoy 1983, 50, 141). In fact, according to Lovejoy's figures, approximately half of all African slaves brought to the New World arrived during the eighteenth century. Given that the Atlantic slave trade lasted approximately 420 years (1450–1870), this means that the colonial powers transported half of the total number of slaves to the New World during one-quarter of the slave trade period. It is not surprising that slave revolts reached a fever pitch during the eighteenth century in Jamaica, Haiti, Cuba, the Lesser Antilles, and elsewhere as colony demographics gradually shifted to reflect the large influx of Africans. Oruno Lara (1979, 103), in fact, views the history of the slave trade as a sequence of revolts, and Michael Craton (1982, 11–17) notes that slave revolt was a fundamental component in the structure of the colonial system. In a chronology of revolts in the colonies of Providence, Barbados, Bermuda, Jamaica, Antigua, St. Kitts, Guyana, the Bahamas, Belize, Grenada, St. Vincent, Tobago, Dominica, Tortola, St. Lucia, and Trinidad during the period of 1638–1837, Craton (1982, 335–39) lists seventy-five different events involving anywhere from "dozens" of people to "many thousands."

The situation deteriorated to the point where some colonists hired aboriginal peoples and even former slaves to fight the uprisings. In fact, by 1800 a British-led militia of Africans was in full operation in the Caribbean to defend the colonial plantation system against rebellious slaves (Buckley 1979, 140–41). The notion of the passive, obedient slave was, like many other claims made by Europeans, a myth that served only to assuage their guilt and justify their economic endeavors. Some runaway slaves were moderately successful in their attempts at establishing self-governing communities (Price 1973, 12). But because the manufactured goods they needed (such as guns and tools) could be obtained only from the plantations, they were never able to break free entirely, and this proved to be their undoing.

Although it is true that rebellions and revolts virtually defined colonist-slave relations in the New World, especially toward the end of the eighteenth century, the situation in Trinidad was somewhat anomalous. While other large Caribbean islands such as Haiti and Jamaica were suffering revolt after revolt, only one such threat of any consequence occurred in Trinidad during the slave period—the alleged Christmas "plot" discovered by the increasingly suspicious British in 1805—but no rebellion or revolt actually occurred (Brereton 1981, 48–49; Craton 1982, 235). In fact, with the exception of the tyrannical six-year reign of Governor Thomas Picton (1797–1802), the relatively humane slave policies of the Spanish (pre-Picton) and a growing humanitarian sentiment of the British Empire (post-Picton) largely defined and characterized relations among slaves, freed slaves, and Europeans in Trinidad.

The colonist/slave dynamic in its various New World forms was a significant factor in the development of African-derived religions. For example, Haitian Vodoun in its "hot" or Petro aspect reflects the revolutionary and survival-oriented sentiments of its early adherents; the Petro *loa*, or spirits, and their corresponding rites are part of a complex of beliefs and practices that can be termed aggressive and potentially malevolent. The structure and organization of the secretive Vodoun religion in Haiti toward the end of the eighteenth century provided the framework and foundation for a successful revolt (Laguerre 1989). Indeed, it was the "Petro cult" that provided the moral justification and organizational structure for the successful revolt against the colonizing French, beginning in 1791 (Deren 1991, 62).

In a general way, the Orisha religion in Trinidad shares many traits with the "cool" or Rada side of Haitian Vodoun but virtually none with the Petro side. Certainly, the relatively peaceful relations between Europeans and African slaves in Trinidad was a contributing factor to the differential development of Vodoun and Orisha: Haitians were forced to look outside the African religious tradition — a tradition characterized by centralization, compromise, syncretism, and eclecticism — for a religious system that incorporated the principles of decentralization, exclusivity, and malevolent aggression; Trinidadians were not.

The two possible sources of the Petro aspect in Haitian Vodoun, Native American religion and European Kabbalah, were present in Trinidad as well. The borrowing and subsequent incorporation of elements from those traditions may have been beneficial and perhaps even necessary for Vodoun, but such was not originally the case for Orisha. Interestingly, however, practitioners of the Orisha religion have recently begun to practice various Kabbalistic rites as well, many of which have malevolent or aggressive overtones (see Chapter Seven).

One reason for the relatively peaceful relations between Europeans and African slaves in Trinidad is that the duration of slave labor on the island was relatively brief: colonists did not begin plantation-style cultivation of sugar until the late 1700s (Hoetink 1979, 23), and complete emancipation occurred in 1838. The Spanish, French, and British imported approximately 22,000 African slaves into Trinidad (Curtin 1969, 68), the majority arriving at the end of the eighteenth century. In the 1600s there was a lucrative tobacco industry in Trinidad, followed in the 1700s by a successful cacao industry that gave way to cotton in the 1780s; none of these used slave labor to any great extent. Then the sugar industry began its ascendancy, and sugar cane soon became the primary cash crop. Sugar production was bolstered in 1784 by the "first wave of French immigration" — mainly from Martinique, Dominica, and Grenada — which transformed Trinidad into "virtually a French colony" comprising mainly "French planters, French free coloureds and African slaves whose cultural orientation was French West Indian" (Brereton 1981, 22).

The arrival of the French and Africans greatly affected the demographics of the island. For example, in 1782 there were only 2,811 people in Trinidad, of whom 126 were whites, 295 were free people of color, 310 were slaves, and 2,080 were aboriginal Indians. Seven years later the total had jumped by 464 percent to 13,053, of whom 1,432 were aboriginal Indians, 5,170 were whites and free people of color, and 6,451 were slaves (John 1988, 40). The slaves were concentrated in the northwestern and west-central areas of the island, the region around Port of Spain having the greatest number (Higman 1984, 90).

According to B. W. Higman (1979, 44), 40.5 percent of the African-born slaves in Trinidad originated in the Bight of Biafra coastal area; for the period 1813–27, fully 41.2 percent with 19.1 percent hailing from west-central Africa. The only other area to claim more than 10 percent was Senegambia (12.2 percent) in extreme western Africa. In 1813, when the Igbo and Moco near the Bight of Biafra and the Kongo of west-central Africa accounted for approximately 20 percent each, the Yoruba (from Nigeria) made up only 1 percent or so (Higman 1984, 127, 132). During the period 1838–70, however, a significant number of Africans emigrated from Sierra Leone and St. Helena to the New World, and the Yoruba "constituted a significant percentage of the liberated Africans [freed from slave ships by the British] coming to . . . Trinidad" (Trotman 1976, 2). Of all the African peoples in nineteenth-century Trinidad, the Yoruba and the Kongolese were the most numerous (Warner-Lewis 1991, 19).[1]

In addition to the African-born slaves in Trinidad, there were also Creole slaves, those born in the New World. In fact, a significant number of Trinidadian slaves were not African-born: in 1813, 11,633 were Creole, and 13,968 were African-born. Most of the Creoles were born in Trinidad, but some came there from other West Indian islands. Beginning in 1813, Governor Ralph Woodford invited slaveowners from neighboring islands to settle in Trinidad with their slaves (Brereton 1981, 56), and between 1813 and 1816, 2,000 slaves were brought in from the surrounding area, most from Grenada (324), Dominica (167), and Guadaloupe (159) (John 1988, 48, 46).

Though not complete, these figures do give some idea of the makeup of the slave population in Trinidad. The slaves were approximately equally African-born and Creole, the former originating primarily in the Bight of Biafra area and secondarily in west-central Africa. Approximately 60 percent of the African-born slaves were Igbo,

Moco, and Kongolese. The Creoles were mostly Trinidad-born, plus a small number from other islands. The Yoruba were not a significant presence until after 1838, when their numbers grew significantly.

The British abolished slavery in 1834, although apprenticeship continued until 1838, when the slaves were completely emancipated. Emancipation coupled with the influx of significant numbers of *orisha*-worshiping Yoruba during that time probably provided the foundation of the Orisha religion in Trinidad. George Brandon (1989–90, 207) draws a similar conclusion in regard to the early development of Santería in Cuba.

As the numbers of Africans in the New World steadily increased during the seventeenth, eighteenth, and nineteenth centuries, they began to influence dramatically the cultures and societies of Brazil, the Caribbean, the southern United States, and other areas. Perhaps the most salient manifestation of African culture in the New World is found in religion: in Vodoun, Santería, Candomblé, Orisha, and others.

Of the hundreds of ethnic and tribal affiliations represented by the Africans who were shipped to the New World during the centuries of Atlantic slave trade, a few tended to exert more cultural influence in the New World than others. In the domain of religion, the influence and prevalence of the following groups have been noted: the Fon in Haiti, Brazil, French Guiana, and the United States; the Yoruba in Brazil, Cuba, Trinidad, and the United States; the Fanti-Ashanti in Surinam, Jamaica, and French Guiana; and the Kongolese in Brazil and Haiti (Bastide 1972; Brandon 1990; Herskovits 1941, 1966; Mulira 1990; and Simpson 1965, 1978, 1980). With the exception of the Kongolese, all these groups are found in the eastern portion of West Africa from Ghana eastward to southwestern Nigeria.

As we have seen, most of the Africans imported to the New World originated more or less equally in west-central Africa and the area stretching roughly from Ghana to Cameroon. Consequently, the stronger influence of ethnic or tribal groups from Ghana to Nigeria on the African-derived religions of the New World, relative to that of west-central African cultures, seems rather puzzling. (Kongolese elements are found in Afro-American religions but do not appear to be as prevalent as those of the Yoruba, Fon, and Fanti-Ashanti.) But the figures are problematic only if we assume that the demographics of

African-born slaves brought to the New World correlate positively with subsequent cultural influence (see Bastide 1972, 11). It is significant that the Kongolese, unlike the Yoruba, Fon, and Fanti-Ashanti, are generally not polytheistic; in fact, only certain ritual experts among them recognize a class of "mysterious spirits," or *bisimbi* (Thompson 1983, 107). The lack of a prevalent or salient Kongolese influence in the African-derived religions of the New World can, perhaps, be attributed to the absence of a complex and widely recognized pantheon of gods, an absence that precluded or at least impeded syncretism or association with the Catholic saints.

It would be misleading to speak of "an African religion" or even "a West African religion," as though a coherent and strictly defined corpus of religious beliefs and practices existed. As a family of religions, however, those in West Africa, particularly in the area ranging from Ghana to Nigeria, do share a number of general or basic beliefs and practices. The Asante or Ashanti (McLeod 1981; Parrinder 1970), the Fon (Argyle 1966; Parrinder 1970), and the Yoruba (Awolalu 1979; Bascom 1969; Ellis 1894), for example, all share a belief in a withdrawn high god, intermediary deities, and lower or earthbound spirits. All three groups practice blood sacrifice, spirit possession (generally interpreted positively as the manifestation of a deity in the body of the worshiper), ancestor worship, and herbal healing based on similar beliefs and practices. All these elements are found in various Afro-American religions in similar form: Vodoun in Haiti (Haskins 1978; Lowenthal 1978; Metraux 1972; Simpson 1945), Orisha in Trinidad (Herskovits and Herskovits 1964; Houk 1986, 1992; Mischel 1957; Mischel and Mischel 1958; Simpson 1962, 1964, 1965), Santería in Cuba (Brandon 1989–90), Umbanda in Brazil (Bastide 1972, 1978), and Batuque (an offshoot of Umbanda) in Belém, Brazil (Leacock and Leacock 1972).

West African and Afro-American religions are similar in many ways, even when specific elements are compared.[2] The deities of the Yoruba religion in southwestern Nigeria and the Orisha religion in Trinidad and the beliefs associated with them, for example, are often virtually identical.

The notion of a supreme being is represented in the Yoruba religion by Olodumare. He is considered to be the creator or at least the oldest of the deities, but there is no specific shrine or group of worshipers associated with him. The Yoruba believe that Olodumare has a particular sphere of influence and is not a force in areas thought to be out of his domain. They also believe that Eshu (discussed below) can contact Olodumare on the worshiper's behalf. Although Olodumare was not found in Trinidad by the other researchers noted above, he was in fact popular — by that name — among the *orisha* worshipers I interviewed. As among the Yoruba, he occupies the central position in the supreme godhead and is considered to be the first of the *orisha*, giving rise, at least indirectly, to the other deities. Because of his lofty standing and his perceived remoteness from the sphere of everyday activity, there are no shrines or worship activities for Olodumare in Trinidad, but, as in Nigeria, Eshu is thought to mediate between Olodumare and humans.

In the Yoruba religion, Eshu (also called Elegba, Elegbara, or Eleggua; I provide the alternative names of deities in each case) is considered to be the divine messenger who mediates between man and the higher deities such as Olodumare. Eshu is a trickster and a general troublemaker, responsible for the misfortunes of man and deity alike. In Nigeria, not surprisingly, Christians and Muslims associate Eshu with Satan or the devil. In Trinidad, Eshu is virtually identical to his Nigerian counterpart; in fact, I heard all four of his names used at one time or another. He is a messenger to the other deities and a trickster who has the capacity to do great harm if he is not placated. He is also identified as Satan by some (but only a few) *orisha* worshipers, a tendency no doubt left over from the strong influence of the Catholic church in earlier times.

Other Yoruba deities also found in Trinidad include Ogun, the Yoruba god of iron, steel, and war; Shango, the Yoruba god of fire, thunder, and lightning; Odua (Odudua, Oduduwa), the creator of the earth; Shakpana (Shopona, Sopona, Sakpata), the Yoruba god of smallpox and other diseases; and Oshun, a Yoruba water goddess. These are referred to in Trinidad by the same names and are thought to have similar functions and abilities. Clearly, although specific rituals and practices may vary, Yoruba deities have been transported across the Atlantic relatively unscathed. This cultural persistence is also apparent in the lexicon of the Orisha religion in Trinidad.[3]

The sub-Saharan religious beliefs and practices that were brought to the New World combined with the Catholicism and Protestantism of the European colonizers, as well as New World aboriginal religions, to give birth to a variety of religious forms. Despite their diversity, all Afro-American religions exhibit at least some degree of syncretism involving African and European religious elements, and virtually all practice spirit possession. Syncretism and spirit possession are, perhaps, the two most important and salient characteristics of Afro-American religions. Syncretism, in fact, perhaps more than any other cultural process, has been the mechanism behind the development of such a diverse and broad group of religions. Some appear to be primarily Christian (such as the Spiritual Baptists of Trinidad and St. Vincent), some primarily African (Vodoun and Orisha), and some heavily spiritualist (Umbanda in Brazil). All, however, can be characterized as at least somewhat African in form.

The most comprehensive typology of Afro-American religions outside South America has been compiled by George Simpson (1978), whose classification includes five types: ancestral, spiritualist, religio-political, revivalist, and neo-African. His examples of the *ancestor cult* category include the Kumina and Convince groups in Jamaica and the Big Drum group of Grenada. According to Simpson (1978, 95), "The ancestral cult consists of a few essentials — the importance of the funeral, the need to assure the benevolence of the dead, and concern with descent and kinship." Afro-American ancestor worship does have an African flavor, but as Simpson elsewhere points out (1976, 293), it is generally less African than forms of worship found among the neo-African groups.

Spiritualist groups are found in Puerto Rico and Brazil. In Brazil spiritualist worship is a result of syncretism between "African religions, American Indian cults, Christianity, and spiritualism" (Simpson 1976, 297–98). In Puerto Rico it is organized around a medium who "attempts to deal with a vast range of problems, including disorders of personality in the broad, nontechnical sense of the term, by summoning, interrogating, and manipulating spirits of the dead" (Simpson 1978, 124).

Two *religio-political groups* in the Caribbean are both part of the Ras Tafari movement (Simpson 1978, 126, 129). The Rastafarians in Jamaica have six basic doctrines that generally focus on the ethnic and racial superiority of Africans and their eventual return to their homeland, Ethiopia (Simpson 1955, 134–35). Simpson notes that there are Rastafarians in Dominica as well, where they are known as Dreads. Rastafarians are also quite active in Trinidad (where they are called

"Rastas"), although most do not concern themselves with the issue of racial superiority, and few aspire to return to Ethiopia. Their philosophy is generally one of passivity, love, and tolerance for all peoples and their ideologies. The Rastas play an integral role in *orisha* worship in Trinidad (see Chapter Nine).

Revivalist groups are found primarily in Jamaica, Trinidad, St. Vincent, and Grenada. In Jamaica, for example, Pukumina (or Pocomania) recognizes a broad pantheon including "Old Testament prophets, New Testament saints, angels and archangels, Satan, Rutibel, and beings from the de Laurence books on the occult and magic"; its beliefs and practices with an African flavor include the "West African concept of multiple 'souls,'" the "ritual uses of stones, blood, and leaves," and the "use of drums and rattles, handclapping, and dancing" (Simpson 1976, 295–96; 1978, 111). At one end of the spectrum are the Spiritual Baptists, or "Shakers," of St. Vincent, whose beliefs and practices contain few African-derived elements. At the other end of the spectrum are the (nonorthodox) Spiritual Baptists of Trinidad, whose beliefs and practices contain many African-derived traits.

The Spiritual Baptist religion of St. Vincent is a fundamentalist Protestant sect thought to be an outgrowth of an early Methodist influence on the island. But like so many other Afro-American religious groups in the Caribbean, Brazil, and the United States, the St. Vincent Spiritual Baptists practice a form of worship that is an admixture of many different religious traditions:

> Shaker [Spiritual Baptist] beliefs and practices seem to be an eclectic blend of elements borrowed . . . from Anglicanism, Catholicism, and Pentecostalism; . . . traditional African elements that have been redesigned or retained; and unidentifiable elements, perhaps invented — all of which have been added to, and mingled with, the selected Methodist elements. (Henney 1974, 23)

The greater Africanization of the Spiritual Baptists in Trinidad, especially the nonorthodox, can be attributed to the presence there of a highly Africanized religion in the form of *orisha* worship; no such group exists in St. Vincent (Henney 1974, 84). I have found that the relationship between the Spiritual Baptists and *orisha* worshipers in Trinidad is indeed quite intimate; in practice, it is sometimes difficult to separate the two.

The religions of *neo-African groups*, as the name implies, contain many "Africanisms" and have a wide distribution in the New World, particularly in the Caribbean, Brazil, and the United States. Examples include Vodoun in Haiti and Louisiana; the various forms of Yoruba-derived *orisha* worship in Trinidad, Brazil, and Grenada; Santería in Cuba, Puerto Rico, and the United States; and Candomblé in Brazil. These are found in areas that have had a long association with the Catholic Church, beginning in colonial times. Consequently, the association or pairing of African gods and Catholic saints has occurred to varying degrees in virtually all these neo-African groups, although the associations are not equivalent from group to group.

Simpson's typology is informative and comprehensive; it does, however, have the drawback of throwing together some types that have almost nothing in common. For example, Simpson's revivalists include the orthodox Spiritual Baptists of Trinidad (the highly "Protestantized" faction), the Spiritual Baptists of St. Vincent, Pukumina in Jamaica, and certain African-American churches in the United States that are essentially Protestant, as well as the nonorthodox or Africanized Spiritual Baptists in Trinidad, who are highly African. And although the scheme purports to typologize Afro-American religious groups, it includes some which, like the spiritualists in Brazil, are hardly Africanized at all.

After reviewing the classifications constructed by Simpson and by I. M. Lewis (1971), Stephen Glazier concluded in 1979 that "a typology of Caribbean religions is [not] very useful at this time" because they "are in a constant state of flux; the dynamics of Caribbean religion should command most of our attention" (1979, 9). It is true that Afro-American religions are actively eclectic and syncretic, still undergoing change, and consequently difficult to categorize, but I do not agree that we should abandon the enterprise entirely. We should, rather, strive to improve on the work that has been done thus far.

A typology should be more than simply descriptive or heuristic; it should provide the foundation for a greater understanding of the things being typologized. In devising a typology of Afro-American religions, therefore, we should not overlook the obvious: the intermingling of Africans, Europeans, and aboriginal peoples in a colonial context has resulted in the development of a variety of religions that all include among their beliefs, practices, and paraphernalia certain African-derived traits in forms that may be highly reinterpreted, syncretic, or virtually unchanged. That is, it makes sense to develop a typology of

Afro-American religions based on their degree of Africanness, since such a classification emphasizes the primary link or connection among all the types. The religious groups that exhibit African-derived elements lie on a continuum ranging from the highly Christianized on one side to the highly Africanized on the other, with a significant amount of clustering at each end. For the purposes of this book, then, I propose that we designate those Afro-American religions that are highly Africanized—for example, Candomblé in Brazil, Vodoun in Haiti, and Orisha in Trinidad—as Type I groups (see Table 5). Type II would designate those that are highly Christianized—for example, the Spiritual Baptists in St. Vincent and Trinidad (the orthodox variety), the Revivalists in Jamaica, and the various African-American spiritual and pentecostal groups found in the United States.

The groups in each category seem to be linked by common threads, especially in regard to spirit possession, symbology, and syncretism. Most significant in this regard is the fact that the degree to which a particular group is Africanized or Christianized greatly influences possession behavior, descriptions of the spirit world, and the use of particular symbols.

The Type I groups, for example, were initially almost exclusively African. African religions (with the exception of the Kongolese) are highly polytheistic and thus easily syncretized with Catholicism, given its rich pantheon of saints and spirits. Possession in Type I groups—Vodoun in Haiti (Bourguignon 1970; Lowenthal 1978; Muñoz 1974), Candomblé in Brazil (Bastide 1978; Gordon 1979), and Orisha in Trinidad (Houk 1986, 1992; Simpson 1965)—have certain characteristics in common (see Table 5). Since worshipers attribute possession to various anthropomorphic spirits, a complex system of interpretation has developed so that particular spirits can be identified. Each spirit has its own character traits, and the association of spirits with distinct behavioral attributes in turn affects dissociative behavior, which must be somewhat standardized and animated if the possessing agent is to be identified. Finally, there is an individual orientation, because all possessions are potentially meaningful, involving as they do the manifestation of one of many different spirits. Individuals who become possessed usually become the focus of ritual activities and group attention.

The presence of Type II religious groups in the New World is largely the result of European and American missionary activities. Although many such groups have incorporated a few African elements

TABLE 5
A Typology of Afro-American Religions

Type I: Highly Africanized	Type II: Highly Christianized
RELIGION (LOCATION)	
Orisha (Trinidad)	Spiritual Baptists (Grenada,
Kumina (Jamaica)	Trinidad, St. Vincent, New York,
Candomblé (Brazil)	Montreal)
Umbanda (Brazil)	Revivalists (Jamaica)
Vodoun (Haiti, U.S. South)	African American Spiritualist (U.S.
Santería (Cuba, Puerto Rico, Miami,	South)
New York, New Orleans)	
SYNCRETISM	
strongly African	strongly Protestant
moderately Catholic	traces of African
POSSESSION	
anthropomorphic spirits	nonanthropomorphic spirit
standardized behavior	erratic behavior
animated behavior	behavior only somewhat animated
individual orientation	group orientation

into their worship, these are generally regarded as symbols having no necessary reference to African polytheism. For example, the chalk drawings of the Spiritual Baptists can be traced back to Kongolese cosmograms; libations of water, oil, milk, and so on interpreted almost entirely from a Christian perspective. The generally monotheistic tone of Protestantism has, of course, served to temper any assimilation of African polytheism. Possessions that occur in these Type II groups — for example, the Spiritual Baptists of St. Vincent (Bourguignon 1970; Henney 1974), the orthodox Spiritual Baptists of Trinidad, Jamaican Revivalists, and African-American Pentecostal groups in the United States (Griffith, English, and Mayfield 1980) — are characterized by certain common attributes (see Table 5). There is ordinarily only a single possessing agent — in almost all cases, the Holy Spirit, thought to be extremely ethereal and thus highly nonanthropomorphic (although a few unorthodox Spiritual Baptists do recognize possession by certain saints and Old Testament prophets, sometimes collectively referred to as "Baptist powers"). Since the identity of the possessing agent is virtually always known, there is no need for behavior in each case to be standardized or distinct. Finally, possession is "group oriented" because if each event is attributed to the same spirit, all individuals are, of course, possessed by this one spirit.

The possession attributes for each group are all manifestations of one general underlying notion: the group's perception of the spirit or spirits that are doing the possessing. In Type I groups, the possessing agent can be any one of a number of spirits who are thought to have different personalities, likes and dislikes, and characteristic abilities. Because a particular spirit may manifest itself only once on a given night, the individual who is possessed is the focus of attention during the possession. Since individuals in Type I groups are often possessed by the same spirit repeatedly, through time they become associated with that spirit by the rest of the group.

In the Type II groups, the possessing agent is a mystical entity that cannot be comprehended in everyday terms. On the one hand, there is no need for standardized possession behavior, because identification of the possessing agent is agreed upon and, thus, is not an issue. On the other hand, perhaps the reason the spirit is not conceived of anthropomorphically is that the chaotic and nonstandardized behavior of the possessed individual does not easily lend itself to characterization along these lines.

The beliefs and rituals of the Type I and Type II groups are largely affected by their respective conceptions of the spirit(s) they worship. The perceived Africanness of the spirits — that is, the degree to which this quality is thought to be present or absent — is undoubtedly the most significant factor in this regard, the highly Africanized groups being polytheistic and the highly Christianized groups tending toward monotheism.

FIVE

Catholicism and the Orisha Religion

O*n Easter Sunday,* March 26, 1989, I attended a prayer session in an Orisha shrine north of Chaguanas in the west-central part of Trinidad. The focus of activity was a small church at the rear of the compound. In the center of the church was a large table set elaborately with candles, cakes, liquor, milk, honey, crystal, candies, and other items. In some ways the table appeared to be ready for a Spiritual Baptist "thanksgiving" (an annual prayer ceremony), yet it also resembled the Kabbalah table that serves as the focal point for Kabbalah "banquets."

The first part of the session involved the "feeding of the children," a standard ceremony at many Spiritual Baptist gatherings, in which worshipers recite and sing Christian prayers and hymns. Near its conclusion the shrine head and his assistants distributed food among the children and sent them on their way. This part of the prayer session was symbolically and ritually homogeneous, and the proceedings were almost exclusively Christian in tone. After the children's prayers, however, the tone of worship changed, giving way to songs and supplications not only to *orisha* saints and Spiritual Baptist powers but also to Kabbalistic entities and Hindu deities.

As if to prepare those in attendance for what was to come, the shrine head began the second part of the session by speaking of the various powers represented in his compound. He told the Baptists in attendance that they should not be afraid of what they might see. He explained that the ceremony was an "open" one and that any number of powers or spirits might manifest themselves. During the next fourteen hours or so (5:00 P.M. to 7:00 A.M.) worshipers beat drums and sang songs to the *orisha*, said prayers to Hindu deities, sang hymns to Baptist powers, and recited incantations to Kabbalah entities. At least one spirit or power from each tradition manifested itself.

61

Prayer sessions such as this one are not uncommon. Indeed, many worshipers have grown accustomed to dealing with what appears to outsiders a bewildering religious system. The African, Catholic, Protestant, Hindu, and Kabbalistic traditions and their accompanying beliefs, practices, and paraphernalia have not been thrown together haphazardly, however. The present form and structure of the Orisha religion and the more general Afro-American religious complex are the result of a specific historical process that over a period of approximately two hundred years has brought together as many as six religious traditions on one small island. Only one of these, Islam, is not a major component of Afro-American religion in Trinidad.

While African, Catholic, Protestant, Hindu, and Kabbalistic components are all present in one way or another, the nature and form of the respective contributions of these traditions differ from case to case. Catholic elements were incorporated into the Orisha belief system sometime during the early developmental period of *orisha* worship in Trinidad; hence, the relationship between these two traditions is much more intimate than that obtaining between the Orisha religion and the other traditions. This chapter traces that relationship. The Spiritual Baptist religion, which claims a relatively large number of adherents on the island, can and does function independently of the other traditions; its links to the Orisha religion are discussed in Chapter Six. The incorporation of Hinduism and the Kabbalah has been recent, and their influence is weak at present, but appears to be growing, especially in the case of the Kabbalah; these developments are discussed in Chapter Seven.

The Catholic Church was already in place when slaves began arriving in large numbers during the latter part of the eighteenth century. The growth and development of the Catholic Church on the island has been, not surprisingly, intimately linked to the often volatile and shifting sociopolitical context of historical Trinidad, as the Spanish, French, and English were all culturally dominant at one time or another during the colonial period.

The first recorded Church activity in Trinidad involved two Dominican missionaries from Hispaniola in 1513; the aboriginals accused the missionaries of collaborating with a belligerent Spanish ship captain and executed them. Other attempts at evangelizing Trinidad were made in 1530, 1567, and 1569 by Dominicans and Franciscans, but the combination of a recalcitrant native population and a sometimes difficult terrain ultimately frustrated their efforts. Two Jesuit missionaries also arrived in Trinidad in 1567 but soon left for the more promising Guyana (Harricharan 1981, 8, 12–13, 14). Finally, sailing under the Spanish flag out of Bogotá in 1592, Domingo de Vera made his way into the interior along the Caroni River and established the settlement of San José de Oruña (known today as St. Joseph), which became the first seat of government in Trinidad and the site of the first church (Brereton 1981, 1–2).

In 1596 twelve Observantine missionaries from Spain landed in Trinidad, but disease and an unfamiliar environment soon took their toll, and those who did not perish left for Spain or the South American mainland. The arrival in 1687 of Capuchin missionaries from Catalonia, Spain, ushered in a short period of economic prosperity. The Capuchins established missions primarily in the west-central region of the island and utilized aboriginal labor to produce a variety of crops, including maize, bananas, and cacao (Harricharan 1981, 15, 20–21). But their proselytizing was not appreciated by a rebellious and increasingly intransigent aboriginal population, and subsequent events led to bloodshed. Adding to the woes of the Capuchins was the attitude of other Spanish planters, who became disgruntled with an arrangement that allowed the missions to dominate the agricultural market through a steady supply of good labor. The government stepped in and arranged a more equitable production system; the Capuchins, dissatisfied with the new arrangement, left the island in 1707 (Leahy 1980, 2).

The Church suffered gravely until the late 1700s. There was only a handful of priests to serve the Christian spiritual needs of the entire island during the first half of the century. To compound matters, the cacao crop failed in 1727, ushering in a period of economic depression and a drastic decline in population (Leahy 1980, 3). In 1758 a new group of Capuchin missionaries arrived from Aragon, took over some of the existing missions, and founded six new missions, of which some survived (Harricharan 1981, 25).

In the latter part of the eighteenth century, Trinidad underwent a drastic change. The *cédulas* (governmental decrees) of 1776 and 1783 opened the door to foreign settlement for those who were willing to profess allegiance to both the Spanish Crown and the Catholic Church (Williams 1964, 41). As a result, French planters flooded in, eventually transforming the island into a de facto French settlement. The Catholic allegiance proviso notwithstanding, among those settling in Trinidad during the latter decades of the century were a number of Protestants, and Freemasons as well (Harricharan 1981, 26).

During this time only four parish churches existed in predominantly French Trinidad, all served by Spanish-speaking clergymen (Harricharan 1981, 27). The linguistic alienation that resulted from placing Spanish-speaking clergymen in predominantly French-speaking settlements would lead to further problems for the Spanish-based Church, but Roman Catholicism retained its favored status, since it was the church of choice among the French, who had become the dominant social group.

For the Spanish, their long period of proselytization among the aboriginal population of Trinidad produced few positive results. The Spanish colonial period did, however, leave its mark on the sociocultural landscape of Trinidad in the form of two Catholic-Amerindian syncretized festivals, La Divina Pastora and Santa Rosa.

The lack of a suitable clergy continued to affect the Church's efforts in Trinidad adversely. Toward the end of the eighteenth century, for example, only ten priests served 15,000 Catholics (Harricharan 1981, 37). By 1802 only eight Spanish-speaking priests remained, five of whom worked in the northwestern region, and in 1817 only six functioning churches existed on the island, some no more than simple huts (Leahy 1980, 32, 37). Sir Ralph Woodford, the governor of Trinidad, noted that "the quarters of Diego Martin, Carenage, Chaguaramas, Couva, Carapichaima, Savanetta, Point-a-Pierre, South Naparima, Oropouche, La Brea, Guapo, Irois, Hicacos, Toco and Guayaguayare are without any spiritual assistance" (Colonial Office Records, Public Records Office, London; cited in Leahy 1980, 34–35). These "quarters" covered much of northwestern, southern, and northeastern Trinidad. By 1820 the situation had scarcely improved: only eight priests worked the entire island (Leahy 1980, 197–98).

The addition of a large number of African-born and Creole slaves to the population of Trinidad in the early part of the nineteenth century gave the Church yet another problem to deal with in its evangelizing program. Nevertheless, from 1820 to 1844 the Church gradually expanded, laying the foundations for further development on the island. The colonists established the first Catholic public school in Arima, in north-central Trinidad, in 1826 and built additional Catholic-based schools soon thereafter (Harricharan 1981, 82).

Since the Church was by this time deeply ingrained in the sociocultural fabric of Trinidad, it managed to weather two of the most serious problems it had ever faced there. The first was the schism touched off in 1826 by Francis De Ridder, the first black West Indian priest; in the spirit of emancipation then sweeping the colonies, he demanded that free blacks be awarded the same rights and privileges as whites. The conditional emancipation in 1834 and complete emancipation in 1838 eventually assuaged hostilities, and the schism came to an end in 1841 (Harricharan 1981, 102–4). The second problem was the program of Anglicization put into effect by the British colonial government. When the Anglican Church became the state church by virtue of the Ecclesiastical Ordinance of 1844 (Brereton 1981, 121), the French Creole–based Catholic Church brought its considerable wealth, prestige, and political clout to bear and eventually managed to gain equal status with the Anglican Church. Catholicism in Trinidad gained considerable prestige with the creation of an archbishopric in 1850 (Harricharan 1981, 133), an event that firmly established the Church on the island once and for all and essentially ended its developmental period.

Catholicism was most influential on the Orisha religion during the earliest years of the development of *orisha* worship in Trinidad. Its present-day influence is practically nil, but Catholic beliefs, practices, and paraphernalia are still important components of the Orisha belief system. A survey of fifty-three shrines around the island revealed that fourteen showed a heavy Catholic influence; that is, statues, lithographs, posters of Catholic saints, and other Catholic paraphernalia were prominently displayed. One gets the impression, however, that the physical and symbolic presence of Catholicism can be largely attributed to syncretism that occurred long ago rather than to current influence. In fact, some practitioners of the Orisha religion are now expunging Catholicized aspects in an attempt to regain what they believe to be authentic Yoruba *orisha* worship. Frances Henry (1983, 65) observed less enthusiasm for Catholic prayers during Orisha rites in 1978 than in her earlier visits to Trinidad in the late 1950s and early 1960s, a trend that appears to be continuing today.

Historically, *orisha* worshipers have shown a preference for particular Catholic beliefs and practices. Much of the dogma of the Church — for example, transubstantiation, Mariological doctrines, eschatological theology, and papal infallibility — has been virtually ignored by *orisha* worshipers. Far more significant are the Catholic saints and the doctrines and beliefs with which they are associated.

Chapter Thirteen looks at the nature of the association between the *orisha* and the saints, most prominently, Peter, Raphael, Anne, Philomena, Catherine, Michael, Francis, John, Theresa, Jerome, Anthony, and Jude. The *orisha* that are syncretized with Francis and John are multi-aspectual and are appropriately associated with the many saints called Francis and John.

In Chapter Three I pointed out that a quarter of the *orisha* worshipers I surveyed claimed some sort of affiliation with the Catholic Church. Many of these were older worshipers whose early training and exposure to Catholic hagiography had "preadapted" them for a later acceptance of *orisha* mythology with its pantheon of anthropomorphic deities. The importance of Catholicism in the personal belief system of one shrine head in her seventies, for example, was obviously due to her childhood involvement with the Church:

First of all, I had a vision when I was young, and I followed the vision. . . . I grew up in the Catholic Church. . . . I grew in prayer as a young child. . . . The lady that raised me, she was from Africa. She believed in prayer, and she prayed the rosary. . . . I moved to Port of Spain and I grew in the Catholic faith with my godmother. She taught me to pray to the saints. From that tradition, praying to the saints, I got gifted as a child. . . . Praying, I used to see the saints appearing and showing me things. (Interview, San Fernando, December 14, 1988)

Another shrine head in her sixties revealed the importance of a Catholic "preadaptation" for her understanding of the *orisha*:

The Orisha [*orisha* worshipers] carry on their Catholic prayers, because it says about "I believe God our Father." . . . That is why I love [those] prayers, the Catholic prayers. It tell you . . . it make you believe. It tell you about the saints and all these things. It's like if someone died and a child did not know that person and they just see a picture — by seeing the picture they will know the person. (Interview, southwestern Trinidad, December 14, 1988)

In contrast to the well-documented accounts of the early period of Catholicism in Trinidad, we have little information concerning the early developmental period of *orisha* worship. Early travelers' accounts (e.g., Day 1852, and Kingsley 1871; both cited in Simpson 1980, 13–14) describe religious ceremonies incorporating what they perceived to be African drumming and singing, but is it not clear whether those involved were *orisha* worshipers or practitioners of some other African traditions. Perhaps because of the lack of data and documentation, historians of early Trinidad (e.g., Black et al. 1976; Brereton 1981;

Carmichael 1961; Williams 1964; Wood 1968) have little or nothing to say concerning the origins of African folk religion. Thus, any discussion of African-derived religious worship during the colonial period is speculative, based on the considerable information we do have regarding the demography, provenience, and ethnic affiliations of Africans in early Trinidad, as well as the social and cultural setting of the island during the eighteenth and nineteenth centuries.[1]

Virtually no African cultural or demographic presence existed until about 1790, when the sugar plantations became a salient part of the socioeconomic landscape of Trinidad. As noted earlier, although many of the slaves hailed from southern Nigeria and the surrounding area, by 1813 only about 1 percent of the African-born slaves in Trinidad were Yoruba. Since the Orisha religion in Trinidad is certainly Yoruba-derived, it appears likely that the practice of this religion began later than that date.

As David Trotman (1976, 2) notes, there was a significant influx of Yoruba into Trinidad beginning in the 1830s and lasting until 1867; during this time approximately 9,000 liberated Africans from the free settlements of St. Helena and Sierra Leone migrated to Trinidad. Since over half of the liberated Africans in Sierra Leone (by far the larger of the two settlements) were Yoruba, this ethnic group was probably well represented among those who came to Trinidad. As noted in Chapter Four, the coincident combination of Yoruba immigration and the emancipation of slaves probably led to the establishment of the Orisha religion on the island around 1840.

By the early nineteenth century the colonists were exposing Africans to the teachings, beliefs, and practices of Catholicism. On Sundays, for example, Africans "were taught the Lord's Prayer, the Belief, [and] the Litany" (Ottley 1974, 60). The slaves' participation in Church activities was generally "peripheral" and "limited," but they were clearly involved:

The participation of slaves in the life of the Catholic Church . . . [included] the reception of Baptism, the Sunday observance, the acquisition of an elementary knowledge of the Faith, the recitation of certain fixed prayers and the celebration of the four great annual Holy Days of Christmas, New Year, Good Friday and Corpus Christi. (Harricharan 1981, 54)

The large number of slaves baptized by Church officials is an indication of the Africans' affiliation with the Catholic Church: according to

C. R. Ottley (1974, 61), almost 15,000 of the approximately 17,000 slaves in Trinidad in the 1820s were baptized Catholics. The fact that many of these baptisms were conducted en masse, however, calls into question the quality of the Africans' involvement in the religion.

Though it is difficult to ascertain the degree to which Africans assimilated the beliefs and practices of the Church, *orisha* worshipers did syncretize various Catholic saints with their own *orisha*, a process facilitated by certain perceived similarities in mythology and iconography. The religious figures of Catholicism and the Orisha pantheon are both regarded as potential mediators between a high or supreme god and humans; the saints and *orisha* are both (for the most part) thought to be historical figures and are thus conceived of in anthropomorphic terms; Eshu is believed to possess at least some of the attributes of Satan, although Eshu, unlike Satan, is not unmitigated evil but a mischievous trickster god.

Among those who have noted the general similarity of the two belief systems, Roger Bastide writes that the "infiltration" of Catholic elements into Afro-American religions can be attributed to what he refers to as "parallels" that are found "in both traditional West African religions and Catholicism":

1. The structural parallel between the Catholic theology of the saints' intercession with the Virgin Mary, the Virgin's intercession with Jesus, and the intercession of Jesus with God the Father and African cosmology of the *orixas* [sic] as mediators between man and Olorun [or Olodumare].
2. The cultural parallel between the functional conception of the saints, each of whom presides over a certain human activity or is responsible for healing a certain disease, and the equally functional conception of the *voduns* and *orixas*, each of whom is in charge of a certain sector of nature and who, like the saints, are the patrons of trades and occupations, protecting the hunter, the smith, the healer, etc. (Bastide 1978, 262)

It is clear, then, that the similarities noted above provided the opportunity for a meaningful syncretism of particular elements of the two religious systems. The existence of such a potential does not, however, explain why such syncretism occurred.

Some of my informants believe that their ancestors in Trinidad used Catholicism as a sort of camouflage behind which they hid their own religious beliefs and practices. Leader Scott illustrated this stratagem by way of example:

You see, long ago you had to practice Christianity, you couldn't practice Orisha. They [the Africans] would put a little "stool" in the yard, and the man [white men] would come by and say, "What is that there?" They would say, "I pray to St. John." He didn't know what you meant. They [the Africans] might pray to Oya, but when they [the white men] come around, they say St. Catherine. (Interview, Basta Hall, June 13, 1985)

Another shrine head explained that when the white men came around to a slave cabin, the Africans would take down their statue of an *orisha* and replace it with a statue of a Catholic religious figure.

Bastide tends to agree with the "camouflage theory" and notes that this practice was especially important in the development of the associations made between the Catholic saints and the African *orisha:*

Syncretism by correspondence between gods and saints is the most basic of these processes, and also the best studied. It can be explained in historical terms by the slaves' need, during the colonial period, to conceal their pagan ceremonies from European eyes. They therefore danced before a Catholic altar; and although their masters found this somewhat bizarre, it never occurred to them that these Negro dances, with their prominently displayed lithographs and statuettes of the saints, were in fact addressed to African divinities. (Bastide 1972, 156)

Other scholars disagree, however. Trotman writes that "the predominant Catholic religion served as a transcultural belief, in that it provided sufficient continuity in perceived religious belief to bridge partially the cultural gap and soften the dislocation caused by migration." He finds two objections to the camouflage interpretation. Since the first attempt by the authorities to prohibit African religious practices did not occur until 1883, there was plenty of time for the Yoruba religion to take root without need for such subterfuge. Moreover, "the public nature of Yoruba worship and the distinctive ritual, paraphernalia, language, drumming, dancing, and sacrifice of animals could in no way be mistaken for Catholicism." He concludes that, "rather than serving the function of fooling the authorities, Catholic saints were a conscious and deliberate inclusion of the Yoruba" (Trotman 1976, 9, 13). Melville and Frances Herskovits's position (1964, 330) is similar to Trotman's; they argue that some aspects of the incorporation of Catholicism into the religious beliefs of transplanted Africans could have been due to reasoned analogy.

When we consider the sociocultural context of colonial Trinidad, it seems that both the camouflage theory and the "voluntary incorporation hypothesis" may be valid, each one perhaps associated with a particular time period. Trotman's point that the Africans had little reason to camouflage their religious system after emancipation in 1838 and before the anti-drumming ordinance of 1883 is well taken, although Africans in colonial Trinidad only one generation removed from slavery no doubt continued to suffer from some form of discrimination. If the Orisha religion was present at least in some incipient form during the period of enslavement, camouflage may have been necessary then. But if indeed the Orisha religion had its beginnings in Trinidad around 1840, the incorporation of Catholic elements may have been voluntary at first, only later giving way to the camouflage stratagem as the government began to legislate against African religious practices.

In any case, the Catholic aspect of *orisha* worship was probably firmly in place by 1900 or so. A short time later, however, there was another period of change and adjustment as Africans embraced the Spiritual Baptist religion in increasing numbers. There are many theories regarding the origins and early development of the Spiritual Baptist religion in Trinidad; whatever their validity, it is clear that the Spiritual Baptists had established themselves on the island by 1920.

SIX

The Spiritual Baptists

The Spiritual Baptist religion is found throughout the Western Hemisphere with churches in many areas, including St. Vincent, Grenada, St. Croix, Venezuela, Guyana, and large urban areas of North America such as Toronto, Miami, New Orleans, and New York City. Many of these churches appear to have been established as the result of movement to and from as well as inside the Caribbean.

The relationship between the Spiritual Baptist and Orisha religions is much more pervasive and marked than that involving Orisha and Catholicism, Hinduism, or the Kabbalah. For one thing, the Baptist and Orisha religions often share members. Spiritual Baptist churches may also be found in the same compounds as Orisha shrines, one person being responsible for overseeing the activities of both. Because of the marked interrelatedness of the two groups, organizational, ritualistic, and theological aspects of the Spiritual Baptist religion have greatly influenced the Orisha religion and vice versa.

The origins and early development of the Spiritual Baptist religion in Trinidad are not well known. Researchers who have dealt with this topic (e.g., Glazier 1981, 1983; Parks 1981; and Williams 1985) have resorted to synthesizing bits and pieces of historical information in an attempt to produce a coherent account. Because of the scattered and lacunal nature of the data, the different versions that have resulted are equally unsatisfactory, but four basic accounts of the origins of the Spiritual Baptist religion in Trinidad can be identified, placing its roots in Africa, St. Vincent, North America, and Grenada respectively.

The African sources are difficult to document. Glazier, who worked extensively among the Spiritual Baptists in Trinidad, notes the popularity of the belief in an African provenience for the religion. A Dahomean diviner, Robert Antoine (his adopted French name), established a

71

Rada compound[1] in Belmont near Port of Spain in 1855 (Carr 1953, 37), and some of Glazier's informants claimed that religious activities at this compound inspired similar forms of worship elsewhere on the island, including Spiritual Baptist and *orisha* worship (Glazier 1981, 38–39; 1983, 34). As Glazier points out, however, there are differences between Dahomean traditional religion and Yoruba-derived *orisha* worship, as well as other problems with this particular origin "myth":

> Differences between Shango ritual and that of Rada constitute only one possible objection to this origin myth. Even if the transition from Rada to Shango [the Orisha religion] were clear, the transition from Rada to the Baptist faith is problematic. Some Shangoists claim that Baptist ceremonies once served as a "cover" for African practices. In order to avoid government persecution, Shango leaders called their religious centers Baptist "churches." The problem, however, is that there is no evidence that Spiritual Baptist churches were better accepted by the authorities than forms of African worship. The decision to adopt Baptist ritual as a "cover" would not seem to have been a very good or logical choice. (Glazier 1983, 35)

Some Spiritual Baptists and *orisha* worshipers contend that the present-day Spiritual Baptists are actually an offshoot or derivation of the "Shouters" who came from Africa. They note that some elements of Spiritual Baptist worship — for example, ebullient shouting and loud rhythmic breathing — are Kongolese traits; we might also add the Kongolese-derived chalk drawings noted in Chapter Four. Mother Joan agrees with the African-derivation theory for the Spiritual Baptists and, in fact, argues that the Orisha and Spiritual Baptist religions share a similar developmental history:

> We must not confuse ourselves by making the Spiritual Baptist a separate entity from the Orisha practice. . . . The Kongos . . . practice shouting, screaming, and whistling . . . [and have] icons and paraphernalia similar to Orisha worship, all of which has permeated the greater part of the Spiritual Baptist religion, blended and intertwined with the Christian phenomena. You cannot, therefore, separate when dealing with the intricacies of the religions one from another simply because each unit identifies itself as a separate entity. (Personal correspondence, October 4, 1991)

A third African-derivation account claims that the "Shouter Baptists" are of West African origin:

Although the history and origin of the faith are vague and have not been studied in detail, the faith is said to have evolved from West Africa or Yoruba and without the assistance of any strong revivalist movement.

Yoruba is said to be the denominational resource for the spread of this African method of worship both in the United States and the West Indies. Congolese, Ibos, Dahomeans, and Mandingoes also joined the faith. The religious beliefs of the Shouter Baptists are directly influenced by West African concepts and procedures. (Thomas 1987, 30)

The Spiritual Baptists in Trinidad have retained a few beliefs and practices that are probably of African derivation. But unfortunately, the religion's propensity to change through time (which would eventually mask the original nature of the trait in question), combined with the lack of reliable historical documentation, makes the notion of African origin difficult to substantiate. Besides, many Spiritual Baptist churches are quite Christian in character, and some are pointedly anti-African in regard to ritual and belief.

Some scholars (Bourguignon 1970, 91; Henney 1974, 81), find the roots of the Spiritual Baptists in the influx of fundamentalist Protestant "Shakers" from St. Vincent (not related to U.S. groups called by that name) during the early part of the twentieth century. Jeanette Henney makes a good case for a St. Vincentian origin by noting the similarity of beliefs and rituals in the worship services of both groups:

Herskovits and Herskovits (1947, 305–9) have discussed the Africanisms they found among the Shouters of Trinidad. Some of the features that they consider African are also found among the Shakers: the importance of the center pole, the removal of shoes during worship, chalk markings on the floor, sprinkling the corners and center pole three times with water, "talking in tongues," the wearing of white dresses by women initiates, the "mourning" period of seclusion, hand clapping and foot tapping as rhythmic accompaniment, and the rhythms of the hymns. (Henney 1974, 80)

Mervyn Williams, who also conducted fieldwork among the Spiritual Baptists, reports that some of his informants spoke of the arrival of immigrants from St. Vincent:

Some older informants relate that some time around the period of World War I a religious group known as the "converted" came to Trinidad from St. Vincent. The most prominent among them seemed to be a man called Taffy. These persons conducted services in make-shift structures called "tents" or "praise-houses" and were known as "Shakers." Due to their behavior during religious services (shouting) they became known locally as "Shouters." (Williams 1985, 26)

Similarly, Glazier (1983, 37) writes that twenty-two of his Spiritual Baptist informants claimed to have come to Trinidad from St. Vincent between 1913 and 1928, a period during which the Spiritual Baptist church in Trinidad underwent significant growth. Alfrieta Parks (1981, 24) argues for a St. Vincentian origin as well and notes that an older informant described the activities of a new religion in Port of Spain around 1915.

History gives some support to this interpretation. In 1917 the Legislative Council of Trinidad and Tobago passed the "Shouters Prohibition Ordinance," apparently for reasons specified in the following comments of the Attorney General:

Unfortunately, a condition of affairs has arisen in the colony by reason of the practice of a sect or body calling itself the Shouters which has, so far as the Government sees, made it necessary to come to this House and submit proposals for interference in the practices of that body. Apparently the Shouters have had a somewhat stormy history from all I have been able to learn regarding them. They seem, if they did not arise there, to have flourished exceedingly in St. Vincent, and to have made themselves such an unmitigated nuisance that they had to be legislated out of existence. They then came to Trinidad and continual complaints have been received by the Government for some time past as to their practices. (Quoted in Herskovits and Herskovits 1964, 343)

Some researchers have looked to North America for the source of the Spiritual Baptists in Trinidad. A. B. Huggins (1978, 27, 32) notes the existence of four Baptist sects on the island — the London Baptists, the Independent Baptists, the Spiritual Baptists, and the Fundamental Baptists — and implies that they all derived from North American Baptists who arrived during the early part of the nineteenth century. According to popular accounts, the British recruited African slaves to join in their fight against the Americans during the War of Independence in the 1770s, promising them freedom in exchange for their assistance. In the early 1800s, after their defeat, the British sent six "companies" of slaves and their families to Trinidad. Five of these settlements — called First Company, Third Company, Fourth Company, Fifth Company, and Sixth Company — still exist today in south-central Trinidad (according to Huggins [1978, 4], some researchers argue that the Second Company was blown off course and wound up in Jamaica). These settlers, who are sometimes referred to as 'Merikins, brought their Baptist faith with them, so the story goes, and gave rise to the various Baptist groups in Trinidad today. Parks (1981, 22) and Donald Wood (1968, 38) also refer to the arrival of black Baptists from North America but write that they were part of the British militia in the War of 1812. The British resettled the former slaves in Trinidad, where Baptist missionaries from the United States provided them with assistance; then, after the Americans lost interest, English missionaries stepped in. As Parks explains, however, a schism in 1901, caused by the refusal of some London Baptists to work with whites from England, eventually gave rise to the Independent Baptists (Huggins 1978, 42; Parks 1981, 22–23).

Viola Gopaul-Whittington offers the fourth and final theory to account for the origins of the Spiritual Baptists. She argues that during the nineteenth century some of the "Yarouba" in Trinidad converted to the Baptist faith and as a result came under fire both from those who chose not to convert and from the Catholic Church. To escape persecution, these "Yarouba" fled to St. Vincent, where they suffered a similar fate, causing them to migrate to Grenada. The discovery of oil in Trinidad around 1910 brought many of them back to the island in search of work in the oil fields (Gopaul-Whittington 1983, 9). This resettlement resulted in the construction of small churches in southwestern and, later, northwestern and north-central Trinidad.

The argument for a St. Vincentian origin seems to be the strongest in that it can be best substantiated by historical and ethnographic data. This does not mean that such an interpretation is correct, nor does it preclude an ultimate African basis for the St. Vincent–based religion itself.

Although all these accounts trace the source of the Spiritual Baptist religion in Trinidad to foreign soil, the religion has obviously undergone a high degree of indigenous development in Trinidad. Whatever its original source, it has developed into a unique and quintessentially Trini institution. Apparently the Shouters' Prohibition Ordinance of 1917 did little to extinguish the religious fervor of the Spiritual Baptists. Eudora Thomas, who is both an Orisha shrine head and the "Mother" of her own Spiritual Baptist church, has traced the beginnings of some churches back to the end of the last century and the early part of this century (1987, 39–40). The prohibition of 1917 (finally lifted in 1951) simply forced the Baptists underground, and even today one can still find churches in remote and virtually inaccessible locations.

Little or no historical information is available regarding the connection between Spiritual Baptists and *orisha* worshipers, but given their similar sociohistorical backgrounds, the interrelationship of the two groups is not surprising. Both have been, until recently, exclusively African and have thus shared a similar historical tradition and socioeconomic class affiliation. Both religions endured a long period of state oppression during which the government banned their practices, forcing their respective members underground. It is not unlikely that relations between the two groups intensified during this time.

The most important factors contributing to the interrelationship are, perhaps, almost exclusively social, for the two religious systems — one primarily Protestant, the other African and Catholic — appear to have had little in common in ideology or practice (beyond the notable exception of spirit possession), especially when we compare Orisha with the orthodox branch of the Spiritual Baptist religion. And, in fact, virtually no syncretism involving the two religious systems has occurred; any mixing in ideology or practice involves a juxtaposition of the two rather than a blending.

Further, the influence of the Spiritual Baptists on the Orisha religion does not appear to be uniform geographically. The Orisha shrines in and around Port of Spain and elsewhere in the north generally appear to be highly Catholicized, while the Baptist influence seems strongest in the south (there are, of course, exceptions). In the south-central area of Trinidad few full-blown Orisha shrines exist; most of the shrines there consist simply of flags and, in some cases, small stools for the *orisha*. Often the flags represent Spiritual Baptist powers instead of, or as well as, Orisha powers. Typically, there is no *palais* or *chapelle* (structures ordinarily found in an Orisha compound), and worshipers associated with these shrines generally do not hold a standard Orisha feast. For example, one female shrine head in south-central Trinidad holds prayers in November, accompanied by a "feeding of the children," but she does not beat drums or sacrifice animals. I was told that she is a typical "Moruga Road Baptist." Moruga Road is the main road in south-central Trinidad, an area that has been the focus of strong Baptist activity throughout the years; every Baptist denomination in

Trinidad has at least a handful of churches on and around Moruga Road. It appears, then, that a strong Baptist influence has tempered *orisha* worship activity in this area.

The Spiritual Baptist religion in Trinidad shares many of the practices of African American spiritual and pentecostal churches in the United States, including glossolalia, possession by the Holy Spirit, and ebullient and often extemporaneous singing, praising, and praying. The beliefs and practices of some Spiritual Baptist churches in Trinidad, especially the nonorthodox churches, resemble those of the Orisha religion: for example, the libations of oil and water, the planting of flags for particular spirits, and the recognition of the *orisha* as important spiritual forces.

Today, the Spiritual Baptist religion in Trinidad is flourishing. Since the government has never included the Spiritual Baptists in its census, one can only guess how many churches and members exist on the island, but by multiplying the assumed number of churches by the assumed average number of members affiliated with each church, we can obtain a rough estimate (see Appendix A). There are, according to my calculations, approximately 11,000 Spiritual Baptists in Trinidad. Among these, worshipers recognize four denominations: the National Evangelical Spiritual Baptist Faith Archdiocese (NESBFA), the National Ecclesiastical Council of Churches Spiritual Baptist of Trinidad and Tobago, Inc., the West Indian United Sacred Order of Spiritual Baptist Churches, Inc., and the Ambassadors for Christ Spiritual Baptists, Ltd. In 1965 the NESBFA became the first incorporated Spiritual Baptist body to be recognized by the government, and—although there are no figures available—it appears to be the largest of the four denominations. There are, in addition, a significant number of Spiritual Baptist churches (25 percent?) not affiliated with any of these organizations.

Organization on the church level can be complex if the congregation is large; Glazier (1983, 52–54) counts twenty-two ranks or positions (possibly because one church in which he conducted research had a congregation of 280, an extraordinarily large number for a Spiritual Baptist church). As Williams (1985, 36–37) notes, however, not all Spiritual Baptists recognize or are aware of so many. Among the more important and widely recognized ranks are Leader, Mother, Shepherd, Pointer, Nurse, Prover, Captain, and Teacher. The duties and privileges of these positions can differ from church to church, but "Leader"

and "Mother" generally designate the highest-ranking male and female members, each of whom, more often than not, has his or her own
church and sometimes an Orisha shrine as well.

While it is true that a Leader is generally the highest-ranking member of a church, some Leaders, as Leader Scott explained, have the
authority to conduct a wider range of rituals than others:

You have different kinds of Leaders. One you have they call a Pastor, one who
can come and conduct a service in the absence of one who is really authorized
to do so. He would be a Leader at a lower rank. Then you have another
Leader, a Leader who is a baptizer, a Leader who has the authority only to
baptize. . . . Then, you have another Leader, another category, which would be
called a Teacher. He is authorized to point you [guide one spiritually] for
baptism, and point you for mourning [described below]. And you may find a
Leader who is authorized to point you for baptism, and point you for
mourning, but may not be authorized for baptizing. . . . There are also
Leaders who can do everything. So, therefore, a Leader is one who is
authorized to carry on a particular vocation or all vocations in the ritual
system of the Baptists. (Interview, Basta Hall, December 8, 1988)

The different positions and duties are achieved rather than as-
cribed; almost without exception, worshipers acquire them during
"mourning," a process involving sensory deprivation and isolation in
which the worshiper undergoes a series of spiritual "travels." This
ritual is perhaps the most important in Spiritual Baptist worship (some
of the symbols involved are shown in Photo 2). It is an important
source of knowledge of religious matters for the Orisha religion as
well, although Baptist Leaders or Mothers generally direct the ceremony even when *orisha* worshipers are mourning.

The ritual can last from as few as three days to seven days or more.
Worshipers typically go through the ceremony more than once. When
I mentioned that one of my contacts said he had mourned twelve times,
Leader Scott observed that that was not unusual; some people, he said,
are "born mourners." The length of the ritual requires that a number
of people be present to assist, but a minimum of two people can carry
out the ceremony: the Pointer conducts the ritual and assists or provides spiritual direction for the "pilgrims" (there is usually more than
one) in their spiritual travels, and the Nurse tends to the pilgrims'
physical needs and comforts. Leader Scott and Mother Joan, for example, once conducted a mourning ceremony themselves when other
assistants were unable to attend.

Worshipers use many terms in speaking of mourning and the area in which it takes place: "throne of grace," "praying ground," "court," "room of seclusion," "dark room," "mourning ground," "the grave," "the tomb," and "ground of sorrow." Most of these are fitting epithets for the most important aspect of the mourning ritual: the symbolic or spiritual death and subsequent rebirth of the mourner. Spiritual death and rebirth occur only during a mourner's first experience; during the second and subsequent mourning experiences—sometimes referred to as "building"—the worshiper simply continues her or his travels in a quest for additional spiritual knowledge.

Mourning actually has four parts: the "pointing," the spiritual travels, the "rising," and, finally, the "coming out." During "coming out," nurses and other assistants bring the pilgrims into the church, generally during a Sunday service, to describe their spiritual travels. Worshipers may travel spiritually to a number of places. Some describe the experience as "dreamlike"; others say they actually leave their physical bodies. During the coming-out rituals that I attended, the pilgrims often mentioned having gone to Africa, India, China, and occasionally to Egypt, the United States, and elsewhere in Trinidad as well. At some point during the spiritual travels, spirits may give a worshiper instructions for building a church or a small shrine, or admonish the worshiper for a way of life not befitting a spiritual person. One woman near Port of Spain, who is now a Mother with her own church and Orisha shrine, told me that the first time she underwent mourning the spirits told her to change her life-style and "behave properly."

Perhaps the most important information received by the mourner is the new status he or she has attained: the worshiper may be given any of the positions noted earlier. Occasionally, of course, since a worshiper naturally desires a prestigious ranking, a pilgrim claims a position that he or she has not actually been awarded during spiritual travel. Leader Scott felt, however, that although mourning may seem personal and subjective, a Leader or Mother who is intelligent and wise spiritually can discern whether the pilgrim is being truthful. Another Leader told me about a young man, once a member of his church, who left one day to direct a church in Port of Spain, even though he had never received instructions to do so. When I remarked that surely such a situation would eventually cause confusion, he explained that the church was not without ways to deal with the problem:

Well, some people go to mourning with something already in their mind. When they come out from there, some of them have antics in their movements. . . . We have what you call a Prover, [and] Search and Warrant. . . . These are the most dangerous positions in the church. . . . The Prover will know if you are talking the truth, yes or no, and he is going to make you shame [if you are not telling the truth]. A Search and Warrant will search you out, and will tell you flat out if you lie. (Interview, St. Joseph, February 18, 1989)

It is important to note that the Leader or Mother directing the mourning ceremony does not induce the trance state pharmacologically. Worshipers claim that the trance comes from a combination of the sealed bands (pieces of colored cloth upon which special symbols or seals are drawn) that are tied around the mourner's head, the mourner's state of mind, and the actions of the Pointer and assistants. Obviously a large degree of skill is involved; I have seen experienced Spiritual Baptists such as Leader Scott put mourners "down" and "bring them up" virtually at will.

In addition to the important mourning ceremony, Spiritual Baptists practice and recognize a number of other rituals and activities, including baptism, thanksgiving, and the weekly services. My own baptism, described in Chapter One, was fairly typical. The ritual generally involves an extended service in the church, followed by a trip to a body of water in which the initiates are immersed three times. The worshipers then conclude the rite back at the church. During the ceremony, the Leader or Mother gives the initiate a secret word and handshake. Most worshipers consider baptism to be the first step toward a formal affiliation with the Spiritual Baptist faith.

When a person is baptized, he or she becomes the spiritual son or daughter of the Leader or Mother who directed the ceremony, whom the initiate thereafter refers to as his or her spiritual father or spiritual mother. In some cases, a person may have male and female sponsors present during the ceremony, the spiritual godfather and godmother. When the same Leader or Mother baptizes a number of individuals, they become spiritual brothers and sisters. In the case of the older and more experienced Leaders and Mothers, this fictive kin network can become quite extensive. The relationships are based solely on an analogy of consanguinity, which is fitting, given that the spiritual father or mother has in a spiritual sense given birth to the initiate. Spiritual Baptists do not recognize affinal ties; for example, they do not acknowledge spiritual in-laws.

Orisha worshipers recognize a similar fictive kin network. A person who undergoes a baptism "on the Baptist side" and head washing and incising "on the African side" will have two sets of fictive kin if the baptizing Leader or Mother is not also functioning as the Orisha priest or priestess. In my case, Leader Scott and Mother Joan performed the baptism, and Elder Biddeau and his wife, Lydia, directed the head washing and incising. Although Leader Scott, as an Orisha priest, could have conducted the Orisha rites at his shrine as well as the baptism, it was my desire to involve both him and Elder Biddeau in my initiation. Consequently, I have spiritual parents and numerous spiritual kin on both the Baptist and African sides.

Another important Spiritual Baptist ritual is the "thanksgiving," a ceremony that many Leaders and Mothers perform on an annual basis and on special occasions as well. A thanksgiving generally involves services for both children and adults. The "feeding of the children" is an important part of this ceremony; in fact, the worshipers often refer to the thanksgiving ceremony in those terms. A thanksgiving I attended in Enterprise, west-central Trinidad, in January 1989 was directed by Leader Scott; a woman had asked him to preside. (In these situations, the individual sponsoring the ceremony generally compensates the visiting Leader or Mother, in either cash or goods.) The worshipers had set a large table with colored candles, wine, honey, cakes, candies, flowers, milk, and olive oil. While his assistants lifted the tablecloth, Leader Scott used white chalk to draw Baptist "seals" at the four corners and the center of the table. He then addressed the forty or so children in attendance, explaining, among other things, why we should give thanks to God. One of his assistants read from the Bible, and another worshiper lit the candles. As the children gathered around the table, Leader Scott rang a hand-held brass bell while his assistants poured libations at the appropriate points, and the rest of the worshipers sang Baptist hymns. Then those present recited various Christian prayers — for example, the Lord's Prayer — and the Apostles' Creed. Next, a group of six women made libations at various points in the immediate area and inside the house as well. Leader Scott threw dried corn about, then knelt and prayed for a few minutes. Following this, the worshipers sang hymns and recited prayers.

Two Baptist manifestations (possessions attributed to the Holy Ghost) occurred about this time. The woman of the house and a Baptist neighbor then knelt and prayed together. One of Leader Scott's assistants read Psalm 103, after which worshipers recited prayers and

Leader Scott gave a short sermon. Next, there was a short ceremony involving the woman of the house, her son, a neighbor, and a plate containing certain liquids and candles. The woman of the house then knelt and prayed.

A bit later, the children gathered around the table and prayed, following Leader Scott's lead. Leader Scott threw dried corn over the table and performed a short ritual involving a loaf of bread. He then ceremonially broke the bread and fed it to those present. The children circled the table in both clockwise and counterclockwise directions. Finally, the sponsor of the ceremony and her assistants served food to the children and then to the adults. Leader Scott and his assistants later gave the children additional food in brown paper bags and sent them home, thus concluding the ceremony.

Of the forty or so children present, ten were East Indian. At another thanksgiving I attended in Malgratoute (in west-central Trinidad) in June 1985, twenty-five of the ninety children present were Indian. This is not unusual; the Baptist who is holding the thanksgiving simply invites children in the immediate neighborhood, at least a few of whom will generally be Indian. The Indian children (and their parents as well) are welcomed by the Spiritual Baptists. In fact, the Baptist woman who sponsored the thanksgiving described above was herself Indian, as were many of those in attendance. The woman's Indian husband, who was not a Spiritual Baptist, was present for only a short time and did not actually participate in the ceremony, but it must be noted that the other Indians did take part in the proceedings, sometimes enthusiastically.

The Spiritual Baptist thanksgiving is a celebration of gratitude directed to Christian spirits: God, Jesus, the Holy Spirit. The rite is somewhat obligatory, since, according to Leader Scott, worshipers hold a thanksgiving in bad times as well as good:

Some people feel that they have labored throughout the year, and they have done well or maybe they have not done well. But they thank God for small mercies. They will set aside a day and time when they will call their brothers and sisters. They come together and they have prayers, and they set a table with food, cakes, and whatnot. (Interview, Basta Hall Village, January 13, 1989)

Worshipers generally hold their weekly services on Sunday, although some churches will also have services during the week. An assistant of the Leader or Mother typically opens the service by ringing a brass bell at the altar, the "center area" of the church, the four corners of the structure, and the entrances. The other assistants then light candles at these points, and a procession of usually three or more people visit each point, pouring water, oil, and perfume and dropping "dry food" such as peas, rice, and flour. Often the worshiper ringing the bell will lead the procession. The Mother or Leader of the church then typically makes a few opening remarks.

What follows is a lengthy session of what I call "pray-praising." In this activity, one or sometimes two worshipers kneel at either the center area or in front of the altar; holding a candle in one hand and sometimes a small brass receptacle containing flowers and water in the other, they recite a rather standard liturgy in a call-and-response pattern involving the rest of the congregation. The typical "pray-praiser" will often recite prayers or lead songs. Pray-praising is generally performed by the higher-ranking worshipers, but on occasion Leaders or Mothers will ask for additional volunteers if they feel that more prayers are needed.

When the pray-praiser is done, she or he will begin a hymn and then engage in ritual handshaking and touching with everyone present. There is both intergroup and intragroup variation in the handshaking ritual, but generally the pray-praiser grasps the hands of another worshiper and stretches his or her arms out to the side, after which each person may touch the side of the head to the same part of the other's head three times, alternating sides. The gestures vary from simple handshakes to elaborate versions of hand and head touching. There seems to be a general relation between the prestige (real or perceived) of the worshiper and the complexity of the ritual.

The pray-praising part of the service is noisy and active, and most of the possessions occur during this time. When the Leader or Mother determines that a sufficient number of worshipers have pray-praised, there follows a somewhat more subdued period (Photo 3) during which the Leader or Mother gives a sermon and makes announcements involving church activities. Worshipers sing, hum, clap, and tap their feet almost continuously during the entire service. A typical service may last as long as four or five hours.

The worshipers do not necessarily hold their ceremonies in religious structures per se. Many of the rites associated with baptism, including those that are generally held in a church, can be performed on the beach. I once watched a group of Leaders and Mothers "construct" an altar by delineating a fifteen-foot square area in the sand and placing Bibles, candles, bells, and other items at various places inside it. Worshipers often hold thanksgivings in impromptu structures built for the occasion or in private residences. Leaders and Mothers can conduct the weekly services outdoors as well; Spiritual Baptists often hold abbreviated public services in Woodford Square and elsewhere.

Such practices have probably permitted greater access to the religion among people who traditionally lacked the resources to build separate structures for worship. In the recent past, however, the popularity of the Spiritual Baptist religion has grown, and its members are now drawn from the upper socioeconomic class as well as the lower. Many churches are small and simply furnished, but some are well financed and very elaborate. A simple structure typically consists of brick, wood, or cement walls, a tin roof, and an earthen floor; it usually has a small altar in front facing a handful of small wooden benches and can generally accommodate fifteen to twenty-five worshipers comfortably (Photo 4). Larger churches, on the other hand, may have finely finished walls, a high ceiling, permanent pews, and an altar decorated with fine cloths, candelabras, and other ritual paraphernalia.

At roughly the center of most churches, whether they are simple or elaborate, is what I call the "center area" (Photo 5). It might be only a vertical pole around which worshipers have arranged Bibles, candles, flowers, bells, and other items. At one church the center area contained a small white structure resembling a three-tiered wedding cake, which served as the base for a small cross. In many ways, it is this center area and not the altar that is the most important ritual location in the church. The altar itself is sometimes no more than a place to store ritual paraphernalia.

Spiritual Baptist churches can range from the conservative or Protestant (the orthodox churches) to the very eclectic, containing materials and symbols from a variety of religious traditions (the nonorthodox churches). For example, Mother Jesse's small church in D'Abadie, in north-central Trinidad, contains small statues of Hindu deities and other Hindu paraphernalia. One can find Catholic, Orisha, and sometimes Kabbalistic symbols and objects in some Baptist churches as well (see Photo 6).

As I pointed out earlier, Spiritual Baptist churches are sometimes found inside Orisha compounds. In some cases the church functions as an Orisha *palais* during the annual feasts; often, however, the church and the *palais* are separate structures. Worshipers associated with such a compound are virtually always members of both the Orisha and Baptist religions; they go to church on Sundays and attend the annual Orisha feasts and other Orisha ceremonies during the week—one of the more salient examples of the interrelatedness of the two groups.

Although the Spiritual Baptist and Orisha religions overlap or interact in a number of domains—organizational, liturgical, and demographic—many Spiritual Baptists, especially those affiliated with the orthodox churches, distance themselves from the more Africanized *orisha* worship. Such worshipers generally do not attend any Orisha functions. At the other extreme, nonorthodox Spiritual Baptists are heavily involved with the Orisha religion and its more Africanized style of worship and generally follow the activities of both their church and their shrine. For them, the terms "Spiritual Baptist" and "*orisha* worshiper" can be used interchangeably; only the context dictates which one is proper at any given time.

Worshipers who affiliate with compounds that contain both Spiritual Baptist churches and Orisha shrines are often called "Shango Baptists" by those outside the circle of Afro-American religion in Trinidad. I prefer not to use this term, for although many Trinis and some writers and researchers refer to the Orisha religion as "Shango" or the "Shango cult," the worshipers themselves take umbrage at the "Shango Baptist" appellation and view it as another sign of the general public's ignorance of their religion.

SEVEN

Hinduism and the Kabbalah

B*y 1950 or so,* various Catholic elements had long been part of the Orisha religion, and the interrelationship between Spiritual Baptists and *orisha* worshipers was no doubt quite advanced. Sometime during the 1950s, for reasons explored below, Hinduism began to make its presence felt in the already highly eclectic Orisha religious system. About twenty years later, many *orisha* worshipers began to practice the Kabbalah as well. These are the two latest additions to the Afro-American religious complex.

Hinduism

Hinduism has been present in Trinidad ever since Indians began arriving about 150 years ago, and it has become one of the island's major religions. Its two main organizational sects (although others do exist) are the Sanatan Dharma Maha Saba, with headquarters in St. Augustine, and the Divine Life Society, with headquarters south of Chaguanas in west-central Trinidad.

Apparently, however, *orisha* worshipers only recently began to incorporate Hindu elements into their belief system. I base this claim primarily on two pieces of evidence. First, researchers observing both the Spiritual Baptists and the Orisha religion before the 1980s (e.g., Herskovits and Herskovits 1964; Simpson 1964, 1965, 1966) and even Parks (1981) make no mention of the presence of Hindu elements in the religious systems of either group. Frances Mischel (1958, 98) does note in passing that one shrine head recognized an Indian god, but that is all she has to say regarding Hindu elements in the Orisha religion — and she implies that Indians were not present even demographically: "Membership [in the Orisha religion] is exclusively composed of lower class, black-skinned Negroes" (1958, 52). Glazier (1983, 3, 29), mentions the influence of Hinduism on the Spiritual Baptist but not the Orisha religion. And Leader Scott and other worshipers have themselves said that not until 1960 or so did they begin to notice Hindu elements in Orisha compounds. Second, except in a few isolated cases, the incorporation of Hindu elements into Orisha has not yet involved syncretism; much of what has occurred thus far is simple borrowing, which suggests that there has not been sufficient time for syncretism to occur. In other words, given enough time and the perception among *orisha* worshipers that the large, anthropomorphic pantheon of Hinduism is similar to their own (a perception that, as we have seen, facilitated the syncretism of *orisha* and Catholic saints), the absence of syncretism involving Hindu and Orisha deities outside a few isolated cases suggests that *orisha* worshipers have only recently become aware of Hinduism in any meaningful way.

The fact that the two religious traditions coexisted in relative isolation from each other for so long can be partly attributed to ethnic factors and to the historical context. The Hindu-Orisha association, unlike that obtaining between the Spiritual Baptists and the Orisha religion, involves two groups who do not share a common ethnic or geographical heritage and who came to the New World under different circumstances.

It is difficult to say exactly why Hinduism has recently become part of the Orisha religion or, for that matter, why it is present in *orisha* worship at all. Historically, of course, both Indians and Africans have suffered from poor working conditions, whether in the sugar cane fields or the oil refineries, and their collective inferior social and economic status has greatly hampered their social mobility. Poor working conditions resulted in the labor riots of 1937, and the inferior socioeconomic status of non-Europeans played a major role in the Black Power Movement of the early 1970s. Certainly, both Africans and Indians have experienced a general feeling of oppression, and according to Leader Scott, the result was to improve relations between them, so that Indians began to consult African spirit men, or "obeahmen," in times of sickness or spiritual need, and Africans began to open up to Hinduism as well. Daniel Crowley (1957, 822) agrees, noting that in the early 1950s Africans visited Hindu *pundits*, and Indians sought the help of African obeahmen. But the late 1950s and early 1960s were also marked by ethnic-based party politics and heightened racial tension

(Oxall 1982, 155–56; Ryan 1972, 171). Given the atmosphere of dis-
trust and resentment that has existed between Africans and Indians to
some degree virtually since the arrival of the latter, it seems unlikely
that the incorporation of Hindu elements into the Orisha religion can
be attributed to harmonious ethnic relations.

It is more probable that the polytheism of the two religions had a
lot to do with the addition of Hindu elements; *orisha* worshipers look at
the Hindu deities and see much that is familiar. Also, *orisha* worshipers
are well aware that Hinduism is one of the "great" religions, that it is a
legitimate, publicly respected, and officially recognized form of worship. The Orisha religion would obviously benefit from allying with
such an organization, since the widespread public acceptance and recognition accorded the Hindu pantheon would give credibility by association to the Orisha pantheon, which many Trinis do not consider
socially acceptable.

As with other borrowings, the incorporation of Hindu elements
into the Orisha belief system characteristically takes different forms
around the island. Worshipers usually simply superimpose the borrowed elements onto Orisha beliefs and practices. Typically, one finds
at an Orisha shrine a small area devoted to one or more Hindu deities.
This area generally contains statues, statuettes, and large poster representations of the deities and an assortment of Indian brass receptacles,
candles, incense, and other materials.

Among the Hindu deities most commonly found in *orisha* worship
are Hanuman, Mahabir, Lakshmi, and Rama. Because virtually all the
Hindu deities borrowed by Orisha are popular figures in many public
Hindu festivals and ceremonies in Trinidad, even the most uninterested African will have some familiarity with them. Hinduism also
manifests itself to a small degree in the form of Osain (also referred to
as Osanyin or Osa), who clearly has Yoruba origins and can be found in
Orisha compounds all over the island but whose shrine is often surrounded with Hindu religious materials. Osain, sometimes referred to
as "the Indian man," is, however, formally syncretized with Saint Francis (see Chapter Thirteen).

Although Hindu-Orisha syncretism is rare, a few of the more
knowledgeable worshipers do speak of an association between particular Hindu deities and African *orisha*. The perceived similarities of the
gods of both groups allow for a syncretism similar to the association
worshipers have made between the Catholic saints and *orisha*. Leader

Scott noted the following pairings (the *orisha* are listed first): Ogun/ Mahabir (or Hanuman), Osain/Mahadeo, Oya/Parvati, Oshun/Lakshmi, Mama Lata/Pahrmisar, Shakpana/Durga, Eshu/Dee, and Obatala/Ganesa. Noorkumar Mahabir and Ashram Maharaj (1989, 194) also mention syncretisms involving Ogun and Hanuman or Mahabir, and Oshun and Ganga Mai.

Nevertheless, in regard to the group as a whole, the relationship that exists at present between the Orisha religion and Hinduism is not a purely syncretic one. Only a few *orisha* worshipers, such as Leader Scott, recognize a syncretism involving specific African and Hindu deities. Personal conceptions of relationships between various gods and spirits, involving as they do the association between concepts and beliefs of different religious traditions such as Catholic and African, or Hindu and African, reflect a sophisticated understanding of different belief systems as being functionally equivalent on some level.

In addition to "mainstream" Hinduism, there is another form of Hindu worship in Trinidad which resembles *orisha* worship: the Kali-Mai ("black mother") sect also practices ritual possession and animal sacrifice. The Kali-Mai sect tends to be associated with the darker-skinned Madras peoples, and mainstream Hindus consider such worship "primitive" and "uncivilized." According to William Guinee (personal communication)—a folklorist who worked with Hindus in Trinidad—as well as Leader Scott and many of the older Hindus, Kali-Mai worship was village-based at one time, and its practice was widespread. Through time the sect gradually lost its appeal but has begun to make something of a comeback, although probably in altered form. For example, a large and elaborate temple in St. Augustine, only recently constructed by Kali-Mai worshipers, draws two to three hundred people every Sunday.

It is interesting to note that although African participation in mainstream Hinduism is virtually nil, some 7 or 8 percent of those attending Kali-Mai services are African. It may be the strong emphasis that the Kali-Mai sect puts on healing that attracts the Africans. At the four Sunday services I attended, it appeared to me that the Indian worshipers welcomed the Africans with an openness that is apparently uncommon at the ceremonies of mainstream Hinduism.

There is little or no actual association between the Kali-Mai sect and the Orisha religion, but worshipers from each group are supportive of or at least sympathetic to the religious practices of the other.

Such mutual sympathy can probably be attributed to a common history of discrimination and social disapprobation. Local tabloids that often blame *orisha* worshipers and Spiritual Baptists for bizarre incidents frequently give the Kali-Mai sect the same treatment, especially if the incident occurs in a predominantly Indian area. Mahabir and Maharaj mention a number of beliefs and practices that are common to Orisha and Kali-Mai, but they point out that these similarities are either incidental or can be attributed to transmutation (1989, 196–98, 192).

The Kabbalah

By the 1970s, while the ranking heads and elders of both the Spiritual Baptist and Orisha religions were incorporating the deities, paraphernalia, and symbolism of Hinduism into their churches, shrines, and worship activities at an ever increasing rate, yet another religious tradition, the Kabbalah, was establishing itself as an important component of the Afro-American religious complex. Its influence, not only on the Afro-American religious complex but on the worshipers themselves, was, and still is, strong and pervasive.

The Kabbalah is an esoteric corpus of mystical and religious knowledge that is thought by its practitioners to contain essential teachings regarding the spiritual mechanics of the cosmos. The term "Kabbalah" is derived from the Hebrew *qabbala*, which means a "receiving," and has also come to be translated as "tradition" (Schubert 1967, 1031). (Many orthographic forms of the term exist — Qabbalah, Kabala, Kabbala, Kabbalah, Cabala, Cabbalah — but I use "Kabbalah" as one of the more popular variations.)

By tradition, the Kabbalah was given to Moses by God and has been handed down through the ages as the esoteric counterpart to more conventional Jewish and Christian religious knowledge (Schaya 1971, 19; Sheinkin 1986, 9–10). Only a select few were aware of the Kabbalistic teachings; practitioners generally passed along their Kabbalistic lore orally until the Middle Ages, when scribes finally began to record it (Sheinkin 1986, 12). The transition from Mosaic Judaism to medieval Kabbalah is unclear, however. Although there seems to be a general similarity between early Jewish mysticism and later Kabbalistic teachings, there is little or no evidence of a transition of any kind from one to the other during the intervening 1,500 years. In fact, "when the first Kabbalistic circles began to appear in Provence and Spain in the

Middle Ages, their symbols and terminology, as well as their concept of the divine world, seemed to be completely novel" (Dan 1986, 4).

Whatever its origins and early development, it is clear that the Kabbalah as it is known today first became popular during the latter part of the twelfth century in Spain and southeastern France. It underwent significant development until the end of the fifteenth century, when the Spanish banished the Jews from the Iberian peninsula. Kabbalistic scholars and practitioners subsequently carried their knowledge and lore to Italy, Turkey, and the Arabian peninsula (Wigoder 1989, 514). The Kabbalah was popular in England by the seventeenth century (Werblowsky 1983, 386).

The Kabbalah today contains elements of Jewish mysticism, Gnosticism, Neoplatonism, Christian doctrine, neo-Pythagoreanism, and hermeticism (writings attributed to Hermes Trismegistus) (Idel 1988, 40–41; Schubert 1967, 1031–35; Wallman 1958, 17; Wünsche 1908, 326). It is an esoteric and arcane cosmology that utilizes a unique symbolic and mathematical hermeneutic to apply basic theosophical and theurgical principles to the problems of human existence.

It appears that some of the colonizing Europeans—Spanish, French, and English—brought the Kabbalah to Trinidad. It had been practiced in Spain and France since the latter part of the twelfth century and had spread to England by at least the seventeenth century, so it is not unreasonable to assume that the Kabbalah was brought to the New World during the period of European colonization. This is admittedly only an educated guess, for there is little or no documentation on its transfer from the Old World to the Caribbean (as far as I know, the only other work on Afro-American religions that mentions the Kabbalah by name and identifies it as being an integral part of religious worship is Souza and Pinto 1976). It is interesting that many of the Kabbalists in Trinidad refer to the Kabbalah as "white man's magic," and many of the Kabbalistic entities are thought to be white and European.

The Kabbalah has apparently been practiced in Trinidad since early colonial times, but only in the last twenty or so years has it become openly associated with the Orisha religion. Two prominent Kabbalah practitioners told me that before 1970, Kabbalah banquets were almost exclusively private and closed affairs. Because of its diabolical overtones and the fact that most *orisha* worshipers themselves consider the practice to be evil, Kabbalists even today, I am told, tend to practice in private and somewhat restricted settings. A growing number of banquets seem to be open to the general public, at least technically, but attendance is often controlled by formal invitations.

Just exactly why Kabbalah worship went public is difficult to say. I was told that a particular shrine head in south Trinidad, Isaac Lindsay, was the first to open his banquet, sometime around 1970. While it is true that there are many heads and many banquets, *mongba* Lindsay was the ranking Orisha priest at the time, and his popularity extended far beyond the circle of worshipers in the Afro-American religious complex. It is certainly possible that this one man's influence could have legitimized Kabbalah worship for *orisha* worshipers as a group. In addition, the increased popularity of Kabbalah banquets in 1970 coincided with the emergence of the Black Power Movement, which ushered in feelings of black pride and a widespread interest in things African. Perhaps the opening of Kabbalah banquets was simply a by-product of a period in which Afro-American religion experienced at least a temporary surge of popularity and public support. (The Kabbalah is, of course, not part of the sub-Saharan African cultural tradition, but many Trinidadians associate it with Africans and the Orisha religion.) Whatever the reasons behind the movement of Kabbalah practices from secret to open and public settings, it is clear that although the ranking heads and elders in the Afro-American religious complex have only recently begun to incorporate Kabbalah ritual, entities (the term used to refer to Kabbalah spirits), symbolism, and paraphernalia into their belief system, this practice is becoming increasingly common.

Kabbalah worship in Trinidad seems to be primarily an African activity. One of my contacts noted that since some Africans worked closely with the colonial Europeans as domestic servants, they were privy to the religious practices of the Europeans, some of which were probably Kabbalistic. Perhaps another important factor was the virtual absence of a popular form of Indian religious worship in Trinidad that practices spirit possession and mediumship, both important aspects of Kabbalah worship. (The Kali-Mai sect is an obvious exception, but it appears to have had a relatively small number of adherents; the total of current worshipers probably does not exceed five hundred. Further, it is not clear that spirit possession was an integral part of early Kali-Mai worship in Trinidad.) Thus, to return to a biological analogy, since the Indians had not been "preadapted" to Kabbalah worship, they apparently were not drawn to it; indeed, they would have had to make a major spiritual leap to adjust to the practice. The Africans, by contrast, have a long tradition of spirit possession–based worship in Trinidad and could easily make the transition to at least the theurgical aspect of the Kabbalah, which is the primary characteristic of its Trinidadian form. In fact, the Trinidadian emphasis on the theurgical aspect of the Kabbalah may be of African derivation: spirit possession, mediumship, and invocation are important in the Afro-American religious complex, especially in the Orisha religion; consequently, the Africans would tend to borrow from the Kabbalistic system that which was most familiar to them.

Yet though it is true that Trini Kabbalists emphasize spirit manifestations and working with the entities, some worshipers also own extensive libraries of occult literature covering the broad range of beliefs and practices that make up the Kabbalah. Perhaps the most popular work in Kabbalistic circles in Trinidad is *The Book of Black Magic and of Pacts* by Arthur E. Waite (1972). Originally published in 1898, this text has been through a number of revisions (in 1911, 1961, and 1970) as *The Book of Ceremonial Magic* (Waite 1970); both versions are still in print. Worshipers often read directly from this work during Kabbalah banquets.

Having access to various works on the Kabbalah has undoubtedly contributed to the development of a more general understanding of this esoteric tradition among those who practice it. A number of Kabbalistic practitioners in Trinidad are familiar with its various aspects, and their understanding and practice of the Kabbalah are quite sophisticated. Elder Biddeau, for example, one of the more prominent and erudite Kabbalists, has devoted roughly half of his shrine to the Kabbalah. The Kabbalists in Trinidad, then, may have begun their practice with an emphasis on the familiar theurgical aspects and only later developed a more generalized and sophisticated understanding of the Kabbalah as they gradually gained access to occult literature.

Trinidadians consider the Kabbalah dangerous, recognizing its diabolical as well as its positive side. The Kabbalists themselves regard many of the entities as demonic beings who are irascible, mercurial, and indifferently amoral. The worshipers maintain that the entities are powerful and will work quickly when handled by a skilled Kabbalist. But as Elder Biddeau explained, neophytes or unskilled dabblers put themselves at a serious risk, since the proper practice of this "art" requires considerable training and knowledge:

A person must be very knowledgeable to handle the Kabbalah. For one, you have to be able to understand everything you read. Not only understanding what you read, but you have to know exactly [what you are doing]. . . . You must be able to work with figures. You must be able to have some sense of alchemy, because you are dealing with things on a scientific basis, and if you don't handle them properly, they won't work. So, you have to make this [the Kabbalah] a study; you can't just wake up in the morning and say you are a Kabbalist. You must devote plenty of time to it, and you must be guided by an elder or a teacher. The self-taught man who is handling the Kabbalah is always in danger.

Because you are dealing here with intelligence . . . there is no room for mistakes. Once it is done, it is done, and the outcome is either negative or positive. So, you have to be careful. (Interview, south of Matura, December 17, 1988)

Many Kabbalistic practitioners are also Orisha *mongba*, *iya*, and shrine heads, and practically all are members of the Orisha religion (in fact, as far as I can tell, little if any Kabbalah is practiced outside the circle of *orisha* worshipers). These individuals will usually have areas set aside in their Orisha shrines for flags or other materials devoted to Kabbalistic entities. A typical Kabbalist will work with the entities in both a personal, informal, and impromptu context and in a public and formal context. The former generally involves spiritual work done on behalf of a client; the latter involves the banquet, the most popular Kabbalistic ceremony in Trinidad.

There are different types of banquets, but they may be generally divided into two groups: "closed" and "open" banquets. During a closed banquet, particular entities are dealt with for specific reasons; attendance at this banquet is restricted. The open banquet is an annual affair during which any Kabbalah entity may manifest itself. The mood is usually festive, and a large table set with cakes, cigarettes, cigars, wine, liquor, and candles is the focus of activity (Photo 7). The entities are expected to make their presence known, interact positively with those in attendance, indulge in their favorite tobacco and drink, and then depart. Such is not always the case, however, and this is where the "operator" becomes important.

The three most important people present during a banquet are the medium, the operator, and the conjurer. (Any one of these positions can actually be filled during one night by more than one individual.) The medium is the person through whom an entity manifests itself

(Photo 8) and is often the "sponsor" or "owner" of the banquet. The conjurer will invoke the entities verbally, often by reading from Waite's *Pacts* (1972) or some other work, or sometimes by reciting a liturgy from memory. The operator has perhaps the most important role, since he or she is expected to conduct the proceedings and to control the potentially harmful entities when they manifest themselves.

I was present on one occasion when an operator lacked the experience to deal competently with a manifesting entity, who began to give orders and to act as he pleased. This unruly behavior caused quite a bit of confusion, since the operator is expected to maintain full control over the proceedings. This particular entity was a potentially violent one, but before it could do much damage another operator stepped in and brought things under control.

Few Spiritual Baptists seem to be involved in the Kabbalah, although I have on occasion seen Spiritual Baptist leaders wearing Kabbalah medallions. There are, however, some interesting parallels between elements of the Kabbalah and Spiritual Baptist worship; during my fieldwork I observed the use of similar chalk-drawn seals or spiritual symbols, the singing of Christian hymns (although the Kabbalah hymns tend to be dirges), the invocation of spirits, the elaborate setting of tables as the focus of spiritual activity, and the use of a "wand" or pointing stick to rap either on a table (Kabbalah) or the earth (Spiritual Baptist). These ritual similarities, of course, may simply be the result of parallel development in an Afro-American religious context, or they may be so general as to be insignificant. Nor should perceived similarities mask the major difference between the two worship forms: the general tone of the Kabbalah is negative; that of the Spiritual Baptists, positive. The Kabbalists will deal with familiar or earthbound spirits or even entities recognized as demonic, for example; the Baptists, as a general rule, will not.

The association between the Kabbalah and the Spiritual Baptist and Orisha religions appears to be a recent one—although, as with Hinduism, I have to appeal to the silence of earlier researchers in saying so. But I find it significant that no researchers except Simpson (1980, 55, 88), who makes a few simple references to "circle people" without elaborating, and Mischel (1958, 87), who mentions that several groups in Port of Spain recognized "powers of darkness," have noted the existence of the Kabbalah in Trinidad—and even those two did not use the term "Kabbalah."

Because it appears that the Kabbalah has become a public practice only since the early 1970s, certainly a researcher could spend some time on the island without coming across Kabbalistic worship. It was not until the end of my three-month stay in 1985 that I serendipitously stumbled upon a Kabbalah room in an Orisha compound that I was researching. And it was only after I had become a virtual fixture at Afro-American religious ceremonies that my contacts began to open up to me on the subject. It is not difficult to see how the practice of the Kabbalah in Trinidad might have been overlooked.

1. *Shakpana's calabash.*

2. *The many symbols recognized by Spiritual Baptists inscribed on a board often used during the mourning ritual.*

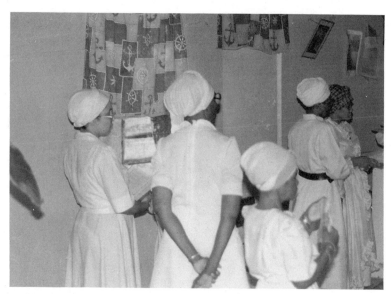

3. *Spiritual Baptists at a worship service.*

4. *A Spiritual Baptist church building.*

98

5. *The "center area" in a Spiritual Baptist church.*

6. *Inside a symbolically complex Spiritual Baptist church.*

7. *A Kabbalah table set for a banquet.*

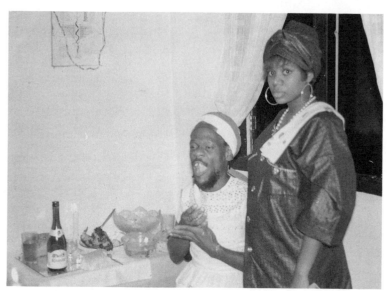

8. *A Kabbalah medium* (seated) *manifested upon by an entity. The conjuror stands by his side.*

9. *Leader Scott's shrine: the* perogun *marked by* orisha *flags* (background); *the tin-covered* palais (right); *flags for personal spirits and Saint Peter* (foreground).

10. *The* perogun *at Henry White's shrine.*

11. *The flags of various* orisha.

12. *Gock, Charlo, and Michael in front of Shaka's freshly painted* chapelle.

102

13. *A Kabbalah tomb at Henry White's shrine.*

14. *Mother Joan* (second from left) *at Hindu prayers.*

15. *Leader Scott directing the flag raising at Eshu's shrine.*

16. *Orisha drummers:* from left, *Po playing the* congo, *Joe the* bemba, *and Dexter the* oumalay.

Part III

EIGHT

Spirits and Spirit Possession

T*he most significant event* in the Orisha religion is the manifestation of an *orisha*. The onset of an *orisha* possession is a startling event: the worshiper who is being manifested upon screams loudly and falls about as if being pushed and pulled by some invisible force. After this initial "settling" period, however, the "horse" dances to the beat of the drums with a beauty that has to be seen to be appreciated.

Although most possessions are somewhat predictable, there is always the possibility that something will happen to disturb the manifesting *orisha*. This sometimes leads to a confrontation between the *orisha* and one or more worshipers. Considering the number of feasts and other ceremonies I attended, the fact that I have had only one major confrontation with an *orisha* is amazing. It is a confrontation, however, that I will not soon forget.

On the night of July 1, 1992, I was deep in the cane country of west-central Trinidad, in Basta Hall Village, attending the first night of Leader Scott's annual *ebo*. I had brought my video camera with me that summer, and Leader Scott had given me permission to videotape the ceremony. After taping the opening prayers inside the *chapelle*, I placed my camera and tripod just outside the *palais*—where the drumming, singing, and most of the possessions would occur—at a point from which I could survey the entire structure while remaining outside the area itself.

By 2:00 A.M., I had footage of the drumming and singing but no possessions. A short time later I noticed that Aaron Jones appeared to be in the early stages of possession and trained my camera on him. But in this case, unlike most possessions, it took about half an hour for Ogun finally to settle on him. At that point he directed a nearby worshiper to tie a red band around his head and asked for his cutlass. Ogun

107

danced for about ten minutes and swung the cutlass menacingly over his head, not with the intent to harm but to show that he was totally in control of the proceedings. I was glad to be outside the *palais* during this time, since I am not comfortable with the idea of an individual in an advanced dissociative state swinging a three-foot machete.

Shortly after he began his dance, however, Ogun ordered the drumming to stop. This is seldom a good sign, since it is usually an indication that the *orisha* is upset with something — this time, unfortunately, with me and my camera. Ogun pointed the cutlass at me and began talking in angry tones. I always found it difficult to decipher the speech of manifesting *orisha*, but fortunately, Leader Scott was in the *palais* and could interpret: Ogun was evidently not pleased that I was videotaping his manifestation. After verbally chastising me, however, he called me his child (referring to the fact that he is my patron *orisha*) and told me not to be frightened but to heed his warning in the future. He then went about his business as if nothing had happened, while I turned off my camera and dismantled my tripod. In retrospect, I am still puzzled that Ogun allowed me to keep the videotape.

Although face-to-face confrontations of this sort do occur from time to time, an *orisha* manifestation is usually a cause for joy and celebration. The *orisha* are generally amiable and interact with individuals in a positive fashion. There is very little fear in the *palais* when *orisha* are present. The same cannot be said, however, of the Kabbalah entities.

Kabbalah manifestations can be truly frightening, for several reasons. First, many Kabbalah mediums are domineering, charismatic men who become loudly demonstrative and arrogant when manifested upon by an entity. Second, many of the entities are, according to Kabbalists, demonic and have such names as "Prince of Evil" and "Skull and Cross." Finally, a manifesting entity is totally unpredictable and will harm other worshipers if not properly controlled. Not surprisingly, then, Kabbalah banquets are intense, sometimes terrifying affairs. The entities may growl, grit their teeth, drool, curse madly, threaten others in attendance, and slap or punch anyone who crosses them. I learned that the best way to deal with these possessions, especially if one has no desire to become involved with the entity or in the ceremony itself, is politely and respectfully to refuse any "gift" that may be offered.

It can be difficult, however, to avoid confrontation with a manifesting entity. On the night of January 1, 1989, I was attending a Kabbalah banquet in Claxton Bay, on the western coast of Trinidad. This being my first banquet, I decided to sit just behind what appeared to be a special high-backed chair at the end of a lavishly set table. Around 2:00 A.M. the medium entered and sat just in front of me in the special chair. The singing of hymns was followed by the reading of passages from various books on the Kabbalah and the occult. Eventually, a particularly nasty entity manifested itself on the medium, who began to groan and drool and jerk violently from side to side. Then the medium tried to stand and fell back right on top of me, cursing and spewing saliva. I helped him up and tried to support him, but the others were yelling at me to move away from the entity, since I was apparently upsetting it. I was finally able to extract myself from this very uncomfortable situation, and I never again voluntarily placed myself so close to a manifesting entity.

Spiritual Baptist manifestations are another thing entirely; the possessed individual carries on in almost total isolation from the other worshipers. Those in attendance at the service never interact with manifesting Baptist spirits other than to assist the possessed individuals to prevent them from hurting themselves as they stumble around.

Possessions, in the Afro-American religious complex, then — or, more specifically, the interactions between worshiper and spirit — run the gamut from positive and uplifting, to neutral and indifferent, to negative and dangerous. The experienced worshiper will be equally adept at handling herself or himself in these various contexts.

Because of the richness of sources that have contributed to the Orisha religion, worshipers at an Orisha shrine are overwhelmed or, more accurately, bombarded with a variety of symbols, prayers, songs, and rites. These sights and sounds reflect a corresponding wealth of numinous and metaphysical aspects of worship involving a plethora of spirits, gods, powers, and entities. The pantheon, taken in its broadest sense, comprises the following groups: the Spiritual Baptist powers (primarily the Holy Spirit, but also certain saints and Old Testament characters), the Kabbalah entities (which include the four archangels, Satan, famous deceased local personalities, ancient and powerful spirits drawn from occult literature such as Astaroth, and a variety of chthonic and familiar spirits), Hindu deities, Catholic saints, and *orisha*.

We find a similar accretion of diverse spirits in other African-derived religions in the New World. For example, Umbanda (Brazil) combines the spirits of Euro-American spiritualism, Yoruba religion, Catholicism, Amerindian religions, and local lore (Pressel 1974; Simpson 1978). The tendency among worshipers to consolidate the pantheons and mythical figures from diverse cultural traditions is found in the Old World as well. The *zairan*, for example, recognized by peoples of northern Sudan, include "the spirit analogues of Muslim saints, Turkish administrators, 'Europeans' (including North Americans, Hindus, and Chinese), Ethiopians, Syrian gypsies, West Africans, nomadic Arabs, and Southern Sudanese, in short, of all human groups with whom [Northern Sudanese] have had contact over the past 150 years or more" (Boddy 1988, 15).

While it is true that the Trinidad case is similar to the Brazilian and northern Sudanese examples, the cultural interpretations, not surprisingly, differ. Like the practitioners of Umbanda but to an even greater extent, worshipers in Trinidad respond to their collection of spirits by simplifying the typology and collapsing or relegating the many groups into one or two. This grouping strategy is at least an implicit or subconscious reaction to the multiplicity of gods and powers derived from five religious traditions. The tendency to "lump," rather than to "split," functions much like the Africanization process, which also acts to simplify the eclectic Orisha religion.

During a lengthy prayer ceremony (like the one described in Chapter Five), a number of different spirits may manifest themselves, taking possession of one or more "horses" over the course of the evening. Varied manifestations can also occur in the same individual; in fact, two different possessing agents may appear to inhabit the "horse" at the same time. Shortly after the opening of a ceremony I witnessed in west-central Trinidad on June 18, 1989, two people—whom I shall call Mary and Patrick—both knelt. Patrick prayed first, for almost an hour; then Mary took her turn. As she was praying, another worshiper started to beat a drum, and the chants and rhythms picked up in intensity. There were soon many manifestations. About ten people were "hit" hard for a few seconds; three of them remained possessed for ten to fifteen minutes. These appeared to be Spiritual Baptist manifestations; they were very chaotic. "Darlene" got a Baptist manifestation and spoke in tongues. Mary, however, got a mixed possession—a bit of Shango (an *orisha*) and a bit Baptist. She picked up a large vase holding palm leaves, put it on her right shoulder, and walked around to various points. Leader Scott told me that she was also "hit" by a "being" (a

Kabbalah entity) for a few seconds. About this time Patrick also became possessed, walking around in a daze with his arms crossed in front of his chest to form an X; Leader Scott said that this was the manifestation of a being as well.

Such scenarios are not commonplace, but they are not rare either. The typical worshiper attends two or three ceremonies a month and will likely witness a multiple manifestation several times each year. When I questioned worshipers about their impressions and thoughts regarding these potentially confusing events, I found that experience in and knowledge of the religion correlates positively with the tendency to lump together all spirits (except Kabbalah entities) in one or two categories.

Faced with the task of constructing something meaningful from the bewildering array of spirits, symbols, beliefs, and practices, worshipers often attempt to reconcile or at least integrate the various spirit groups in some way. Some, naturally, are more successful than others. Newcomers in "the faith" and some of the rank and file tend to perceive the pantheon analytically and to differentiate substantively between various spiritual groups. But not a few individuals responded equivocally and ambiguously to my inquiries regarding the interrelationship between the various spirit groups; it was obvious that they had not even thought about the nature of such an association.

One young worshiper in his thirties, who had been attending Orisha ceremonies for over ten years, seemed to have given the nature of the spirits little thought. When I asked him what caused the manifestations in Spiritual Baptist worship and whether or not the possessing agent was the same at Orisha rites, he pondered for a considerable length of time before he answered:

The Spiritual Baptist manifestation doesn't be as deep, and doesn't take hold of the flesh, as when a manifestation from the *orisha* take over. The *orisha* has the body to take charge of at that time. . . . It [the Spiritual Baptist manifestation] just doesn't have that tight hold on you . . . [long pause]. It could be the same force [in each case]. (Interview, near Barataria, December 13, 1988)

He added only that he recognizes distinct Hindu, Catholic, Kabbalah, and Orisha spirits.

The older, more experienced, and more knowledgeable worshipers, however, speak in terms of consolidation and focus on the consonance of the various spirit groups rather than their incongruity. Leader Scott's comments on the relationship between the Yoruba and Hindu religions illustrates this tendency:

One thing you have to consider is that the *orisha* practitioners are open to the spirit world. Therefore, they do not discriminate against one spiritual form or another. We find it easy to communicate with spirits in any form. The Hindu with respect to the Orisha [religion] have certain things in common. For example, the Orisha [*orisha* worshipers] believe that everything comes from the earth and returns to the earth; the Hindu believe that too, that the earth is sacred. In the way that the Orisha consecrate places that must be of earth, in the same way the Hindu must use earth. . . . With respect to libations, there are also things in common — the water, the perfumes, the flowers, milk, honey. . . . The same things that are used by the Hindu are used by the Orisha. . . . The Orisha also recognize the ancestors using chants and drums like the Kali-Mai. . . . So although they may come from different cultures and use different languages, their practice and interpretation are almost the same.

You may say that there are two different groups of spirits because they are worshiped differently. And they are perceived of in different ways because of their whole orientation. [But] even though I am an Orisha, I can deal with the Kali-Mai possessions and relate to them. . . . It may be that in the Hindu way, the manifestation appears to be a little different; the approach may be a result of their own culturization. But when you take it in spirit form, the spirit is performing the same thing in different ways. . . . It is the same spirits operating differently. It is the same God that is worshiped in India and Africa.

Leader Scott explained that Spiritual Baptist powers fall within the same general category of spirits but that problems arise because of mistaken interpretation:

Their [Spiritual Baptists'] whole spiritual intelligence is based more on visions, and communication with spirits. When the Orisha [*orisha* worshipers] say they are going to talk with Ogun or deal with Ogun, they know exactly what they are going to talk to, and they know what they are going to deal with. The Baptists never know exactly what they are dealing with. When they have a manifestation that is unknown, they call it the Holy Spirit. They are trying to identify it with Christianity. It is the Christian influence within the Baptist that wants to recognize the Holy Ghost to keep it in line with Baptist theology. But these manifestations are just *orisha*. (Interview, Basta Hall Village, June 8, 1992)

Leader Scott subsumed the Catholic saints as well under the general rubric. Scott and many other *orisha* worshipers in Trinidad understand the term *orisha* to be roughly synonymous with the term "ancestor." Adherents recognize all but a handful of the Yoruba-derived *orisha* as historical figures that once walked the earth. The Catholic saints fit logically into such a scheme.

Virtually all worshipers, however, from neophytes to experienced elders, distinguish between the Kabbalah entities and the *orisha*. Leader Scott explained the difference:

The *orisha* are the top spirits. They can direct and communicate with other spirits no matter who they are. The Kab [Kabbalah entities] do not have this kind of control, but they can interfere. But they would not do this very long because they know that there is something bigger than them. He [a Kabbalah entity] would withdraw because the water is too hot for him. (Interview, Basta Hall Village, June 8, 1992)

Edmond David (popularly known as "Gock"), a prominent *mongba* and accomplished drummer and song leader in the Orisha religion, explained the relationship between the various spirit groups in much the same way:

All other religions came from Orisha. The Hindu [deities] are the same *orisha* but they have Indian names. Like Lakshmi is the mother of the ocean; we have Oshun; the Spiritual Baptist or the Catholic will say St. Philomena. But it is the same said spirit. It is just that the Indian have their way of worship and their way of doing their thing, and the Orisha [*orisha* worshipers] have their way.

I believe the Catholic saints originated from the *orisha*. I believe that all other religions came from Orisha because it was the first religion on the earth. The Baptist is a breakoff from the Orisha [religion]. It is a mixture of Christianity and Orisha. Because, you see, Christianity came many years after the Orisha [religion].

On the subject of the Kabbalah, however, *mongba* David, like Leader Scott, was careful to differentiate between the entities and the *orisha:*

All the spirits belong in the atmosphere. There are different levels in the atmosphere where these spirits dwell. The *orisha* are at the very top. . . . You see the *orisha* are light, they are light forces. When I say light I don't mean in the sense of weak; when they manifest on you they keep moving. They walk and talk up and down the *palais*. But a Kabbalah force when he manifests has to sit in one place. If he walks, he walks with a weight. (Interview, Claxton Bay, June 19, 1992)

Merlin Hernandez, a woman in her forties, expressed the same sentiments in a more philosophical tone:

A spirit is not something that has a temporal existence. A spirit is an essence, and that essence in India will be given a name; that essence in Africa will be given a name; that essence in Native America will be given a name. And whether you have Oshun in Yoruba or Lakshmi in Hindi, it's the same essence. (Interview, Couva, June 21, 1992)

But Hernandez too was careful to discriminate between the Kabbalah entities and the *orisha*, describing the former as "negative essences" that could "taint" *orisha* worship.

It is true that even some experienced worshipers do recognize distinctions between various spirit groups. For example, Mother Joan and Elder Biddeau contend that such differences, especially between Hindu and African traditions, are more than simply cultural. They state outright that Hindu gods and Yoruba *orisha* are separate categories of spirits. But with these few exceptions, most experienced and knowledgeable worshipers incorporate the Spiritual Baptist, Catholic, and Hindu powers and saints into a broad category subsumed under the general heading of *orisha*. Virtually no one, however, fails to distinguish between Kabbalah entities and the *orisha* and, more generally, between the two religious systems associated with their worship.

But even worshipers who tend to consolidate the powers, saints, and gods of various traditions into the broad category called *orisha* (or, sometimes, "African") nevertheless characterize particular manifestations of these spirits by specific cultural markers. A manifesting spirit is identified as Krishna, Ogun, Ezekiel, St. Catherine, Prince of Darkness, or whatever, depending on its movements, choice of implements, and general comportment. Interpretation also depends on context. Spiritual Baptists attending Baptist services usually attribute possession to the Holy Spirit or other Christian powers rather than to African gods. Likewise, at "sit-down" or Indian prayers held at Orisha shrines, at an Orisha feast, or at a Kabbalah banquet, worshipers usually identify the possessing agents as Hindu deities, *orisha*, or Kabbalah entities respectively. Identification ultimately depends on the behavior of the manifesting spirit and the knowledge of the identifier.

The recognition of a large number of manifesting powers is fairly common in complex societies where spirit possession is practiced; it is apparently instrumental in articulating individuals with their culture and society. A large pantheon of possessing spirits also provides a variety of roles through which individuals may express themselves in ways that mirror the various sociocultural and gender-based roles that exist in the society:

Possession trance, for the most part, involves the impersonation of spirits by human actors. . . . An inspection of spirits represented in possession trance rituals reveals for the most part, it appears, a symbolic rendition of human society. Thus, Gussler [1973] shows us the importance for the Zulu of ancestor spirits, representing the well-defined kin groups into which the society is divided. . . . Leonard [1973] tells us that in Palau, the traditional mediums served the gods of the clans and villages, that is, societal divisions are reproduced and reenacted on the spirit level. In the Umbanda cult of present-day Brazil, Pressel [1973] shows us, possession is by a variety of highly individualized spirits representing different segments of the population. A great many other examples can be cited from the broad literature on possession trance that tend to confirm the view that complex societies offer a great repertoire of roles. (Bourguignon 1973, 22)

It seems plausible that old religions indigenous to a particular area would be associated with many spirits whose personality attributes are socially and culturally meaningful. Articles of faith notwithstanding, the form and substance of religion is largely predicated on a complex assortment of political, social, economic, and historical factors. Thus, it is easy to understand why, say, the Fon peoples of Benin and the Yoruba of southern Nigeria conceive of the *vodoun* and the *orisha*, respectively, in terms that are familiar to them, and that these spirits manifest in culturally meaningful ways by expressing themselves — whether in language, dance, or other activities — in a familiar and culturally appropriate manner. These pantheons are, after all, affiliated with religious systems that have undergone centuries of indigenous development.

But the Orisha religion began in Trinidad only during the last century, and its primary components were borrowed from the Old World. In addition, Trinidadian society is dynamic and richly multicultural, having undergone several major upheavals during the last two centuries. We would therefore not necessarily expect to find a culturally relevant pantheon reflecting the historical traditions, sentiments, and needs of its worshipers — but we do, and there are two primary reasons.

First, the nature of the slave trade and the socially disruptive immigration process of the Yoruba essentially precluded any wholesale transfer of African religion to the New World. There was plenty of opportunity for the transplanted Africans to augment, along lines that were meaningful in their new surroundings, the bits and pieces of Yoruba religion that had survived the passage from the Old World with beliefs and rituals generated locally. Second, the cosmopolitan and "Trini first" attitudes of Africans in Trinidad (noted in Chapter Three) have been instrumental in the willingness of *orisha* worshipers to incorporate into their religious system elements drawn from practically all the major religious traditions on the island. The result is a rich pantheon with the potential to represent any number of personality types. (It is interesting that the predominantly "India first" Indian Hindus of Trinidad have borrowed virtually nothing from the other religious traditions. This is not particularly noteworthy in the case of mainstream Hinduism, which East Indians managed to transfer to the New World virtually intact, but it is significant in the case of the various offshoots of Hinduism in Trinidad, especially the Kali-Mai sect, which practices spirit possession and recognizes a large but exclusively Hindu pantheon.)

Whatever the numbers, sources, and characteristics of manifesting powers, however, there remains a central question: What is the etiology of spirit possession? The answer has eluded social scientists for years, although many scholars have attempted to explain and better understand this phenomenon.

Spirit possession is one specific type of the broader category commonly referred to as "altered states of consciousness." These occur universally, but the forms that specific manifestations take are culturebound: "It must be stressed that although the capacity to experience altered states of consciousness is a psychobiological capacity of the species, and thus universal, its utilization, institutionalization, and patterning are, indeed, features of culture, and thus variable" (Bourguignon 1973, 12).

Anthony Wallace has noted the difficulties that arise from the confusion of the natural and cultural aspects of the phenomenon and clarifies his own definition:

Casual observers and many anthropologists alike use this word [possession] in two very different senses: as a label for some person's overtly observable behavior, and as a label for a native theory to explain this behavior. These two uses are, unhappily, often confused. It may be best to state flatly, at the outset, that I will use the word "possession" to denote any native theory which explains some event of human behavior as being the result of the physical presence, in a human body, of an alien spirit which takes over certain or all of the host's executive functions. (Wallace 1959, 59)

It should be clear that spirit possession, combining as it does both natural and cultural elements, is essentially biocultural. Any treatment of possession, therefore, should at least attempt to explain the physiological aspects of this phenomenon and interpret the cultural aspects. A few, but not all, of the attempts at classifying possession types reflect this strategy.

I. M. Lewis (1971, 31–36) focuses on the difference between possession by peripheral spirits and possession by central spirits. He explains that peripheral spirits are often amoral and originate outside the group in which they are found, whereas central spirits are those found in "state" religions that perpetuate the world view and moral precepts of the community as a whole. Karl Knutsson (1975, 247) makes a distinction between what he refers to as ritual or voluntary possession and spontaneous or involuntary possession. He notes that the former is usually institutionalized, but the latter is not. Colleen Ward (1980, 149) distinguishes between ritual and peripheral possession (not to be confused with Lewis's notion). Ritual possession is amenable to cultural explanation and occurs in particular cultural contexts; peripheral possession is a more individualized and pathological phenomenon. Lewis Langness (1976, 56–64) explores the difference between hysterical psychoses and possession. He writes that "possessions are actively sought and induced," and that "there is a conscious, deliberate intent and attempt to bring about the experience," whereas "the victim of a hysterical psychosis is innocent of such intent, at least at the level of consciousness. There is no attempt to bring it about" (1976, 59).

These classification strategies, with the exception of Lewis's (1971), differentiate between natural and cultural explanations, although the focus in each case is different. The explanatory and interpretive studies, however, tend to be naturalistic, with many leaning toward particularism. The three most popular approaches are psychological, biochemical/physiological, and sociopolitical.

T. K. Oesterreich, approaching the phenomenon from a psychological perspective, writes that "there may be *a priori* two emotional states, parallel and separate, which co-exist." He also explains that the personality may "change in certain pathological conditions and thus constitute a 'second' personality" (1966, 91, 38). Others (Kiev 1961, 137; Mischel and Mischel 1958, 254; Ward 1980, 154) view spirit possession as a medium through which repressed needs and impulses can be satisfied. M. C. O'Connell (1982, 35–36) and Colleen Ward and Michael Beaubrun (1979, 49) postulate a link between stress and possession.

Biochemical/physiological approaches are those that consider biologically pathological mechanisms or other physiological factors. Edward Tylor (1896, 354) observed long ago that convulsions, delirium due to fever, and other phenomena are sometimes mistakenly attributed to possession by an alien spirit. Noting the preponderance of women in groups that practice spirit possession, Alice Kehoe and Dody Giletti (1981, 550) write that possession, at least in regard to women, "may be causally associated with sumptuary rules and economic patterns that limit women's access to adequately balanced nutrition, particularly the nutritional needs of pregnant and lactating women." Lewis (1971, 39) and Lenora Greenbaum (1973, 42; cited in Rouget 1985, 183) argue that music can serve as a physiological triggering mechanism to induce trance and possession. Rodney Needham (1967, 607) notes the connection between percussion and contact with the spirit world.

Also taking a physiological approach, Andrew Neher investigates the link between dissociation, drum-beat frequency, and alpha wave rhythms of the brain; he argues that possession occurs when drum-beat rhythms fall in the range of seven to nine cycles per second, a frequency that corresponds to alpha wave rhythms (1962, 154). Although Neher's work is intriguing and compelling, serious objections to his research design and conclusions have been raised. According to Gilbert Rouget (1985, 172–76), Neher's experiments did not produce actual trance or possession or anything close, and the constant and uniform "auditory stimuli" used in the laboratory did not accurately simulate the drumming and percussion that usually accompany possession and trance.

Sociopolitical approaches tend to focus on possession as the means by which socially repressed persons may improve their plight. Lewis (1966, 318) writes that "women and other depressed categories" use spirit possession to "exert mystical pressures upon their superiors in circumstances of deprivation and frustration when few other sanctions are available to them," an observation made by Seth and Ruth Leacock (1972) as well. In another work Lewis notes that spirit possession can be considered "in terms of manipulative strategies adapted in response to frustration" (1983, 412). Knutsson (1975, 269–70) writes that "the mechanics of possession may offer the individual the opportunity of an adequate course of action which falls outside any expected and legitimate role but still, through the invocation of superhuman authority, becomes both 'legitimate' and efficient." Finally, though not commenting specifically on spirit possession, Victor Turner writes in *The Ritual Process*—his tour de force on ritual and *communitas*—that in rituals of status elevation "structural underlings may well seek . . . deeper involvement in a structure that, though fantastic and simulacral only, nevertheless enables them to experience for a legitimated while a . . . kind of 'release' from [their] lot" (1969, 201).

These notions are all, no doubt, tenable to some degree, but each is deficient in some way. For example, Kehoe and Giletti's (1981) study focuses mainly on women, particularly pregnant women, and is almost exclusively scientistic. Neher's (1962) intriguing work deals solely with the psychophysiological triggering mechanism of possession and says little regarding cultural interpretations of this phenomenon. The sociopolitical approaches emphasize the link between possession and social mobility and argue that the possession experience allows repressed individuals to "legitimize" themselves—to stake their social claim, so to speak—by intimately associating themselves with the gods. Yet the link between the desire to upgrade oneself socially and dissociative behavior is never made. Moreover, how are we to explain possessions in the case of shrine heads and church leaders? The psychological approach may ultimately prove to be the most fruitful, although psychology may be best equipped to deal with the naturalistic or, more specifically, the neuropathological aspects of spirit possession.

Possession and trance states are prevalent among the world's cultures. Erica Bourguignon (1973, 10–11), for example, found that "culturally patterned forms of altered states of consciousness" were present in 90 percent of the 488 societies she surveyed, indicating "that we are dealing with a psychobiological capacity available to all societies." This would suggest that a universal or cross-cultural comparative approach would be productive here, and as we have seen, such studies have been relatively successful.

Still other researchers have approached possession from a more "insider-oriented" perspective (see, e.g., Lambek 1988; Ong 1988). Studies of this type, by giving the worshipers' point of view priority, avoid the smugness that can characterize scientistic and empirico-deductive research on spirit possession. The intent is to understand possession by examining the meaning and significance of behavior and ideology from the worshipers' perspective:

> In contrast to a naturalizing, epidemiological model that considers spirit possession as an expression (however indirect) of social or psychological distress and hence concerns itself with the question of who is vulnerable, the main question here is not which persons or classes of persons are most susceptible to possession but why they become possessed by particular spirits rather than others. This shifts the focus from viewing the possessed as objects and victims, or the detached manipulators, of their condition to an examination of the public and private relevance of their acts for human subjects. (Lambek 1988, 710)

Janice Boddy also argues in favor of a more insider-oriented or culture-specific approach:

> My concern is to avoid viewing possession phenomena in terms that, though our culture finds them accessible, are foreign to [the northern Sudanese] — whether biochemical reactions to nutritional deficiency (cf. Kehoe and Geletti 1981), or women's instrumental efforts to assuage their subordinate status by acquiring goods or garnering attention (cf. Lewis 1971, 1986). Such approaches may prove fruitful in assessing and translating specific cases of possession illness, . . . but since they neither account for possession forms, nor adequately credit the taken-for-grantedness of spirits in the everyday lives of the possessed, ultimately they distort and impoverish what they propose to understand. If the aim of the enterprise is to comprehend the scope of possession phenomena, to situate them in their cultural contexts, ethno-graphers must attend to their informants' experiences of possession and not seek merely to explain them away as something at once less dramatic and more clinical than they appear. (Boddy 1988, 4)

Worshipers themselves typically consider reductionistic explana-tions of possession and trance — whether physiological, sociopolitical, psychological, or whatever — to be particularly demeaning and insult-ing. This is not surprising, given the fact that spirit manifestations routinely legitimize religious belief and help define the roles of spirits vis-à-vis the worshiper. Of course, it is true that research conclusions often run contrary to indigenous sentiment, especially in those cases where the social scientist invokes economic, political, or otherwise materialistic factors in his or her analysis of, say, religion, mythology, or social organization. Though we may consider such results unfortunate (at least when we take into consideration the sentiments of those being studied), ordinarily the evaluation of such work should not be influenced by the degree to which it corresponds to the notions of those being researched. Nevertheless, in the specific case of spirit possession, I believe that one can make a good argument for a culturally meaningful approach. Scientistic or Western-oriented research designs have proved to be fruitful and elegant up to a point, but insider-oriented approaches have also proved successful when applied to specific cases of possession or trance.

Consider, for example, the high incidence of possession reported among female factory workers in Malaysia (Ong 1988, 29–30). Professionals (most of them Western trained) from a number of fields described these episodes as simple hysteria or seizures and usually prescribed conventional medical treatments. Aihwa Ong (1988, 33), however, found that the incursion of modern factories into the sociocultural landscape had disrupted the traditional social boundaries that effectively delimited the range and influence of spirits. For example, the women were reported petrified at the thought of using a Western-style toilet because they felt that swamps and bodies of water were "amoral domains" occupied by evil spirits.

Another reason we should seriously consider the natives' point of view and culture-bound explanations is that enculturation appears to be a significant component of the complex of beliefs, practices, and behavior associated with possession. I first became aware of the role of enculturation during my investigation of spirit possession among the Spiritual Baptists and *orisha* worshipers in Trinidad (Houk 1986, 1992). Others have noted the effect of enculturation on possession as well. Melville Herskovits described possession as a "conditioned reflex" that was a perfectly normal response to familiar cultural stimuli:

Now let us imagine a person who has been brought up in a cultural environment in which there is a profound belief in divinities, and in which he has been taught since childhood that he will receive, or be capable of receiving, one of these divinities; that these deities are summoned by the intermediary of specific drum rhythms and chants, to which they respond by descending upon the heads of those chosen to serve them. There is a good chance that, in the presence of the stimulus constituted by all the factors of a given situation conforming to the indications I have just given, the response will not be long delayed, and that possessions will take place. (Herskovits 1943, 25; cited in Rouget 1985, 177)

Bourguignon noted the importance of enculturation and describes the learning process:

First, the child acquires the basic personality dispositions, such as traits of independence and dependence and attitudes toward the self and the body. Next, the child learns the basic structure of the universe, the existence of spirits and their behavior, and the manner in which their presence may be perceived or induced. This prelearning is requisite before a ritual ASC [altered state of consciousness] may be experienced successfully. (Bourguignon 1979, 267)

During the eighteen months I spent in Trinidad, I witnessed hundreds of *orisha* possessions. Only once did I observe a possession of someone younger than fifteen years of age (the exception occurred in July 1985 at a feast in north-central Trinidad, when a twelve-year-old girl ran screaming and crying hysterically about the compound). And on only a handful of occasions did I observe possessions of young people under the age of twenty; these were virtually always characterized by uncontrolled and hysterical behavior, as were possessions among adults who had only recently converted to the religion. Most of the possessions I observed involved worshipers who were twenty-five and older. An important part of enculturation involves learning the attributes and ritual significance of the many spirits that are worshiped. The sheer complexity of the pantheon makes this process a difficult one, especially for the younger and less experienced worshipers — a factor that no doubt has some bearing on their chaotic dissociative behavior.

I found no significant difference between the number of possession events involving young to middle-aged people and those among persons aged fifty or more. The older group did differ dramatically from the other age groups in one respect, however: their possessions came and went quietly, and their behavior was "smooth" and appeared to be well controlled throughout — although I do not mean to imply here that the worshiper was totally conscious of her or his activities at the time.

It appears that age (or, in the case of adult converts, experience) is important, correlating positively with the propensity to undergo a possession experience at least up to the age of twenty-five or so, when the number of possession events per age group stabilizes. Of the possible explanatory factors for this correlation, I believe that enculturation is perhaps the most significant. Until individuals reach a certain level of sophistication in regard to cultural knowledge, they do not have the ability or capacity, consciously or otherwise, to effect an acceptable possession episode. As they mature, however, their level of cultural understanding increases to the point where they have mastered even the ideological subtleties of the local culture, resulting, perhaps, in possession events that fall within the range of what is considered to be socially proper. (For other accounts of the relationship between age and dissociative behavior, see Crapanzano 1987, 16; Rouget 1985, 32; and Zaretsky and Shambaugh 1978, xvii.)

Let us also not forget the positive correlation spoken of earlier between experience in the religion and the tendency on the part of the worshiper to consolidate the various spirit groups. Perhaps we could consider this a "leveling mechanism" of some sort that acts to ameliorate the natural confusion of dealing with such a diverse array of spirits and powers. While it is true that on the level of the community of adherents the manifesting spirits display a variety of cultural markers linking them to this or that tradition, on the individual level the possessed worshiper is at least subconsciously "cognizant" of the potential unity rather than the diversity of the various possessing agents. In fact, worshipers tend to associate particular individuals through time with one or, at most, a handful of particular possessing agents, referring to an individual as, say, "Ogun's horse" or "Shango's horse." Links of this sort are, perhaps, merely another consequence of the desire among worshipers to minimize the potentially bewildering effects of embracing an eclectic religious system.

I would not venture even a guess at this time about how much of this enculturation and manipulation occurs on an explicit or conscious level and how much occurs on a more implicit, subconscious, or even unconscious level. A. R. Tippett (1976, 147) writes that spirit possession episodes are neither spurious nor psychopathological but prima facie genuine. I am inclined to agree. After observing hundreds of possessions, I am convinced that they are not feigned. Individuals appear to be totally unaware of what is going on around them; they have no recall of the experience afterward and, indeed, are sometimes embarrassed to find their clothing and hair in disarray and their feet bare and dirty. Thus, at least part of the psychological machinery driving the possession experience is below the level of conscious thought. The worshipers themselves claim that the dissociative behavior observed at religious events is caused by a manifestation of a deity in the body of a worshiper; for the time being, the deity is in control of the physical body. A sophisticated and complex explanatory scheme associates particular possession behavior with particular deities. Asked why the possessions of younger people or neophytes tend to be so much more chaotic and hysterical than those of older and more experienced practitioners, worshipers simply explain that it takes a while (that is, many possession experiences) for a deity to settle itself completely on the head of a particular person.

"Scientific" approaches, though certainly productive, tend to ignore or at least deemphasize the worshipers' point of view. Folk explanations are more meaningful to the people who actually practice spirit possession, but the culture-specific nature of these explanations makes translation to ethnological science exceedingly difficult. It would be presumptuous to argue for the validity of Western, empirically based explanations at the expense of folk explanations — or vice versa. In fact, according to Rappaport (1989), we should assume that each approach is valid in its own way and move on to a synthesis or integration of the two; only then will we arrive at a holistic understanding of spirit possession.

NINE

Social Organization of the Orisha Religion

T
he *Orisha religion* is highly variable when viewed in cross section and dynamic when viewed longitudinally or across time. Whether because of opportunism, desire, or sheer necessity, it is a complex synthesis of a variety of religious traditions. Thus, those who practice the religion must be at least somewhat adept at manipulating an assortment of symbols and ideologies; this is especially true for the elders, shrine heads, *mongba*, and *iya* who construct and maintain the shrines and actively direct the annual feasts and other important rituals.

The shrines of many of the most popular and successful heads in the religion tend to be symbolically complex, an indication of their ability to manipulate the elements of Yoruba religion, Catholicism, the Spiritual Baptist religion, Hinduism, and the Kabbalah. Manipulation of this sort gives rise to island-wide symbolic and ideological heterogeneity and ultimately leads the many shrines to become increasingly distinct from one another. If left alone, this diffusion of ritual and ideology would eventually cause the religion to disintegrate.

There are processes at work, however, that serve to counterbalance this tendency toward diffusion. The first is the annual feast circuit. Although there are over 150 shrines on the island, only thirty-five or so heads actually direct feasts, and only about fifteen of those direct most of the feasts. Thus, each year a relatively small number of individuals disproportionately influence Orisha worship around the island. Second, many *orisha* worshipers are quite mobile, traveling great distances to attend a feast. As a result of these "pilgrimages," worshipers from all parts of the island are in constant contact with one another. A third process is the movement to Africanize the religion by expurgating the non-African or non-Yoruba elements. This relatively recent trend may

125

perhaps be a response to an increasingly confusing religious system more than an expression of a desire to Africanize the Orisha religion: that is, nativism of a pragmatic rather than a sentimental sort.

Finally, the Orisha religion, long disorganized and decentralized, is now becoming less so primarily because of the establishment during the 1970s and 1980s of organizations seeking to consolidate the various shrines and their members. In 1992 there were two such organizations — the "Orisha Movement" and the "Opa Orisha (Shango) of Trinidad and Tobago" — both formally recognized by the government. The latter held its first General Assembly in October 1991.

Although both groups have been meeting for years, neither had much influence on the affairs of the Orisha religion on an island-wide basis until the 1990s. The Orisha Movement has been in existence longer, but the Opa Orisha (Shango), which practices and endorses a broad, eclectic philosophy of worship, has been more successful thus far in its attempt to incorporate a number of shrines in Trinidad into one unified body. One of the most knowledgeable and respected *mongba*, Clarence Ford, long considered the spiritual head (*baba olorisha*) of the Orisha religion in Trinidad, is affiliated with the Opa Orisha (Shango), lending considerable credibility to the group. The *iya olorisha* or ranking female of the Opa Orisha (Shango) is Mother Gretel of Claxton Bay.

The Opa Orisha (Shango) has begun to flex its political muscle, so to speak, since being officially recognized. In 1992 the government invited members of the organization to attend the inauguration of the new parliament, the first time the government had ever proffered such an invitation to representatives of the Orisha religion. The *baba olorisha*, Clarence Ford, attended the National Day of Prayer on behalf of the Opa Orisha (Shango) and recited various Orisha prayers. The group was also represented, by Elder Ford and Mother Gretel, at the government-sponsored International Woman's Day Interfaith Service.

The centrifugal forces that facilitate change and variation, then, are tempered by the centripetal mechanisms of mobility, day-to-day contact, centralization, Africanization, and the fact that a small number of heads exert a disproportionate influence on religious practice. The centrifugal tendency, however, seems destined to maintain the upper hand for two reasons. First, if a shrine head, *mongba*, or *iya* is to become popular or successful, he or she will have to display an aptitude for working with a variety of religious traditions, thus guaranteeing the continued presence of a complex assortment of religious symbols and ideology. Second, fierce competition among heads for members and recognition gives rise to the development of unique religious styles. Although it appears that the activities of the Opa Orisha (Shango) could eventually consolidate the various shrines, the Orisha religion as a whole is loosely organized. It remains highly personalized, as the large variety of shrine designs and worship practices indicates. Many worshipers build shrines in response to dreams and visions or instructions received during the mourning ritual. Each shrine is an independent entity with its own core members, although inexperienced worshipers who have been instructed to give a feast will seek the help of other shrine heads or elders when constructing their shrines or holding a feast.

Given the lack so far of island-wide consolidation and organization, there are no officially recognized positions within the religion with the exception of the *baba olorisha* and the *iya olorisha*. The result is that the Orisha structure and hierarchy have been formed largely by consensus. The hierarchy of the religion is basically four-tiered. At the top (which we can call level one) are the *mongba* and the *iya*. At the next tier (level two) are shrine heads who are not part of the first group, and those who assist the shrine heads, *mongba*, and *iya* and play important roles during the annual feasts: for example, song leaders, drummers, and slayers. Level three includes those who attend a number of *ebo* during any given year and actively participate in the Orisha rites and ceremonies. Finally, there are the interested bystanders (level four), who are not recognized as being members of the religion.

Although it is difficult to tell exactly how many *mongba* and *iya* there are in Trinidad, I estimate their number to be thirty-five. *Mongba* and *iya* direct the *ebo*, a responsibility that includes leading songs and prayers for the *orisha* and overseeing the various ritual activities. Some direct only their own *ebo*; a few direct ten or more in a given year. There are many more shrines in Trinidad than there are *mongba* and *iya*, since one may own a feast yard and sponsor a feast yet not have the knowledge and ability to direct an *ebo*. Thus, an individual may be a shrine head but not be a *mongba* or *iya*; such an arrangement, in fact, is commonplace. On the other hand, my friend Aaron Jones attained the title of *mongba* years ago but did not acquire his own shrine until 1992.

It is the community of Orisha worshipers that determines, on a consensual basis, which individuals will be designated *mongba* or *iya*.

Thus, potentially, anyone can assume these titles; in reality, however, only the most experienced and knowledgeable will attain that status. One must be able to lead a variety of Yoruba prayers and songs, conduct a number of rituals and ceremonies, and, in most cases, have a sophisticated knowledge of Spiritual Baptist, Catholic, Hindu, and Kabbalistic beliefs and practices. Since there are so many ways to interact with the *orisha* and varying levels of knowledge and ability, practically no two *mongba* or *iya* will work in exactly the same manner.

Virtually all *mongba* and *iya* have their own shrines; given the expense of constructing and maintaining a shrine, economics is a factor that should be added to the list of criteria for membership in this elite group. But, as noted above, many who finance and construct shrines or sponsor feasts on their own property never attain the position of *mongba* or *iya*. For example, spirits or powers can instruct a Spiritual Baptist (usually during mourning or through dreams) to hold an *ebo*. It is not uncommon for such an individual to bring in a *mongba* or *iya* to assist with the festivities, though it is possible that feast sponsors may eventually attain a level of knowledge sufficient to conduct an *ebo* themselves. On occasion a sponsor will even invite an individual who is not a shrine head or *mongba* or *iya* to direct the feast. Such an individual is often a rapidly rising star in the religion, one who possesses an ability to guide and oversee the various Orisha rites and ceremonies. If the initial venture is successful and he or she continues to direct feasts, such an individual will eventually be recognized as a *mongba* or *iya*.

The overwhelming majority of those who direct the annual *ebo* are men. I estimate the number of *iya* to be no more than five or so; thus, *mongba* outnumber *iya* about six to one. An implicit gender bias may be at work here, although economic or other factors could be responsible. A cultural explanation may also apply. *Orisha* worshipers were traditionally lower-class Africans whose culture in Trinidad was characterized by highly transient single males and matrifocal households. Thus, male worshipers traditionally enjoyed a life-style that permitted them a larger range of movement and greater opportunity than women to participate in the affairs of the Orisha religion, with its dusk-to-dawn ceremonies and an annual feast schedule that involves a large number of shrines all over the island.

One might expect that having strong family ties in the religion would be advantageous to those who seek to become *mongba* or *iya*. There are, after all, no formal classes or standardized written works regarding beliefs and practices, and no generally recognized body to evaluate and otherwise sanction the activities of the various religious functionaries. These factors and the emphasis on the oral transmission of religious knowledge should produce a relatively higher incidence of level one membership among individuals in Orisha families than among the general public. The data do, in fact, reflect this tendency. Of the twenty-three *mongba* and *iya* I interviewed, seventeen were "traditional" worshipers who had been involved in the religion since childhood and had substantial familial ties to *orisha* worship. Typically, each one's mother or father was a *mongba*, *iya*, or shrine head. The remaining six "nontraditional" leaders had virtually no familial or hereditary ties to the religion, and most had converted to Orisha after adolescence. The relatively high proportion (26 percent of my sample) of nontraditionalists at the top of the religious hierarchy suggests that the religion is flourishing and that although proper family ties may confer an advantage on the aspiring *mongba* or *iya*, they are not essential to achieving this status.

Because of the large variety of shrine styles, religious affiliation, and personal ideologies that exist in the religion, there is no such thing as a typical *mongba* or *iya*. Even so, by looking at the involvement of a particular *mongba* (whom I shall call "Arnold") and a particular *iya* ("Barbara"), we can get a general idea of the individuals who are members of this ranking category.

Arnold holds a number of activities at his shrine, including weekly Spiritual Baptist services, an annual thanksgiving, Easter prayers, a Kabbalah banquet, and an *ebo*. He is a nontraditionalist: his family has no history of participation in the Spiritual Baptist or Orisha religions, and to this day only one other family member is involved in either one.

Arnold explained that practically everything he has learned about his "work" he obtained through mourning, which he has done on an annual basis for the last thirteen years or so. He first mourned when he was a young boy, soon after being baptized into the Spiritual Baptist religion. Through his affiliation with the Spiritual Baptist church, he became interested in the Orisha religion. Eventually, he received instructions (while mourning) to hold a small annual ceremony at the sea in honor of the *orisha*. After some five years, the powers and spirits he encountered during mourning instructed him to carry on a full four-day *ebo* at his shrine. More recently, his spiritual guides have given him Kabbalistic work to do, which he does, although somewhat reluctantly.

Arnold's shrine is symbolically rich and complex, containing shrines, flags, and other paraphernalia for Spiritual Baptist, Hindu, Orisha, Catholic, and Kabbalistic powers and spirits. It is not unusual for spirits from any or all these categories to manifest themselves during ceremonies held at his shrine. For example, at one Easter Sunday prayer service, spirits from all these categories appeared. Arnold is typical of that group of *mongba* and *iya* whose involvement in the religion has contributed to the gradual expansion of its corpus of beliefs and practices and the concomitant increase of symbols and paraphernalia. Because his shrine is popular and his annual ceremonies are well attended, he will probably continue to exert a strong influence on the Orisha religion for years to come.

Barbara is an elderly woman whose mother introduced her to the Spiritual Baptist religion when she was a child. When she was ten years old, her mother died, and Barbara gradually drifted away from the religion. As she noted, however, the spirits are strong, and "after a while, they does call you"; at the age of forty she began to construct her own church and to mourn on a regular basis. She has been conducting Spiritual Baptist rituals and an annual *ebo* on the same spot for many years.

Like Arnold, Barbara received her work through mourning. She said that though she was already somewhat familiar with the Baptist side, she obtained her knowledge of the *orisha* (and of Hinduism) almost exclusively from her spiritual travels during mourning. When I asked whether or not she had received any instructions involving the Kabbalah, she replied that Kabbalistic knowledge cannot be obtained during mourning. (Arnold and others disagree.) In fact, she strongly denounced the Kabbalah: "You can't hold God in this hand and the devil in this one. That is the other side. . . . It is evil."

Because she lives in a crowded area, the various parts of her shrine and her residence are contiguous. The primary features are a Spiritual Baptist church, a small area containing flags and paraphernalia for the *orisha*, and Hindu paraphernalia prominently placed throughout the shrine. Despite her age, she is still active in the affairs of her church and regularly conducts the various rituals of both the Spiritual Baptist and Orisha religions.

Individuals who, like Barbara, have years of experience in the Orisha religion as a *mongba* or *iya* have necessarily withstood any number of attempts on the part of their colleagues to disrupt their religious activities. Worshipers attach considerable prestige to the titles of *mongba* and *iya*, and the individuals in this ranking group are in constant competition with one another; disputes, both public and private, are not uncommon. In fact, to maintain the position of ranking functionary in the religion, one must be able to weather successfully the spiritual assaults of others and the many conflicts that often arise between *mongba, iya,* and even shrine heads. At one particular *ebo* in west-central Trinidad in July 1989, for example, there were four *mongba* in the *palais* at the same time, all attempting to deal with the powers that were present. The "horse" for St. Anthony/Dada (see Chapter Thirteen) was crying and sobbing and behaving in a manner that suggested extreme sadness. A young *mongba* who attempted to console him was soon embroiled in an argument with a popular elder. The conflict was not resolved until the elder, apparently not wishing to be involved in a public dispute with a young *mongba*, simply left the *palais*.

Such confrontation and conflict frequently entail spiritual warfare and, typically, the use of magic, or "obeah." For example, in July 1989, on a Friday afternoon preceding the last night of an *ebo* in the west-central part of the island, the shrine head (who was also acting as a *mongba*) conducted a ritual at Eshu's shrine. He used Kabbalah paraphernalia in a ceremony that involved lighting small alcohol-fueled fires and ritually working with four eggs, which he later threw north, south, east, and west. During the ritual the Kabbalah entity Prince of Evil unexpectedly manifested itself on one of the worshipers, but the shrine head quickly dismissed it, later explaining that someone had attempted to disrupt his *ebo* by sending Kabbalah entities to invade his yard. A special place for Eshu is an important component of any compound but can act as a conduit of sorts for Kabbalah entities — which is, for some worshipers, an unfortunate byproduct of enshrining Eshu. Throwing the four eggs in the four directions symbolized sending out Eshu to ward off the entities. In another case a *mongba* who was preparing for a baptism sensed the intrusion of negative powers during the ritual by the sea (at the time he was acting as a Spiritual Baptist leader). To counteract this spiritual assault, the *mongba* laid the novitiate down inside an outline of a coffin that had been drawn on the sand and then ritually lifted him out before baptizing him.

Disputes and confrontations of this sort extend to Kabbalistic functions as well. During one Kabbalah banquet, as we saw in Chapter Seven, the operator lost control of the proceedings, and the manifesting entity seized the moment by ignoring the operator and carrying on as it pleased. A visiting *mongba* who was also a Kabbalah practitioner attempted to take over the ritual, and although he was able to restore some semblance of control, the shrine head and sponsor of the banquet resented his intrusion. An open dispute followed, and the visiting head finally left.

As these examples illustrate, incessant confrontations occur between ranking members of the religion. Those who best survive challenges to their authority year after year eventually become respected ranking heads. These elders are, not surprisingly, knowledgeable in the affairs of all the various religious traditions that are practiced. When I asked forty-two worshipers to rank the heads of the religion, their top five *mongba* and *iya*—four males and one female—were also among the most prominent and experienced. The *baba olorisha*, Clarence Ford, was the most popular. The one woman, Melvina Rodney, was the *iya olorisha* or ranking female spiritual head in the Orisha Movement. The other three, long-standing figures in the religion, were all knowledgeable and personable, one of them an Indian who yearly holds one of the most popular *ebo* on the island.

When asked why they chose a particular *mongba* or *iya*, respondents' reasons (they could select more than one) included "knowledge of the rituals and beliefs" (98 percent of those polled), followed by "stress on discipline and proper behavior" (50 percent), "ability to lead songs" (45 percent), "family background" (29 percent), "age" (21 percent), "personality" (5 percent), "sex" (5 percent), "size of the *ebo* the *mongba* or *iya* carries on or directs" (2 percent), "presence of Hindu elements at the shrine or church" (2 percent), and "presence of Kabbalah elements at the shrine or church" (2 percent). Clearly, one must be adept at dealing with a variety of beliefs and practices in order to be successful and popular. The five most popular *mongba* and *iya* all had considerable knowledge regarding the Orisha religion, Catholicism, the Spiritual Baptist religion, Hinduism, and the Kabbalah. Such variety is reflected in their shrines as well: all five are symbolically complex. It is interesting to note that the worshipers' responses reveal little concern about whether specific religious elements (such as Hindu and Kabbalah) were displayed at a particular shrine; actual behavior, however, indicates otherwise, since ranking heads and elders are respected in proportion to their religious expertise in the various traditions. Perhaps worshipers consider such expertise (minimally) necessary but not sufficient.

The fact that "stress on discipline" was the second most frequent reason given by respondents for their choices clearly reflects a concern on the part of some members that young worshipers do not show the proper respect for the behavior codes of the religion. The "ability to lead songs" is, of course, a necessary attribute for anyone who hopes to direct a feast successfully, since the singing of songs for the *orisha* goes on for hours each night of the *ebo*. "Family background" underlines the importance of a hereditary link to the religion, which apparently provides the individual with a certain amount of prestige that aspiring "nontraditional" members must work to achieve, a point that Mischel (1958, 112) also noted. Age, the only other characteristic chosen by at least 20 percent of the respondents, no doubt reflects the fact that those who have considerable religious knowledge are usually the older practitioners.

Clearly, the Orisha religion reflects the multiethnic and pluralistic characteristics of Trinidadian society, not only in its symbolically complex and religiously eclectic beliefs and practices but also in the emphasis worshipers place on the multicultural expertise of their *mongba* and *iya*. The Africans proudly view the combination of different ethnic groups and their traditions on the island as something uniquely Trinidadian, another manifestation of their "pro-Trini" attitude. The amalgamation of beliefs, practices, and paraphernalia drawn from a variety of religious traditions to form an Afro-American religious system is merely a specific manifestation of this cosmopolitan, pro-Trini mindset. Not surprisingly, then, it is those worshipers who are most adept at manipulating a variety of religious symbols and ideologies who become the most respected and successful ranking members of the religion, for these individuals come closest to affirming the worshipers' notion of an ideal Trini society.

Shrine heads, drummers, song leaders, slayers, and assistants to shrine heads, *mongba*, and *iya* constitute level two in the group hierarchy. Some drummers and song leaders are *mongba* and *iya* as well, since both positions involve considerable skill and knowledge. All but a handful of the drummers and song leaders are men, but the women who do engage in either of these activities are well known and respected. A shrine head is anyone who owns a shrine. All Orisha shrines are located on private property, almost always on property owned by the shrine head. Most shrine heads are not *mongba* or *iya*, but, as noted above, practically all *mongba* or *iya* are shrine heads. About half the drummers are Rastafarians. The involvement of Rastafarians in the religion as a whole is demographically low: I made head counts at thirty different feasts and found that on the average they made up about 6 percent of those in attendance. Since the participating "Rastas" are virtually all drummers, however, they have attained considerable prestige as a group.

The Rastas who affiliate with the Orisha religion usually do not associate with any of the various Rastafarian organizations on the island — for example, the Twelve Tribes of Israel (an international group), the Niyabinghi, or the Rastafarian Brethren Organization. These groups meet regularly for religious services and social gatherings, and some plant flags, say prayers, and beat drums. But according to my Rasta contacts in the Orisha religion, these practices reflect primarily a Judeo-Christian rather than African influence. I would guess that the heavy Yoruba influence on the Orisha religion in Trinidad and the opportunity to worship African gods are persuasive factors for most of the Rastas who become members.

The *orisha*-worshiping Rastas do maintain some of the sentiments of traditional Rastafarianism (not those, however, involving racist doctrines) and continue to dress and to wear their long hair ("dreadlocks") in traditional Rasta form. Not surprisingly, some worshipers, especially the Rastas, claim that one of the *orisha* is a Rastafarian: according to Edmond David, the popular Rasta drummer and *mongba*, Dada (in Christian terms, St. Anthony), who is sung to when bread is broken and children are fed at religious ceremonies, is a "Ras"; his sacrificial food is a sheep or a white cock, "just like Shango."

Since it is the drums that call the *orisha*, the task of drumming is not taken lightly. According to a few elders, drummers must undergo a specific initiation before they can perform in the *palais* during an *ebo*, but many drummers have not been so initiated. Still, considerable skill is involved because drummers may be called on to play as many as twelve different rhythms, although many of these are rarely heard today. A few drummers, such as Elder Biddeau, know a large number of rhythms drawn from West Africa, the Rada tradition in Trinidad, Haitian Vodoun, Santería, and other African-derived religions in the New World; most are familiar with only a handful, but the drummer should be able to play at least the most important rhythms. The two most basic and popular (the two that I myself play) are those associated with Ogun and Mama Lata.

Many song leaders are also drummers; in fact, the individual playing the center or lead drum (the *bemba*) will often lead the songs as well. Theoretically, anyone in attendance can lead a song, but only those individuals who have a thorough working knowledge of the large number of songs and melodies will actually do so. Slayers (also referred to as *ashogun*) perform the sacrifices and may direct the cleaning of the animals and the preparation of the food offered to the *orisha*. They are often appointed by *orisha* that manifest themselves at an *ebo*. Again, this position requires considerable skill and knowledge of exactly when and how sacrifices are to be done. The various assistants perform a number of tasks, including tending to the spirits when they manifest themselves, sweeping out the *palais*, cooking and serving food. Often, these individuals are relatives or close friends of the *mongba*, *iya*, or shrine head.

The active participants (level three members) constitute by far the largest group, and most possessions involve individuals in this category. These members, especially the women, position themselves inside the *palais* during an *ebo* and support the singing and clapping that accompany the songs for the *orisha*. Some active participants are also assistants during the *ebo* at the shrine with which they are affiliated; that is, in this limited context they would be classified as level-two members. Typically, they travel to other feasts in their area as well, although on the whole they do not travel as often or as far as members of the first two groups.

Finally, the interested bystanders (level four) are curious onlookers at a neighborhood feast. *Orisha* worshipers welcome these individuals as long as they dress and behave appropriately. Many of them are Indians from the immediate area, who typically attend one or two nights of a nearby feast each year.

These four groups tend to segregate themselves spatially during festivities in a somewhat concentric circular fashion. The shrine head or *mongba* or *iya* (level one) typically directs and oversees ritual activities from inside the *palais* (the focal point of *ebo* activities). The drummers and other assistants (level two) sit or stand inside the *palais* as well. Active participants (level three) position themselves around the perimeter of the *palais*, sitting on benches or standing just outside, while curious bystanders (level four) observe the activities from the outermost perimeter of the gathering.

The relative degree of contact between the worshipers and the *orisha* greatly influences the nature and form of this concentric pattern.

One of the primary functions of the *ebo* is to create a context conducive to *orisha* manifestations. Members of levels one and two, because of their knowledge and experience, enjoy a highly intimate form of contact with the *orisha* and interact with them in a way that is not unlike their everyday behavior toward friends and family—behavior that is by no means disrespectful but is surprisingly nonchalant. Level-three worshipers—the rank and file, as it were—are attentive and obsequious in the presence of manifesting *orisha;* their contact with the spirits seems formal and ceremonious rather than intimate. Curious bystanders usually have little or no contact with the manifesting *orisha*, neither desiring nor seeking it.

I remained a curious bystander during my first summer of fieldwork in Trinidad, but when I returned for a year-long stay, I gradually moved into the active participant group. After my initiation and once I began serving as a drummer, I moved up to a level-two involvement in certain contexts. During rites and ceremonies at Leader Scott's or Aaron's shrine, for example, I played the drums, put out Eshu's food (the significance of which is explained later), lighted candles, and assisted the manifesting *orisha*. My movement from the fringes to near "center stage" occurred as my knowledge of and experience in the religion grew.

The multitiered nature of the religion and the varying levels of participation in its activities make estimations of group membership somewhat difficult. Virtually the only time *orisha* worshipers come together as a group is during the annual feasts. No researcher has ever officially or systematically counted Orisha worshipers. Henry's (1983, 64) estimate of one hundred shrines and 10,000 members is one of the few available in the literature, and she makes no mention of her demographic methodology or the quality of her sample. The government does not include either the Orisha or the Spiritual Baptist religion in its census list of religious choices, no doubt in part because of the general ignorance that exists in Trinidad regarding the nature of the two groups; some consider neither to be a valid or legitimate religion, and others confuse the two. My own counts—11,000 Spiritual Baptists and approximately 9,000 *orisha* worshipers (see Appendixes A and B)—indicate that each group can claim 1 percent or more of the population, and both appear to be flourishing.

According to figures I obtained in head counts at thirty different shrines during a particular night of an annual *ebo*, 51.6 percent of those in attendance were female and 48.4 percent male. Approximately 12 percent were children and teenagers, and 11 percent were over fifty years of age.

Traditionally, the Orisha religion was almost exclusively African; as late as the 1950s, the involvement of non-Africans was virtually nonexistent (Mischel 1958, 112). Today, however, the Indian presence is significant, a trend that apparently began in the 1970s (Mahabir and Maharaj 1989, 191). In the head counts I made at eighteen feasts, approximately 10 percent of those in attendance were Indian; many of these were only interested bystanders, but some actively involved themselves in the *ebo* festivities. One Indian known as Panco, for example, is a popular drummer. One successful shrine head, Ralph Frank, is also Indian, as are many others who play prominent roles in the Orisha rites and ceremonies.

It is probably no coincidence that the recent incorporation of Hindu elements has been accompanied by an influx of Indians into the religion. Although it is the predominantly African shrine heads, *mongba*, and *iya* who actively engage in this borrowing, the fact that the Hindu and Orisha religions have been displayed and discussed as religious counterparts by *orisha* worshipers has not been lost on the Indians.

The basically loose and decentralized structure of the religion, the autonomous shrines, and the importance of consensus in determining rank and status is complemented by the manner in which individuals formally affiliate with the religion. Potential members may follow any of a number of tracks. Adherents recognize three basic initiation ceremonies — baptism, *desieni* (head washing), and *singbare* (head incising) — but potential *orisha* worshipers are not necessarily required to participate in any of the three. Most worshipers are Spiritual Baptists before they affiliate with the Orisha religion. Typically, one "travels" to Africa while mourning, or is otherwise given African work to do. The mourner often receives instructions regarding, for example, what animal donations should be made to feast givers, what stools should be put down, what color the flags should be, and when he or she should hold a feast.

Given the prior Baptist involvement of most *orisha* worshipers and the interrelationship of the two religions, it is not surprising that many adherents consider a Christian type of baptism to be an important first step. As Leon London, a *mongba* and one of the most skilled and respected drummers on the island, explained:

Baptism is requisite. . . . It don't bound to be [a Spiritual Baptist baptism]. But anyway you do baptism regardless to what, you are a follower of Christ, you understand, because Jesus Christ [was] baptized. . . . There is only one Baptist in the universe and that is St. John the Baptist. (Interview, Fyzabad, February 19, 1989)

The significance of the last statement lies in the fact that St. John is syncretized with Shango, one of the most prominent deities in the Orisha pantheon.

The *desieni* or head washing ritual formally designates one's membership in the Orisha religion. The *singbare* or head incising prepares the worshiper for possession; it is said that her or his head is "seated" for a particular *orisha*. Again, participation in these rituals is not necessary to establish oneself as a member of the Orisha religion; in fact, some worshipers have no history of Baptist involvement, have not been baptized, and have not had their heads washed or incised. My impression, however, is that most will eventually go through one or more of the three rituals.

An initiate typically begins with the baptism, followed by the head washing and, finally, the head incising. The three ceremonies may be spread out over a long period of time, or they may be performed within the space of two weeks or so. My baptismal ceremonies at Leader Scott's shrine, for example, concluded one week before Elder Biddeau washed and incised my head. A Spiritual Baptist leader or mother (who may also be a *mongba* or *iya*) will usually direct the baptism, and a *mongba* or *iya* will perform the head washing and incising.

When a person is possessed for the first time, he or she is sometimes washed and incised on the spot or only a short time later. One does not necessarily have to undergo head washing and incising after the first possession, but it is customary and expected of worshipers who intend to continue their affiliation with the religion. The individual is usually washed and incised "under" or in the name of the possessing *orisha*.

Sometimes, however, the spontaneous and impromptu nature of such possessions, in which an *orisha* unexpectedly overwhelms the unsuspecting neophyte, leads to an unsatisfactory pairing. Emmanuel Pierre, for example, a shrine head and elder near Port of Spain, "fell" (became possessed) during an *elefa* offering when he was seven years old, and the elders in attendance promptly washed his head. "Elefa" is regarded by some worshipers as an *orisha* but understood by others as a type of offering to Obatala, one of the primordial *orisha* and considered to be very powerful; such offerings are conducted only by the most experienced *mongba* and *iya*. Mano (as Emmanuel is popularly known) said that because of his young age he could not deal with and relate to such a strong *orisha*, so he subsequently "washed" under Emanje.

In my case, I deliberately chose Ogun as my patronal *orisha*, although I received considerable input from Leader Scott, Mother Joan, and Elder Biddeau and his wife, Lydia, my spiritual fathers and mothers on the Spiritual Baptist and African sides.

TEN

The Orisha *and Their Abodes*

We did not go into a feast because we want to, . . . we did not
enter in this [*orisha* worship] because we want to. You see we were
asked in a dream or a vision that we supposed to put down the
flags and the color of the flags. . . . So we obey the powers that
come to us. And by obeying, we really see them around us . . . and
we can have a spiritual understanding with them. And by that,
you can understand if you are going on the right road or not.

If you are on the right track, you will get prosperity. Because
you don't have to get rich in money. . . . Some people do this
thing [*orisha* worship] and they don't really get [financially]
rich, . . . they are spiritually rich. Some people have homes
because they don't want to see you always looking down [on
them]. Because the spirits like to see healthy and look nice places.
So they help you get a nice place so they themselves can dwell
among us. . . . [When] they come around and see your place is
down, they help you get a proper place that they can stay,
because . . . they don't want to stay in filthy places.

— Interview with Leader Coker, Pinto Road, north-central
Trinidad, July 18, 1985

O*risha shrines vary greatly* in layout, size, and complexity, but all
share certain characteristics. First, they are "earthy." Virtually the entire shrine has a dirt floor, especially the more sacred areas;
when individuals enter the sacred areas, they are expected to remove
their shoes. There are various implements, utensils, candles, and so on
stuck here and there in the ground; medicinal and religious plants
growing in the compound; and pens holding chickens, goats, and other
animals. Second, Orisha shrines are active. Candles burn constantly,

and spiritual work is done almost daily in some compounds. Finally, shrines are historical. The remnants of past feasts and ceremonies — goat horns, morocoy (tortoise) shells, chicken feathers, and globs of melted wax — can be seen under the flags for the *orisha*. While there is nearly always some spiritual activity taking place at an Orisha shrine, the typical shrine head expends only minimal effort during the year tending to the physical upkeep of the various structures in the compound. In preparation for the annual feasts, however, the shrine is cleaned and painted, buildings are mended, and grass and weeds are cut. The *ebo* is, after all, that special time of the year when the *orisha* visit a particular shrine. And, as Leader Coker said, "the spirits like to see healthy and look nice places."

Worshipers in Trinidad recognize thirty to forty *orisha*, although most are familiar with only about half that number. Worshipers believe that a few of them have always been spirits but that most were humans who came to be recognized as *orisha* after their deaths. Virtually all the *orisha* are conceived of anthropomorphically, and human character traits are displayed when they manifest themselves.

The *orisha* are personable and accessible, often interacting intimately with worshipers when they appear in the form of a possessed individual, but they can become aggressive and punitive if they are not treated with respect and honor. For example, Leader Scott recalled that a drummer some time ago had sexual relations during a feast, and later that night Osain forced him to use a cheese grater on his penis. In another case, the same *orisha* (Osain) chopped off the fingers of a worshiper who would not move away from the corner of the *palais* as he approached it. Leader Scott added, however, that Osain eventually healed both these worshipers. During a feast outside of Chaguanas, Ogun doused a young woman with olive oil because she did not have her head covered and was dressed in a way that was considered improper by other worshipers.

Practitioners regard the *orisha* as powerful spirits and call on them to deal with sickness, financial problems, court appearances, and a variety of other matters. Working with the *orisha* may or may not involve a manifestation. The *orisha* will not work negatively, however, except in cases where redress is sought. Mother Joan noted that she once belonged to a *sou-sou* (a revolving credit club), and when it was her turn to collect her allotment, she learned that someone else had claimed the money. Since she had planned to use the money to purchase a goat for the *orisha* Shakpana, she went to him for help. In a matter of weeks the other woman's house was robbed and her automobile totaled in an accident. Mother Joan noted that she easily managed to collect enough money to buy the goat.

Worshipers believe that all the *orisha*, with the exception of Olodumare, Olorun, Odudua, and Obatala, walked the earth long ago. Not surprisingly, *orisha* worshipers in both the Old and New Worlds associate each *orisha* with a particular life history that at least partly explains the relationships between them, their attitudes, likes and dislikes, and other personal characteristics. Their behavioral attributes, as explained by Leader Scott, are evident during manifestations:

Ogun

Ogun is said to be a warrior and a fighter. He will always engage in battle to defend the house of Obatala. He was in a leadership position. He is also a lookout, like a watchman. But Ogun had a bad habit: he used to drink wine. That is why today we throw puncheon rum and do libations for him. He was engaged in a lot of battles with bloodshed and whatnot. And they felt that Ogun was overstepping his bounds. Because when he drinks and gets vicious . . . he don't care what is in front of him. He started to reconcile with himself that the same energies that were used for fighting and destroying could be used for something that was more positive, . . . to help people.

He is known as the *orisha* of iron and steel. Because the iron and steel are associated with war, you have the sword and these kind of implements. He was also known as a good judge. He carried the scale. . . . Not that he used to try cases, but because of the way he used his intelligence to weigh and balance the situation. He became a power of reason.

He is a man in whom you can confide and speak to. He listens and counsels, and he advises and so on. Now, it is said that all the *orisha* have an Ogun. In other words . . . Ogun plays a part with all the *orisha*, to open the way for them. He comes as [is like] an intermediary spirit. . . .

He is the man that comes and supervises and looks around and sees and clears the way. He is a man of organization. That is why you see so much attention is paid to Ogun. . . . And he directs his own thing. When Ogun comes, he makes sure, "do this, do that." And he looks carefully where you put things. By your own observation you must have seen how detailed he is. . . . Another thing, Ogun likes to be celebrated. . . . He likes attention and so on.

When he manifests he is powerful, rigid. But he has a certain sort of calm about him, once he settles. But when he hits, he hits you rigid. . . . The minute the body is able to balance with him, he could still dance rigid because he has moves, you know. He can be very calm or he can be very rigid according to the situation. He can dance you very cool and full of style.

Mama Lata

Mama Lata, Onile [we sometimes call her], . . . Onile is really the earth, so we pay obeisance to the earth. So we call her Iya Lata, which means "mother of the earth." . . . As old as the earth is, is as old as Mama Lata is. So therefore she is a very old person. Now, when she manifests, it could be the strongest individual in the world, [yet] they have to hit the ground. She will roll from corner to corner; she will roll over and over on the ground. It is one of the powers that really has you out of sense, out of body. All of these powers carry you out of sense really. But when Mama Lata manifests, she is so much out of human reach. . . . When Ogun manifests on a body you can talk to the manifestation in a kind of way. . . . When Mama Lata manifests, you can't call her back so [easily] unless she wants to come.

She goes to her stool and instructs what is to be done in a real motherly fashion. She hardly ever speaks. She works more by signs because she is so old and frail. She may stand, and when she stands she leans on a stick. . . . She is a good medicine woman.

Shakpana

He is a man of ceremony. Like in the child-naming ceremony . . . there is a special ceremony you have for cutting the hair. Shakpana is the main *orisha* in that respect. Shakpana is also a healer. He is a man of the forest. He loves herbs. He is a healer of children's diseases such as smallpox. . . . He is a man that has dealings with the head. . . . But if you get him on the wrong side, he is a very very serious man. . . . When I say the wrong side, if I come into your house to thief from you or to beat you or to take advantage of you, don't you have to respond?

He is also a very good workman, a very good healer. . . . By his stool there is always something for healing. He has his calabash with his medicines. As a matter of fact, those things in that calabash are used to exhaust [exorcise] spirits in possessions.

When he comes, he likes to come with a noise, a shout. . . . You must know when he comes. . . . He dances very nice. . . . Shakpana talks to people, he counsels people. But there are certain things that Shakpana would not do. Shakpana will do the things he wants to do if he finds pleasure with you. Shakpana won't do nothing for you that he don't find pleasure with. He has to have a certain tendency toward you. . . . You see, if you pay obeisance to Shakpana, of course he will probably do you a favor because you respect him. . . . But the point is, let us say you come in to see me about something and I say to myself, "Boy, the man who could really do that work is Shakpana." But when you bring the person to Shakpana . . . [he will] look at the person and say, "You see he, he don't fall in my bag." . . . Sometime you have to do a little thing before he will come and attend to you. He is sort of stubborn.

Osain

Osain is a forest man, a man out on the earth, a man of the river. Mostly the rivers and the forest. . . . He likes to protect the forest. He is a real searcher. He can do a number of things. He can help people in distress, he can find jobs for people, he can feed people. He likes that, . . . to collect seeds and whatnot and to feed people. He is a very good chiropractor. . . . Also, when it comes to sores and whatnot, he is very good. . . . And a next thing, he will carry a lot of people's troubles on his back. If you notice when he manifests, he gives people a ride on his back. . . . He takes your burden on his back.

He is very stylish. He is full of style. He likes people to know he is there and he is something to look upon. . . . As good as he is, he has his bad ways. If he gave you instruction to do certain things and you didn't do them, he is quick to show you why you should do them. . . . He may break your bones, or break up your foot. . . . He likes obedience. He is a very disciplined man. While you could do other things with the other powers and get away with it, not with Osain boy!

He can get things done for people. . . . He is a man that can do all sorts of things. He is a real magic man. (Interview, Basta Hall Village, July 28, 1992)

Clearly, the anthropomorphism here goes far beyond the "God was angry" or "God was pleased" conceptions of the Judeo-Christian god. The worshipers frequently address an *orisha* as "old man," "papa," or "old woman." The *orisha* are stubborn, demanding, moody, proud, ostentatious, stoic, mercurial, loving, caring, concerned, matronly. Some like rum; some prefer water or sweet (olive) oil. When manifesting, some go about their business quietly, without fanfare; others prefer and sometimes demand constant attention. Each one has a special talent or ability, be it healing, counseling, clairvoyance, or whatever. In a word, their personality types are eminently human:

The *orishas* are also seen as representations of human qualities or feeling. In many ways the *orishas* can be seen as archetypes of the collective unconscious. . . . The archetypes have intensely individualistic characteristics and each one controls a different aspect of the personality and/or a different human interest. This definition of the archetypes could just as well describe the functions of the *orishas*. (González-Wippler 1985, 13)

Worshipers associate each *orisha* with particular colors, days, and foods. Colors are important, especially for the flags that mark the stools, worshipers' attire, and, in some cases, the food offering: for example, Ogun takes red and white but not black cocks, and Mama Lata takes brown or black but not white hens. Sacrifices to each *orisha* are performed during the early morning period of particular days.

TABLE 6
Colors, Special Days, and Food of Selected Orisha

Orisha	Colors	Day	Sacrificial Food
Anthony (Dada)	brown and white, brown and red	Tuesday	ram, cocks
Elefa (Elefon)	white	Wednesday	bulls
Emanje (Yemanje)	blue	Thursday	fish, aquatic fowl
Erele (Erinle)	blue, blue and white	Thursday	cocks, guinea birds
Eshu (Elegbara, Eleggua)	black	all	assorted animals
Gurum	red, red and black	Thursday	turkeys, cocks, peacocks
Mama Lata	brown, brown plaid	Wednesday	hens
Obatala	white	Thursday	pigeons, bulls
Ogun	red and white, red and green	Wednesday	male goats, cocks
Osain (Osanyin, Osa)	yellow, yellow and brown	Thursday	morocoys (tortoises), male goats, cocks
Oshun (Osun)	pink, blue, pink and white	Thursday	fish, aquatic fowl
Oya	green	Friday	female sheep, hens
Peter (Agare, Ebeje)	purple, purple and white	Thursday	fish, ducks, cocks
Raphael (Deokuta)	red and green	Wednesday	male goats, cocks
Shakpana (Shopona)	red, red and black	Wednesday	male goats, cocks
Shango (Sango)	red, red and white	Friday	rams, cocks

Table 6 lists sixteen of the more prominent *orisha*, with their colors, days, and food. (I have included Elefa here, since he is recognized as an *orisha* by many worshipers, even though some knowledgeable heads consider *elefa* a type of offering.)

Besides the animals listed, it should be noted that the *orisha* receive "dry food," the term used for any food offerings not obtained from blood sacrifice: corn meal, parched corn, *chilibibi* (made from ground corn and sugar), slush (made with okra), *acra* (made with flour and fish), rice, black-eyed peas, olive oil, honey, and *coocoo* (made with corn meal and okra). Additional foods offered to some *orisha* include rum (Ogun), wine (Oshun), and "ground provisions" (root vegetables and tubers) such as yams and potatoes (Mama Lata).

I have listed more than one name to designate some *orisha*. The first name is the one that worshipers use most often; the names in parentheses are alternative designations recognized by some. Worshipers actually identify three of these *orisha* — Anthony, Peter, and Raphael — as Catholic saints and generally use their Catholic names, seldom mentioning the African equivalents. But although many Yoruba-derived *orisha* have been syncretized with Catholic saints, worshipers still refer to most of them by their African names.

Although *orisha* may descend on particular people ("horses") during *ebo* or other ceremonies, it is through Trinidad's many shrines that the *orisha* make themselves accessible to the community of worshipers. For the purpose of this study, I define an Orisha shrine as a compound that contains *orisha* flags and/or stools and serves as the site for an annual *ebo* lasting a minimum of two days and involving the beating of drums and the offering of food to *orisha*. In all cases, the shrine is privately owned, the shrine head generally residing on the compound.

I found many Afro-American religious shrines that resemble Orisha shrines but in which the flags and stools represent Spiritual Baptist powers. Such compounds are usually Baptist in nature — that is, they are associated with those who affiliate themselves exclusively with the Spiritual Baptist religion — but may be in the process of developing into Orisha shrines, a development typically guided by instructions received while mourning. Some worshipers claim that a few of the Baptist powers are African-derived, but because they do not overtly identify them as *orisha*, I have not classified such shrines as Orisha shrines.

I also discovered a number of religious shrines that had flags and stools for the *orisha* but no longer served as the site of an annual *ebo*. In some of these compounds, passed down from the original head and often quite old, the current shrine head had not planted flags and stools on an annual basis, and it proved to be virtually impossible to reconstruct the original shrine. For research purposes I thought it best to exclude compounds that had been long out of use, though many are, of course, still active in other ways and remain an important part of *orisha* worship in Trinidad.

The Orisha shrines on the island have never been officially or systematically counted. Henry (1983, 64) estimates that there are one hundred shrines, but because she does not explain how she arrived at that figure, I cannot assess its accuracy. Simpson (1980, 77) notes that there are "at least" one hundred but did not conduct a systematic search. My research indicates that the number today is much higher, probably because of the recent resurgence of the religion.

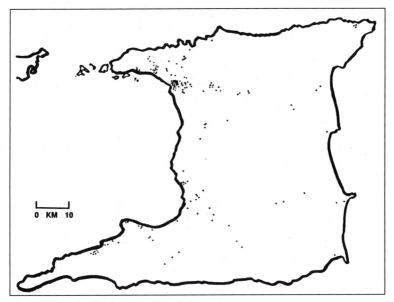

FIGURE 2. *Orisha shrines in Trinidad.*

During my stay in Trinidad, I visited 106 shrines and learned of the location of an additional fifty; among the latter I identified the shrine heads of thirteen. Considering the nature of the data, I believe that 156 is a good estimate. The actual total could be higher, because in and around Port of Spain there are shrines totally enclosed within private residences. Their existence can be partly attributed to a lack of living space in the crowded villages near the city: for example, Belmont and Laventille to the east. Also, many adherents no doubt continue to follow the traditional practice of worshiping in private, a response to the restrictions and prohibitions on Afro-American religious worship that were in effect at one time. Because such shrines cannot be identified externally, I located only a handful. I would guess that there are between ten and forty in the Port of Spain area, but since their existence could not be verified, I will leave the total at 156 and simply note that the actual number may be much higher.

Approximately half the shrines are located in the northwestern quadrant of Trinidad, in and around Port of Spain (see Figure 2). Given the dense concentration of Africans in that part of the island, African

TABLE 7
Orisha *Stools, Flags, and Colors*

Orisha	IO	Flag color(s)	IO
Ogun	37 (100%)	red and white	24 (65%)
		red	11 (30%)
		red and green	2 (5%)
Osain	34 (92%)	yellow	27 (79%)
		yellow and brown	5 (15%)
		yellow (triangular)	1 (3%)
		no flag	1 (3%)
Shakpana	32 (86%)	red	28 (88%)
		red and other colors	1 (3%)
		green and yellow	1 (3%)
		brown	1 (3%)
		gray	1 (3%)
Mama Lata	22 (59%)	brown	11 (50%)
		no flag	7 (32%)
		brown plaid	3 (14%)
		pink	1 (4%)
Oshun	21 (57%)	pink	11 (52%)
		blue	5 (24%)
		no flag	4 (19%)
		white	1 (5%)
Peter	17 (46%)	no flag	7 (41%)
		white	3 (18%)
		blue and white	2 (12%)
		yellow and white	1 (6%)
		purple and white	1 (6%)
		mauve and white	1 (6%)
		yellow and blue	1 (6%)
		purple	1 (6%)
Emanje	15 (40%)	blue	12 (80%)
		blue and white	2 (13%)
		blue with white dots	1 (7%)
Erele	12 (32%)	blue	4 (33%)
		blue and white	4 (33%)
		blue and yellow	2 (17%)
		brown and white	1 (8%)
		green	1 (8%)
Oya	10 (27%)	green	8 (80%)
		green and white	1 (10%)
		pink	1 (10%)
Elefa	8 (22%)	white	7 (88%)
		red, white, and blue	1 (12%)

TABLE 7
Continued

Orisha	IO	*Flag color(s)*	IO
Gurum	7 (19%)	red and black	2 (29%)
		red	2 (29%)
		blue and green	1 (14%)
		red and white	1 (14%)
		no flag	1 (14%)
St. Anthony	5 (14%)	brown and white	4 (80%)
		brown	1 (20%)
Eshu	4 (11%)	black	3 (75%)
		no flag	1 (25%)
St. Raphael	4 (11%)	green and red	2 (50%)
		brown	1 (25%)
		no flag	1 (25%)
Shango	2 (5%)	red and white	2 (100%)
Ajaja	2 (5%)	green and yellow	2 (100%)
Vigoyana	2 (5%)	red	2 (100%)

Source: My survey of thirty-seven Orisha shrine compounds.
Note: IO = incidence of occurrence, in both raw and percentage form, of stools for important *orisha* (col. 2) and of colors in their flags (col. 4). Insignificant differences such as light and dark shades and minor design features, which would introduce needless complication, have been omitted. Color percentages have been rounded to whole numbers.

demographics and shrine density appear to be positively correlated, although other factors must be considered before a causal relationship can be determined. Most of the remaining shrines are distributed along the main thoroughfares extending eastward and southward from this area.

The typical shrine compound has three primary structures — a *perogun*, a *chapelle*, and a *palais* — plus a small concrete pool or "boat" for the water powers and a number of isolated flags and stools (Photo 9). The *perogun*, an uncovered three-sided tin or concrete block structure, partially encloses flags or stools arranged in a linear fashion (Photo 10). Since there are usually three to nine flags mounted on bamboo poles that may reach as high as thirty feet, the *perogun* is an obvious visible marker for Orisha shrines (Photo 11). Because worshipers consider a flag or stool to be a conduit through which an *orisha* may enter, it serves as the focal point of many religious activities. For example, a *mongba* or

TABLE 8
Orisha *Stools in Shrine* Chapelles

Orisha	*IO*
Shango	30 (100%)
Oya	26 (87%)
Emanje	15 (50%)
Oshun	13 (43%)
Obatala	12 (40%)
Osayin	11 (37%)
Erele	11 (37%)
Mama Lata	3 (10%)

Source: My survey of thirty *chapelles* at Orisha shrine compounds.

iya might consult a particular *orisha* regarding a financial matter, sickness, or some other concern by means of divination at the base of the appropriate flag. When one enters a compound, it is customary to "greet" the *orisha* represented in the *perogun* — particularly Ogun — with libations of rum, oil, and water. Most important, worshipers make the blood offerings to most of the *orisha* (two notable exceptions are Shango and Obatala) in the *perogun*.

In my sampling of thirty-seven shrines (see Table 7), the most visible *orisha* was Ogun, whose flag appeared in every shrine I examined. He was followed closely in popularity by Osain and Shakpana. In eleven of the shrines in the sample, one to seven *orisha* not listed in Table 7 were represented. These were either unique to a particular shrine or were rare on the island; only a few shrine heads, for example, were familiar with Olokbo (see Figures 4 and 5), whom they referred to as a "bush man." African-derived powers not identified as *orisha* were occasionally allotted a place (Figure 5): for example, Kitush is a pygmy who can be called on to do virtually any sort of spirit work; Big Boy is a *rere*, a playful, mischievous spirit that may (rarely) take over a "horse" when a possessing *orisha* departs. Finally, I found flags or stools for one to six Hindu deities in ten (27 percent) of the shrines.

The *chapelle* is a small structure that serves as a sanctuary and a place for storing implements for various *orisha*. There is usually a small altar on one wall holding Christian (primarily Catholic) paraphernalia. Stools for various *orisha* are arranged along the remaining walls. Worshipers generally build the structure of wood or concrete blocks and

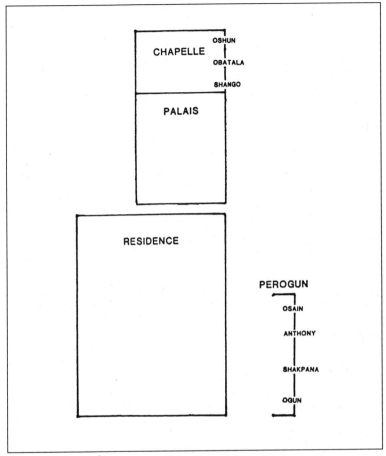

FIGURE 3. *Diagram of an Orisha shrine compound.*

cover it with wood or tin (Photo 12). The floor is virtually always earthen. The *chapelle* is the abode of at least two important *orisha*, Obatala and Shango, and it is in here that the shrine head will conduct Shango's annual ram offering. Smoking is usually prohibited inside the *chapelle*, and worshipers are asked to remove their shoes before entering.

In my survey of thirty *chapelles* (see Table 8), I found that Shango's stool appeared in all of them and Oya's in most. In nine I found stools

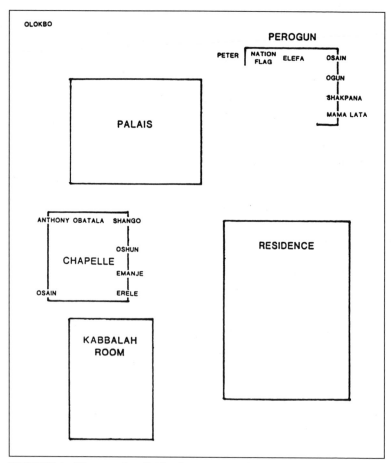

FIGURE 4. *Diagram of an Orisha shrine compound.*

for up to three *orisha* not listed in Table 8 (worshipers identified some of these as saints only), and stools for Hindu deities in four of them. (I should point out here that many worshipers consider the spot on the floor just in front of the base of the altar as a stool for Obatala, whether or not it is overtly marked as such. In my survey, however, the shrine head did not always acknowledge Obatala's stool, so I did not want to assume that it was recognized in all cases.) The *chapelle*, then, is similar to the *perogun* in a few general tendencies: the same two or three *orisha*

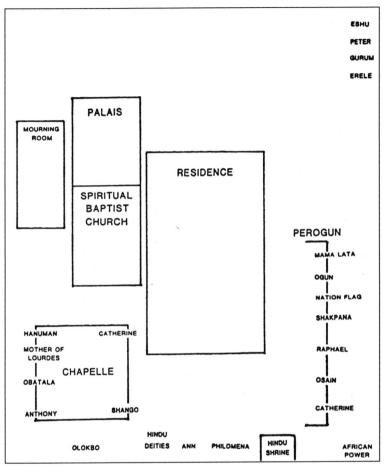

FIGURE 5. *Diagram of an Orisha shrine compound.*

are found in nearly all of them, but, again, the overall impression is one of diversity rather than similarity.

The *palais* is a rectangular structure with sides of fifteen to thirty feet in length, much larger than either the *perogun* or the *chapelle*. The typical *palais* has an earthen floor and waist-high walls, to permit viewing from the outside, and is covered with a roof constructed of tin and wood. There are usually one or two entrances, and benches against the walls on all four sides. During a feast the drummers occupy one entire bench. The *palais* is the focus of activity at an *ebo:* drumming and singing for the *orisha* take place there, as do most of the possessions.

In addition to the *perogun, chapelle,* and *palais,* a shrine head may also include in the compound a Spiritual Baptist church, a Kabbalah room, Kabbalah flags and stools, or occasionally a Kabbalah "tomb" (a sarcophagus of sorts) as a focus of ritual activity (Photo 13). In a survey of fifty-one shrines, eighteen (35 percent) contained a Spiritual Baptist church, sixteen (31 percent) contained a Kabbalah room or Kabbalah flags and stools, and twenty-three (45 percent) contained a flag or stool for at least one Hindu deity. Because I arbitrarily chose one flag or shrine as sufficient to mark a Hindu presence, the numbers are somewhat misleading, especially when compared to those for Spiritual Baptist churches: although well over half the Orisha shrines do not include a Spiritual Baptist church among their religious structures, the majority of shrines do utilize Spiritual Baptist prayers and songs and practice some of the rituals as well. As noted earlier, the Spiritual Baptist component is an integral part of the Orisha worship complex, whereas the Hindu component, so far, remains somewhat superficial.

Given all these variables, each shrine tends to differ from all the others, so it is somewhat misleading to think in terms of a typical or generic Orisha shrine. Plans of three examples appear in Figures 3, 4, and 5.

I also collected data on thirty-four shrines regarding their age.[1] They ranged from one to seventy-five years, the average being about fifteen years. Seventeen of the thirty-four were less than ten years old. Since the Orisha religion in Trinidad is approximately 150 years old, the relatively low value for average shrine age is puzzling but can probably be attributed either to recent relocations or the building of new shrines. (To relocate, all one has to do is ritually destroy the shrine before establishing a new one elsewhere.) In my travels around the island, I noted approximately ten first-year shrines. I have no way of knowing whether or not this figure is unusual, but it is certainly a significant indication of the growing popularity and public acceptance of the religion. A few of the older heads can trace their family's shrines back to the nineteenth century, but even these had been rebuilt from time to time in the same general area, although not always on the same spot. A few of the values I obtained would have been increased considerably if I had used the extended age of the older shrines, but for the survey I used only the ages of existing shrines.[2]

One of the oldest shrines on the island is located in the Belmont area of Port of Spain. Mano (Emmanuel Pierre) is both the shrine head and the *mongba*. He explained that his family has practiced the Orisha religion in Trinidad for four or five generations. The existing shrine, about seventy-five years old, replaced one built in the latter half of the nineteenth century adjacent to the current site. Mano is well versed in the history of African religious worship on the island and is an accomplished Kabbalist as well. His grandfather, Gab Thompson (born sometime in the late 1800s), was one of the most prominent Kabbalah practitioners of his time.

One indication of the age of Mano's shrine is the presence of *orisha* that are only rarely, if ever, found anywhere else on the island, including Wonka, Neoni, Yamela, and Goloshun. The *perogun* also includes a somewhat unusual stool for the "elders" (deceased *orisha* worshipers). Like many of the older shrines, especially in the north, Mano's shrine reflects a heavy Catholic influence.

ELEVEN

The Ebo, *Feast for the Gods*

From Mayaro to Port of Spain,
Las Iros to La Romain,
They come! To the Night of the SHANGO.

The drums are throbbing a wearied note.
The priest is tying the frightened goat.
They come! To the Night of the SHANGO.

The night is dark, frightened dogs bark,
Doctor, limer, and city clerk,
They come! To the Night of the SHANGO.

Some are walking the dreary mile
Through the forest in single file.
They come! To the Night of the SHANGO.

Young and old with faces bold,
Children shivering in the cold,
Yet they come! To the Night of the SHANGO.

The moon is peeping through the trees,
The gods are dancing in the leaves.
Tonight is the Night of the SHANGO.

— Carver Milton Scobie, "Night of the Shango"

Worshipers learn much of what they know about the *orisha* at the many *ebo* that are held during the feast season. Anywhere from a handful to dozens of *orisha* will manifest themselves in the course of a week-long feast. The primary functions of the *palais*, *chapelle*, and *perogun* become clear during the *ebo*, as does much about the liturgy, ritual behavior, and Orisha beliefs.

The *ebo* is without question the most important ceremony in the Orisha religion. It is basically a celebration of food, dance, and song during which the *orisha* manifest themselves and interact with worshipers in a variety of ways. Again, there is no set or standard program that a feast giver must follow, but many *ebo* do reflect a general pattern.

Shrine heads will begin the preparations for their annual *ebo* months in advance, since they need to acquire a number of materials and animals. The most costly materials include olive oil, rum, and candles; one can easily spend $2,000 TT (Trinidad and Tobago dollars; roughly $450 US) on these items alone. The other major expense is the animals. During a typical *ebo* a shrine head will offer at least three goats and a sheep, plus cocks and hens, ducks, guinea birds, pigeons, other fowl, and morocoys (tortoises) to the *orisha*. The goats and the sheep alone can run well over $2,500 TT (roughly $550 US). There are additional expenses as well, since the shrine head must buy new paint for the compound and cloth for the flags, pay the drummers, and feed hundreds of people. The total cost of an annual *ebo* might run between $5,000 and $15,000 TT (roughly $1,100 to $3,300 US).

Only rarely, however, is a shrine head expected to bear the full responsibility for funding the *ebo*. During the weeks before the feast, friends and others affiliated with the shrine will contribute materials and animals; wealthy individuals will often donate cash. Even so, the cost can sometimes be prohibitive; some shrine heads, in fact, reluctantly skip a year every now and then for lack of funds, or are forced to hold only an abbreviated (one- or two-day) feast.

Rituals and ceremonies that are associated with the annual feast but take place before the *ebo* proper are the Hindu prayers (optional) and the "raising" or "planting" of the flags. Many shrine heads do not include the Hindu or "sit-down" prayers, but those who do usually hold them one week before the opening day of the *ebo*. Often a Hindu *pundit* will be asked to direct the prayers, which are generally attended only by the *pundit* and his party and the family and close friends of the shrine head. The *pundit* will typically bless the drums and the drummers, discuss the role of African religion in Trinidad and its similarity to Hinduism, and oversee the planting of Hindu flags when appropriate (not all shrine heads put up flags for Hindu deities). Spiritual Baptist Leaders or Mothers may also direct sit-down prayers, sometimes in the Hindi language (Photo 14).

Between the conclusion of the Hindu prayers and the beginning of the *ebo*, the shrine head and his assistants raise the flags. All the flags in a compound, whether they are Orisha, Hindu, Kabbalah, or Baptist, are planted anew each year (although the Kabbalah flags are not usually planted during this time). The shrine assistants take down the old flags, with the exception of the Hindu, and burn them; the Hindu flags, by Indian custom, are left to deteriorate on their own.

A flag-raising at Leader Scott's shrine on Tuesday, June 23, 1992, was fairly typical. In the early evening Leader Scott opened the ceremony with Yoruba and Christian prayers and songs along the road in front of his compound. His assistants lit small rum-fueled fires at each *orisha* stool and made libations of oil and water at various points around the compound. As they burned the old flags, those in attendance recited Christian and Yoruba prayers in the *palais* and later sang Yoruba songs. Scott directed his assistants in ritually cleansing the bamboo flagpoles, and then everyone moved over to the *perogun*, where the new flags were to be planted. An assistant lit candles of the appropriate colors beside the stools. In each case, before planting the flag, a worshiper placed various materials into the hole made to support the bamboo (depending on the *orisha* in question, these materials include mercury, coins, honey, milk, olive oil, rum, and other "dry" food), and Scott performed a divination with obi seeds to ascertain whether or not the *orisha* approved. (If a "no" answer is received, one keeps making appropriate changes until a "yes" is obtained. If a "yes" is not received in a "reasonable" number of tries—the exact number depends on the shrine head—worshipers simply do not plant the flag for that particular *orisha* at that time.) Leader Scott's compound contains flags for personal spirits (those not generally associated with the Afro-American religious complex but important to him for personal reasons), and his assistants planted these as well. Scott had planted Eshu's flag two days before the others (Photo 15). Because of his whimsical, volatile, and dangerous nature, worshipers spatially and temporally isolate Eshu and his work from other activities.

The *ebo* itself begins on the Tuesday evening following the flag raising and concludes the following Saturday morning. The pattern is much the same from day to day, the primary difference being that worshipers make offerings to particular *orisha* on specific days and make no offering on Friday night and Saturday morning. At approximately 10:00 P.M. each night a Spiritual Baptist leader or mother leads the worshipers in Christian prayers and songs in the *palais*, often holding a candle in one hand and a brass bowl containing flowers in the

other. Later, other worshipers pray and lead songs, a privilege generally reserved for those of high status within the group: visiting leaders,
mothers, *mongba*, *iya*, or respected elders.

Some worshipers see this as an opportunity to increase their
prestige and to test the group's perception of their status, but their
efforts do not always work to their advantage. On a Wednesday night,
for example, just after a ceremony had begun at a shrine in the southern
part of the island, a man made an ostentatious entrance into the *palais*;
he admonished one worshiper for crossing his legs and another for
wearing his hat, and he both sang and prayed loudly in such a way as to
draw attention to himself. When the individual who was praying and
leading songs at the time was done, the new arrival attempted to
take the candle and flowers from him. He was promptly rebuffed by
the *mongba*, however, who forced him to take a seat with everyone
else.

The initial Christian part of the ceremony lasts from fifteen minutes to two hours or more. Many worshipers prefer not to take part in
the praying and singing at this time, choosing instead to "lime" ("hang
out" with friends) outside the compound or at least outside the *palais*
until the African part of the ceremony begins. My head counts during
the Christian and African parts of the ceremony indicated that attendance during the latter was consistently over twice as great. On the
other hand, I occasionally observed certain leaders or mothers leaving
the *palais* for the night at the conclusion of the Christian praying and
singing. Both situations reflect the varying attitudes concerning the
increasing Africanization of the Orisha religion.

Once worshipers have completed the Christian praying and singing, the drummers take their places, and shrine assistants light candles
and make libations on the floor of the *palais*. At this time one of the
more knowledgeable worshipers (usually the *mongba* or *iya* directing
the feast) sings a litany in Yoruba and leads a few Yoruba prayers.

The following typical prayers to Shango and Ogun are taken from a
collection of Yoruba prayers with English translations compiled by the
Orisa (*sic*) Youths Cultural Organization (see Chapter Thirteen) and
reproduced here by permission:

Sàngó o, ó pò l'ọkùnrin	Shango, the powerful one
Papò o fi ṣòkan	Unite us as one
Kabiyesi, ọba kòso	Your majesty, the King who did not hang

Baalè *oba kòso, gba wa ségun òtá wa*	Great King who did not hang, help me defeat the enemy
Atóbájayé *se alabo wa*	Sufficient support in life protect us
Sàngó *maa je ki a l'ìbànújé o*	Shango keep us from grief
Je *ki a maa oosi, maa se je ki a pedin*	Let us increase, let us not decrease
Maa *je ki a se sofi ijoba*	Keep us from breaking the law
Maa *je ki a ri aisàn o*	Let us not see illness
Je *ki a maa ri ikan rere l'aiyé*	Let us have the good things in life
Maa *je ki owo ìkà enia be wa*	Do not let the hand of wicked people reach us
Ba *wa ségun òtá o*	Help us defeat the enemy
Ba *wa wo omo wa*	Protect our children
Maa *je ki a nrin arin fi ese sa*	Do not let us stumble
Maa *je ki a nsoro fi enu ko*	Guide the words of our mouth
Ògún *ò*	Hail Ogun
Ògún Oni're	Ogun, the lord of Ire!
Òkè *nlá kìléhìn* Ìrè	The great mount that stands behind Ire.
A-kó *okolóko-gbéru-gbéru*	You who ravaged other people's farms
Ògún *pa sotúnun*	Ogun killed on the right
Ó *b'òtún je*	And made the right a total destruction
Ògún *pa sosì*	Ogun killed on the left
Ó *bòsì je*	And made the left a total destruction
Ó *pa olómú gògò sójú omi*	He slew the one with very prominent breasts on the waters
Ó *dá ìjà akèn àti eja*	Thus creating a bone of contention between crabs and fish;
Òsìn Imálè	Chief of the divinities!
Onílé Kángun-Kàngun *òde òrun*	The owner of many houses in heaven,
Ògún *onílé owó, olónà olà*	Ogun who owns the store of gold and the path of wealth,
O *lomi sile fèjè wè*	He who has water at home but prefers to bathe in blood;

Ògún *a-wǫ́n-lẹ́yin-ojú*	Ogun whose eyeballs are terrible to behold,
Ègbè *lẹ́hìn ǫmǫ òrukàn*	He who gives support to the orphans
Ògún *ò*	Hail Ogun!

Following the Yoruba litany and prayers, one of the shrine assistants places two small calabashes containing ashes and water, offerings to Eshu, on the floor in the center of the *palais* along with a lighted candle. The drummers then begin beating the drums (Photo 16) and the *mongba* or *iya* leads songs for Eshu. (The singing of songs for any *orisha* follows a call-and-response pattern: the leader sings a verse, which the congregation then repeats.) The song leader may sing as many as seven different songs for Eshu, during which time a few of the worshipers dance in a circular pattern around the calabashes. At some point during this singing, one of the shrine assistants carries the water, ashes, and candle outside the *palais* and places them at Eshu's stool (if there is one) or elsewhere on the outskirts of the compound. When the ritual at Eshu's shrine is completed, the drumming and singing cease. Shrine assistants then put down candles in the corners of the *palais*, and the worshipers begin the drumming and singing for other *orisha*, starting with Ogun.

In virtually all Yoruba-based religious ceremonies in the New World, worshipers deal with Eshu first. He is thought to be very strong and able to stand up to any spiritual force except Olodumare, the supreme or high god. As a messenger of the gods, he has the ability to mediate between humans and any of the other *orisha*. During an *ebo* the worshipers show honor and respect for Eshu by singing his songs first and putting out his food. Those in attendance ask him to watch over the feast and to guard the spiritual "doors" lest unwanted spirits attempt to gain entrance. Elder Biddeau explained Eshu's role this way:

Most people think that Eshu is the devil, but we have no devils in the Orisha religion. What we do have is mischievous spirits who can make things very difficult for you if you should go against [them]. So you find that Eshu is that kind of spirit. But apart from that, in the *orisha* pantheon, he is considered the inspector general, because Eshu is the deity that takes all reports, especially reports of the *ebo*, to Olodumare. And that is the reason why Eshu must be entertained first. You dare not make the mistake of not entertaining Eshu once you are giving an *ebo*. Let's put it this way, the whole *ebo* would be considered null and void, and instead of getting any progress and success,

again he will play tricks on you. It's like "How dare you forget me!" So, you
have to consider him first. (Interview, south of Matura, December 10, 1988)

During the African part of the ceremony, worshipers sing six different types of songs for the *orisha*. Invitation songs ask the *orisha* to
visit the *ebo* and possess one of the worshipers. Acceptance songs are
an expression of gratitude after the *orisha* manifest themselves. Work
songs are sung while an *orisha* is attending to or consulting with someone. Pleasure songs are dance songs to entertain the *orisha* after they
have completed their work. Farewell songs are sung when a power
indicates that he or she is ready to leave. Finally, dismissal songs are
used on the rare occasions when an *orisha* overstays his or her welcome.
Worshipers are obligated to sing for and entertain many powers during
the night, and if an *orisha* lingers in the *palais* too long, those in attendance will, through song, politely and respectfully ask him or her to
leave.

During a typical *ebo*, worshipers may sing five or six types of songs
for each of some thirteen *orisha*; moreover, for a popular *orisha* there
are several songs of each type, so worshipers often sing more than a
hundred different songs in the course of the feast week. The song
leader sings for the *orisha* in a particular order, but since there is no
standard, written liturgy, the order differs somewhat from shrine to
shrine. Generally speaking, the sequence is as follows: Eshu, Ogun,
Mama Lata, Peter (who can also be sung for after Osain), Shakpana,
Raphael, Osain, Emanje, Oshun, Erele, Shango, Oya, Obatala (optional). In practice, however, a song leader may introduce variations:
for example, if Shakpana manifests himself during the singing for
Ogun, and if Ogun is not present at the time, worshipers may sing then
for Shakpana. Thereafter, the song leader goes back to Mama Lata and
restores the sequence.

The large number of songs and the lack of liturgical standardiza-
tion often lead to confusion, as we have seen. Disputes over just what
song should be sung at a particular time are common, at least partly
because of disagreements as to which power is the possessing agent at
that moment. Another problem is the manifestation of Kabbalah entities, which are often difficult to identify because they sometimes
mimic the behavior of a particular *orisha*. Worshipers certainly do not
intentionally entertain Kabbalah entities during an *ebo* but may in-
advertently invite them in. Most *mongba* and *iya* consider the presence

of Kabbalah entities at an *ebo* to be polluting, but they deal with this contingency by constructing spiritual "barriers" that serve to keep the unwanted spirits out, as well as by seeking the protection of Eshu.

Throughout each night of the *ebo*, worshipers beat drums and sing virtually nonstop until dawn. During this time as many as twenty possessions may occur, or there may be none at all. Typically, the possessed worshiper dances with the implements associated with the manifesting *orisha* and provides a number of services for the worshipers, including healing and counseling. Different *orisha* may be present at one time, and different aspects of the same *orisha* may also be present simultaneously.

As dawn approaches, shrine assistants ritually cleanse the animals to be sacrificed that morning while the other worshipers are singing for the appropriate powers. Each animal has a sponsor, the person who either purchased the animal or is tending to it for someone else. The slayer immolates the animals and directs the flow of blood onto the stool of the *orisha*. The slayer leaves some part of the animal (feathers, horns, morocoy shells) at the stool to commemorate the offering. Shrine assistants cook the animals and put a small portion out for the *orisha*; worshipers consume the rest.

On Saturday morning Shango and Ogun customarily conclude the *ebo*. Ogun removes a sword that has been planted in the *palais* since the opening night, a gesture that officially closes the feast. Some worshipers feel that Ogun's presence at this time — but not Shango's — is necessary and sufficient. Yet I was also told that other powers may conclude a feast, or that no powers need to be present at the end. A *mongba* in Port of Spain noted that in the past a feast was not over until Ogun arrived to withdraw his sword, even if that meant continuing the *ebo* indefinitely, but he added that few people today are willing to extend the feast past Saturday.

Most *ebo* follow the pattern described, but exceptions do occur. Not all *mongba* or *iya* begin each feast night with Christian prayers and songs; a few shrines are exclusively African and contain no stools for Catholic saints or Hindu gods and no Christian or Hindu paraphernalia. Worshipers affiliated with these shrines generally do not recognize the Catholic counterparts of the *orisha*. There are fewer than ten such shrines, but this basic tendency toward Africanization seems to be on the rise.

Another variation is that some shrine heads do not sacrifice animals but offer fruit instead. Worshipers may replace blood sacrifice with fruit offerings for moral reasons, since some object to the spilling of blood or at least to the sheer number of animals slaughtered; or there may be financial reasons, since fruit offerings are relatively inexpensive. Or from time to time the *orisha* themselves may issue instructions to discontinue the offering of animals; this is interpreted as a gesture of approval on the part of *orisha* who wish to relieve a shrine head, *mongba*, or *iya* of this burden, usually after years of faithful service. In fact, Leader Scott and Mother Joan had been so instructed and no longer sacrificed animals during their *ebo*. Fruit offerings are not practiced on a large scale, but worshipers consider them a proper and appropriate ritual practice. They include bananas and coconuts, with boiled corn and peanuts, for Ogun; bananas for Shango; mangos and watermelon plus honey for Oshun; and watermelon for Eshu.

According to some of my contacts, feasts that are carried on in the "north" (primarily Port of Spain, but including areas east of the city along the east-west corridor) differ from those in the "south" (the rest of the island but mainly the west-central and southwest portions). Worshipers explained that the manifestations differ behaviorally, that different songs are sung for the powers, and that the closing ceremonies are dissimilar as well. They also noted that only "bamboos" are planted in the north, as opposed to both "bamboos and stools" in the south: that is, in addition to planting the flag, southern worshipers build a small shrine in the earth and mark it with the appropriate implements. Noting "the traditional rivalry between North and South," Henry (1983, 64) writes: "Southerners generally believe that their ritual is more sanctified while Northerners consider those in the South to be backward country bumpkins." My observations generally support Henry's statement; worshipers from both the north and the south often rated their own form of worship as being in some way superior to the other.

My cursory investigation revealed the following differences. I was told that Oya was placed outside in the north but not in the south, where she is found exclusively in the *chapelle*. In my sample of shrines I found Oya outside in ten cases, only one of which was southern. I also found that worshipers did indeed sing different songs at northern feasts, and that the opening Yoruba prayers and songs differed as well. Finally, as I mentioned earlier, northern shrines tended to be more heavily Catholic than southern shrines. My general impression, however, is that the north/south contrasts are neither pronounced nor widespread. Northern worshipers attend and participate in southern feasts and vice versa. Perhaps in the past such differences were more salient, but the movement of people within the island has clouded the distinction. Present-day variations may be interpreted simply as a manifestation of the general variability of worship practices on an island-wide scale; the differences are minor, and both forms of worship fall squarely within the range of religious practices referred to as the Orisha religion.

Although beliefs and practices do vary significantly from shrine to shrine, the mobility of *orisha* worshipers has served to temper or counteract any tendency on the part of particular shrine heads to develop totally unique worship patterns. The religion as a whole, especially when viewed on the level of the shrine and its members, is only minimally integrated at best, so the constant interaction of worshipers from different parts of the island has probably played an important role in maintaining what little cohesion exists.

As noted in Chapter Two, the traditional feast season extends from the Tuesday after Easter Sunday to the beginning of Advent (four Sundays before Christmas Day), a period of thirty-two to thirty-six weeks. (Not all shrine heads, *mongba*, and *iya* recognize the traditional feast-giving period; three of the feasts in a sample of seventy-six were not held during this time.) Since worshipers hold 150 or so *ebo* annually, there are often several feasts taking place in any particular week. Thus, worshipers have the opportunity to visit many different shrines during the feast season, often during the same week.

Worshipers determine feast dates in various ways (see Chapter 2), but most base their decision on Catholic feast days, phases of the moon, and seasonal cycles, sometimes making adjustments to fit a new feast into the existing schedule. It is common for shrine heads in a particular area, for example, to check with the heads of nearby shrines before setting the dates of their own feasts. September, October, and November are especially active: of the seventy-six feasts I sampled, forty-three (63 percent) occurred during these months, the rest being distributed over the remainder of the feast season. The feast days of the Catholic counterparts of four *orisha* occur during the active three-month period: Saint Michael, Saint Francis, Saint Raphael, and Saint Catherine. During this time worshipers also recognize the feast day of Saint John of the Cross, one of the aspects of Saint John/Shango.

Perhaps the occurrence of significant Catholic feast days from September to November explains the large number of feasts during this time. Another possible explanation involves economics: one worshiper noted that many shrine heads who have put off their feast for financial reasons finally hold their *ebo* near the end of the season.

The feast schedule remains somewhat random and unstructured. During some weeks there will be no feast on the island, yet during others there might be four or five; in fact, in one particular week I counted seven. On other occasions, two feasts may occur at shrines so close together that the worshipers and resources in the area are divided. During the third week of October 1988, when two shrine heads held their *ebo* within a short walking distance from each other, the attendance at one appeared to be adversely affected by the presence nearby of an *ebo* directed by a popular *mongba*, Leader Scott.

During a typical feast season, in any case, the worshipers have many opportunities to visit different *ebo*, and my data on forty-two respondents show that they do indeed take advantage of these opportunities, attending from as few as 3 to as many as 50 feasts a year; the average is 14.6. To the question of how far they were willing to travel to attend a feast, the answers ranged from 6 to 130 kilometers (3.7 to about 81 miles), the farthest possible distance separating two shrines in Trinidad; I used this figure for those who said they would travel "anywhere." The mean was found to be 51.79 kilometers (32.16 miles). In some areas of the island, particularly the northwestern portion around Port of Spain and the west-central portion, a 51.79-kilometer radius would include well over a hundred shrines.

Part IV

TWELVE

The Orisha Religion as an Open System

I *have focused considerable attention* thus far on the highly eclectic nature of the Orisha religion. The question naturally arises, what are the transformative processes at work in the religion — that is, those mechanisms of change that have transformed the religious system from a body of knowledge initially drawn from a single cultural tradition to one drawn from a variety of cultural traditions? Several sociocultural processes can act to shift society and culture from one state to another, ranging from nativism on the one hand to assimilation on the other. The ethnocentrism of nativism initially serves to temper any tendency toward radical change, since traditional and preexisting ideologies are emphasized and extraneous ideologies rejected. Nevertheless, a transformation does occur, which results in the ascendancy of dormant traditional notions. Complete assimilation takes place when varying degrees of ethnocentrism give way to conciliation and capitulation in the face of alien intrusion.

According to Seyyed Nasr, the Western world view has instilled in modern people a predisposition toward a kind of intellectual xenophobia that rigidly delimits religious thought and results in the conception of religion along extremely myopic lines:

One of the paradoxes of our age is that the manifestation of religion in different worlds of form and meaning has been used by the already desacralized type of knowledge, which has dominated the mental outlook of Western man in recent times, to destroy further what little remains of the sacred in the contemporary world. Modern man is encountering the other worlds of sacred forms and meaning in their full reality at the very moment when sacred knowledge and an interiorizing intelligence, which would be able to penetrate to [the] inner meaning of alien forms, have become so inaccessible. The result is that the multiplicity of sacred forms, which is itself

169

the most definitive evidence of the reality of the sacred and the universality of the truth that each universe of form and meaning transmits in its own manner, has been employed, by those who deny the reality of the sacred as such, to relativize what has survived of the Christian tradition. The multiplicity of sacred forms has been used as an excuse to reject all sacred forms, as well as the *scientia sacra* which lies behind and beyond these forms. (Nasr 1981, 280–81)

Nasr further notes that this tendency toward secularization is partly attributable to scientific and objective approaches to the study of religion. Much of the reductionism that has been so popular in the academic study of religion also seems to be heavily influenced by philosophical positivism and its deemphasis of the metaphysical.

What, then, do we make of religious catholicity and eclecticism in which individuals not only do not reject "sacred forms" but, in fact, embrace them? Surely all peoples have developed a natural skepticism toward things foreign — if not always for the reasons noted above, then certainly for reasons involving something like a culture-specific logic: that is, ethnocentrism. To address this problem, we should go behind theology and the neat and ordered domain of ideology to the everyday world of capricious, whimsical, and unpredictable behavior that is geared more toward survival and contingency than toward theoretical closure.

I do not mean to imply that the world of human social and cultural interaction lacks any sort of continuity and consistency, but only that *Homo sapiens* will generally compromise theoretical elegance in the name of pragmatism and adaptability. This is, in fact, one of the primary characteristics of syncretism: a compromise between the need to retain those things that give meaning to everyday life and the desire to embellish and broaden that meaning in the context of an ever changing sociohistorical and ecological matrix.

I am making an assumption here that cultural — in this case, religious — systems are in fact susceptible and vulnerable to change. In Orisha we are dealing with a nonliterate religion in the sense that there is no written corpus of beliefs and practices. Worshipers have passed down religious information orally for generations, and the resulting lack of liturgical rigidity has brought about a tendency toward flexibility rather than conservatism. Jarich Oosten notes that nonliterate religions are vulnerable to broader social and cultural considerations:

Since there is no sacred book, the continuity and uniformity of the religion depends on oral traditions that are much more flexible than books. Oral traditions are often sacred and the mnemotechnical skill of the participants is usually considerable, but often political, economic, and other interests cause the participants to adapt their oral traditions, and once they have done that the earlier versions are lost irrevocably. (Oosten 1985, 246)

Another important factor is the likelihood that the Orisha religion was not transplanted intact to the New World. The Orisha religion in Nigeria is a complex system of different shrines, each dedicated solely to a particular deity, which are maintained and managed by a number of religious functionaries. No one group practices the religion as a whole; rather, it is the activities of disparate groups, each focusing primarily on one deity, that combine to make up what we refer to as the Orisha religion in Nigeria. It is highly unlikely that Africans were able to transport the religion to the Caribbean in toto, although they obviously brought with them a rich corpus of lore regarding individual deities. Early worshipers probably merged the bits and pieces of religious knowledge that survived the passage into a moderately coherent form of worship; theological lacunae would eventually be at least partially filled with elements of other religious traditions. In Trinidad, many of my contacts spoke of a division of labor involving the various religious elements that have been incorporated into the Orisha religious system. One gets the impression that we are dealing with what was, in fact, originally an open system: that is, a collection of beliefs and practices which, unlike a fully developed religion, has not yet adequately addressed some of the personal needs and existential concerns that worshipers generally have.

As an open or incomplete belief system is gradually transformed into a richer, more comprehensive corpus of belief, ritual, and symbolism, it seems reasonable to assume that—at least in situations of unforced and passive contact—those individuals actively engaged in the borrowing and incorporation of new religious traits will avoid redundancy and contradiction. For this reason, an eclectic or syncretic religion will in time resemble something on the order of the proverbial "well-oiled machine," its many parts contributing in complementary fashion to the overall effectiveness of the whole. I use the phrase "something on the order of" because theoretical closure is seldom if ever attained by a religious ideology—with the possible exception of the so-called great or world religions that have ancient literary traditions. We can, perhaps, conceive of the process of change and transformation in passive contact contexts in teleological terms as an ongoing struggle on the part of worshipers to attain a closed ideological system. Worshipers in the Orisha religion in Trinidad have integrated the elements of five different traditions into one general worship pattern, and each one illustrates the foregoing comments in its own way. An examination of the ways in which the Kabbalah and Spiritual Baptist traditions have been assimilated is particularly illuminating.

Despite its diabolical overtones and the general negative perception of Kabbalah, it is popular among Orisha adherents. In a survey of fifty-one shrines I found Kabbalah shrines, flags, or rooms in sixteen. In response to a questionnaire, over half (twenty-four of forty-two) of the worshipers said that they had attended a Kabbalah banquet within the last year. It is obvious that at least to some, the benefits of the Kabbalah outweigh the disadvantages. An eloquent Spiritual Baptist leader and *orisha* worshiper in Port of Spain, Leader Ronnie, did not deny the negative aspects of the Kabbalah, but he described Kabbalistic practice in matter-of-fact tones:

All the lower forces are governed by the same four [Kabbalistic] princes. . . . When you work with these forces, you must get a speedy answer, whether good, bad, or indifferent, because they are at your beck and call. They are here to obey you. You are the ruler of this land. God put you here as the ruler of this land, and the forces are there for your assistance.

Most of the time when we call a spirit . . . it will be restless and vindictive because this is what we find from the person who calls it. . . . Remember that the spirit is neither good or evil, hence we call it a demon. . . . Now, whatsoever we have in our minds is what the spirit manifests itself in. If we have evil, the spirits feed on that. If the spirit comes evil, it is because we have hate in us.

In darkness there is an abundance of light. In the absence of light you find darkness, and at the absence of darkness we find light. So the both is equal. We have to put the both of them to use, to make an elevation [in our knowledge]. We have to use them equally and right because understanding means both negative and positive. Without the negative the positive can't work. Without the positive the negative can't work. . . . With the two together we gain knowledge. (Interview, Port of Spain, December 23, 1988)

Elder Biddeau, an accomplished Kabbalah practitioner, likewise explained that the Kabbalah itself is a sort of neutral force but can be manipulated to do either good or evil:

Now, for example, this [Waite 1972] is a book of black magic and pacts. I personally would say that this book contains very good information. There are certain passages or chapters in this book that I would not use; I would not touch them. The reason why is that I believe that the meaning of my being here would be hampered if I should deal with these certain passages. But there is certain information in this book which can help, and by learning and practicing it, you can help your fellow man. For example, if someone is possessed by an evil spirit, what you learn here, you can dismiss this spirit.

But then you find that there are people I know of who . . . would go on to learn that which is negative in this particular book. I personally don't agree with this, but again, to each his own. Anything that can help, I learn. (Interview, south of Matura, December 17, 1988)

Most of those who actively work with the Kabbalah entities describe the Kabbalah in terms similar to those of Leader Ronnie and Elder Biddeau: as a powerful force that can be used both positively and negatively. In this way the practice of the Kabbalah can be defended on the grounds that it takes on negative or evil forms only as a result of the malevolent intentions of the individual practitioner.

Many worshipers, however, refuse to have anything to do with Kabbalah worship because of what they perceive to be its evil and demonic overtones. One shrine head explained that it is contradictory to practice the Spiritual Baptist religion or Orisha worship while being involved with the Kabbalah at the same time. I questioned her about those who had told me that they received their instructions for Kabbalistic work while mourning, but she was skeptical:

You believe that? I don't know that. You can't hold God in this hand and the devil in this one. That is the other side. . . . It is evil. . . . If you can't give them [the Kabbalah entities] a life [in return for knowledge or favors done], sometime they take your life. (Interview, near Port of Spain, January 17, 1989)

Another worshiper described the Kabbalah as spiritually polluting:

I feel as though there was some kind of divine intervention in my coming to the *orisha*, and I don't think I should taint it by deliberately courting what I know to be negative essences. If you invite me to something [a Kabbalah ceremony] I will go, but before I go to a Kab thing I do a whole consecration ritual with myself, so when I get there I feel that I am sanctified and that nothing can touch me. (Interview, west-central Trinidad, June 21, 1992)

Joseph Henderson, a young Rastafarian and a popular drummer, referred to the Kabbalah as "90 percent evil." Although our discussion

made it clear that he had a lot of respect for the Kabbalah, he was quick
to point out the spiritually negative and potentially ruinous aspects of
this religious practice:

What makes the Kabbalah so dangerous . . . [is] the Kabbalah side is of evil. . . .
You will find, now, that Prince of Darkness [a Kabbalistic entity] will sit here
at this table, and you have been hurt by your neighbor . . . and you feel like you
can go to Prince and lick up [physically abuse or otherwise harm] that
neighbor. You will go to Prince and he will gladly do that work for a certain
price. . . . "Give me $10,000 or give me some cigars and I will kill Tom for
you." That is how they function.

Man goes into the Kabbalah because he feels he will get rich overnight:
fast money, jewels, and live a posh life. . . . But he pays for it. He pays for it in
one way only, the evil way. . . . Their time is short. . . . And notice the people
who choose the Kabbalah life and live that life. They get cut off very young.
They get big overnight, and they get plenty material value, but they don't live
very old. . . . The Kabbalah has taken a lot of them early. (Interview, Basta Hall
Village, July 3, 1992)

These overwhelmingly negative opinions notwithstanding, the
Kabbalah is an important part of the complex of religious activities that
center on the Orisha religion. But for reasons that can no doubt be
attributed to lingering perceptions of the Kabbalah as negative and
polluting or, more generally, as something totally distinct from the
Orisha religion, practitioners isolate it from *orisha* worship, spatially,
ritually, and otherwise. As Elder Biddeau explained:

The Kabbalistic order has no place at all in *orisha* worship. This is an order by
itself. It is an old order, one of the oldest in the world. But what you would
find that makes you think it has a place in the Orisha . . . [is that] most *orisha*
worshipers practice the Kabbalah. . . . You find that persons are able to
communicate with the Kabbalistic spirits for very wicked deeds.

Also they can communicate with Kabbalistic spirits for very good deeds. It
all depends on the category of spirits you are dealing with. Whereas with the
orisha, you do good and you don't ever get the deities involved with anything
that is wrong to your fellow man, because that is one of the laws within the
Orisha religion. (Interview, south of Matura, December 10, 1988)

Worshipers consider the Kabbalah powers to be amoral and uncon-
cerned with human affairs. Even those who work with the entities often
refer to them as "wicked," "evil," and "demonic." Worshipers say that
the Kabbalah entities are powerful and work "fast." If someone needs

immediate results, he or she appeals to the Kabbalah entities. If someone wishes to manipulate the natural order so as to benefit unjustly at the expense of another, he or she works with the Kabbalah. In contrast, most adherents contend that the *orisha* work "slow" and, furthermore, will not assist the worshiper in activities that would be considered negative. Thus, practitioners regularly call upon Kabbalah entities to perform tasks that fall outside the domain of the *orisha*.

Worshipers maintain, however, that the *orisha* are more powerful than the Kabbalah entities and that their refusal to engage in negative activities seems to be a matter of taste rather than ability. One gets the impression that the *orisha* are reluctant to do harm but will eventually respond negatively and forcefully if an individual insists on trying their patience. According to one worshiper:

Ogun, Shango, and all of them could do destruction to a full capacity. But that is a last [resort]. Like if you neglect keeping your feast, one year, two year, three year. One day you may fall and break your two foot. . . . Eventually, if you carry it too far you will go home. They will take you. So, there is a limit to how much they will take. If you keep neglecting their instruction, eventually you will get a break foot. He may put you in a bed that [from which] you can never raise again. He may put you in a wheelchair. (Interview, west-central Trinidad, July 3, 1992)

Given the slow response time of the *orisha* and their aversion to negative behavior except in special cases, the *mongba* and *iya* who integrate the Kabbalah into their personal religious system greatly expand their repertoire of magical practices and are then able to meet the needs of a larger clientele. Likewise, the rank-and-file worshipers can then appeal to a much broader pantheon, able to perform any number of tasks.

Clearly, the relationship between the two religious systems involves something more like juxtaposition than syncretism. *Orisha* worshipers have borrowed and utilized Kabbalistic elements but have not integrated them; Kabbalah rituals, paraphernalia, and structures remain, for the most part, independent of and isolated from those of the Orisha religion. For example, shrine heads who include Kabbalah rooms and stools in their compounds will spatially segregate these structures from the rest of the shrine.

There are, however, a few signs of incipient syncretism. The notion that Kabbalah entities could enter an Orisha yard through Eshu's shrine (Chapter Nine) at least implicitly associates Eshu with the Kabbalah powers. But since Eshu protects an *ebo* from unwanted spirits, including Kabbalah entities, it appears unlikely that he will be syncretized with them. A few of my contacts also noted that the *orisha* Shakpana could be used to perform negative tasks, and some equated him with the Kabbalah entity known as Skull and Cross. Leader Scott mentioned an interesting correspondence between Shakpana, the *orisha* Gurum, and the local Kabbalah entity known as J. B. Sohuluman. Kabbalah practitioners "plant" Sohuluman's stool by a tree — the same kind of tree, in fact, from which *orisha* worshipers obtain the stand for Shakpana's medicinal calabash; Gurum (who, according to Leader Scott and others, may be Kongolese-derived) is also planted by a tree, and interestingly, one can dismiss a Kabbalah entity with libations at Gurum's stool. Although Leader Scott did not quite posit a direct connection between Gurum, Shakpana, J. B. Sohuluman, and other entities, it is clear that some sort of association is being implied here. Some worshipers, however, are not aware of or do not recognize any such relationships. I would guess, given the perceived nature of the *orisha* and the Kabbalah powers and the prevailing view that the two religious systems are incompatible, that syncretism on a large scale will not occur.

It seems likely, however, that the Kabbalah will become an increasingly significant part of the worship complex. Its popularity has risen greatly in the last twenty years or so and shows no sign of abating. As pointed out in Chapter Four, the Haitians grafted a "hot" (Petro) form of worship onto the existing "cool" (Rada) side of Vodoun; their expansion of the religious system along those lines facilitated an aggressive, belligerent, and, eventually, successful response to colonial oppression. Orisha adherents in Trinidad seem to be going through the same process, although for much different reasons; Orisha, like Vodoun, appears to have both "hot" and "cool" sides, and although this division is not yet a trademark of the religion as a whole, I predict that it will become more noticeable in the future.

The Spiritual Baptist religion also plays an important role in the Orisha religion. The consensus among many *orisha* worshipers is that Spiritual Baptist worship constitutes a sort of first step or primary level in a process that eventually leads to *orisha* worship. A drummer explained that one "graduates" from the Spiritual Baptist religion and moves on to the Orisha religion. A flag raising south of Princes Town in southwestern Trinidad on April 24, 1989, provides an excellent illustration of this notion.

Carli Rawlins, a *mongba* and Spiritual Baptist leader, directed the ritual. Those in attendance began the ceremony with approximately three hours of Baptist praying and singing, after which Carli and his assistants planted the flags. The flag raising itself resembled a typical Orisha ritual, but I noticed some differences: Carli drew Baptist seals on the flags, he put no materials in the earth before planting the flags, and he made no sacrifices. Carli explained later that these flags were the first to be planted in this yard and that the owners of the property were newcomers to the "faith." Therefore, he had to "cool" the flags a bit, since the neophytes could not handle the power that an *orisha* flag would bring to the yard. He noted that the manner in which powers manifest themselves is related to the nature of the flags that worshipers plant in their honor. He added that eventually the property owners would plant full-blown *orisha* flags. (I should point out that some *mongba* who confine their practices solely to those of *orisha* worship also do this work in graduated stages.)

One more example illustrates the prerequisite function of the Spiritual Baptist religion in the Orisha religious system. Once a year a popular Spiritual Baptist mother in west-central Trinidad holds a one-day session of prayers and singing. When I attended this ritual in the summer of 1985, it closely resembled a Spiritual Baptist thanksgiving. When I attended again in the summer of 1989, there had been a few changes: she had planted *orisha* flags in her yard, placed Orisha implements in the two corners flanking the altar so that her church resembled a *chapelle*, and added an extended session of Orisha drumming and singing to her ceremony after the Baptist prayers and singing. Leader Scott explained that this Baptist mother is working with the *orisha* but does not yet wish to sponsor a full-blown *ebo*. He agreed with my assessment that she appears to be moving in stages from what was initially a Spiritual Baptist function to what may eventually become an Orisha feast.

Many *orisha* worshipers were once exclusively Spiritual Baptists but eventually received instructions for Orisha work through dreams, visions, or mourning. The experiences of one shrine head illustrates this process:

[Baptist] is one . . . foundation of it [*orisha* worship]. Because John the Baptist is one man, but in Shango [*orisha* worship] they call him Shango. He was a man who was keeping the truth in ancient days. . . . Now in the Baptist faith, we use the bell. The bell is the power. . . . And in Shango we use the drums. You see, the Baptist and Shango is one. After some time, they [the *orisha*] give them [Baptists] work to do. . . . It is from the Baptist [during mourning] that I get the feast. In my first mourning I went to Africa and they give me the drums and all the things to use. (Interview, northwest Trinidad, January 17, 1989)

Edmond David, who also mentioned that Orisha work can be obtained while mourning, clearly relegates the Spiritual Baptist religion to subordinate status in comparison with the Orisha religion:

The Baptist is a "breakoff" from the Orisha [religion]. It is a mixture of Christianity and Orisha. Because, you see, Christianity came many years after Orisha. You will find that many of those that have turned to Christianity will sometime return to a *mongba* or *iya* for work. . . . You see, plenty people get Orisha work through the Baptist [religion]. When you mourn you get a gift. (Interview, Claxton Bay, June 19, 1992)

The Spiritual Baptist religion, then, like the Kabbalah, serves to supplement the Orisha religion; the result is, again, a stretching or broadening of the original system. There exists virtually no redundancy or contradiction in that part of the Afro-American religious complex that includes the Orisha and Spiritual Baptist religions and the Kabbalah. Worshipers have merged the Baptist and Kabbalah beliefs and practices with those of the Orisha religion, thereby filling in some of the theological lacunae noted earlier. The addition of the Kabbalah powers to the pantheon gives those worshipers who accept them access to a much larger and diverse group of spirits and permits them to operate not only in a spiritually positive fashion but in a negative fashion as well, should the need arise. The Spiritual Baptist religion provides a safe and proper starting point for those neophytes who plan to affiliate with the Orisha religion eventually or to head their own Orisha shrines in the future.

Some adherents have also added Hindu beliefs and practices to their belief systems, although most have only a minimal knowledge of Hinduism. The fact that a relationship between the Hindu and Orisha religions exists at all may be attributed to the similarity of their pantheons, which contain numbers of anthropomorphized deities: hence the Trini practice of planting flags and stools for the deities of both religions. Many worshipers view Hinduism simply as the Indian counterpart to *orisha* worship. Only a few have syncretized the Hindu and Orisha deities; most are unaware of or do not recognize this association. For the most part, then, Hindu elements have so far simply been borrowed, seemingly in recognition of a popular and pervasive religion practiced in Trinidad. Because the wholesale incorporation of Hinduism into the Orisha religion would result in redundancy, especially in regard to the respective deities and their domains, and because those practicing the Orisha religion are predominantly African and those practicing the Hindu religion are almost entirely Indian, I would guess that the association between the two religions will remain at a superficial level.

The notion of an open versus closed system is merely one way to contextualize a discussion of religious change but is an approach that helps us understand many transformative aspects of the Orisha religion in Trinidad. A discussion of the Catholic component in this context, however, requires special consideration. Many *orisha* worshipers feel that Catholic saints are so similar to the *orisha* that any syncretism involving the saints and the *orisha* would certainly be redundant on some level. Nevertheless, adherents have thoroughly syncretized the two pantheons, and this syncretization is one of the most significant and visible components of the Orisha religious system. Even worshipers who argue that the Orisha religion can stand on its own, that it need not be blended with other traditions, grudgingly admit that the Catholic component has become an integral part of *orisha* worship in Trinidad. To understand the anomalous Catholic case, we must examine the process of syncretism in historical context.

THIRTEEN

Syncretism and Eclecticism versus Africanization

T*he syncretism of Catholic saints* and African gods — *orisha, vodoun,* or others — is one of the more salient and prevalent character- istics of African-derived religions in the New World. It was Melville J. Herskovits, in his research of the highly eclectic and multicultural Afro-American religions, who first popularized the term "syncretism" in the social sciences. Scholars have given syncretism little theoreti- cal treatment, the more notable exceptions being Munro Edmonson (1960), Jay Edwards (1980b), and Herskovits (1948, 1955). The pro- cess itself has been investigated in the field by Bastide (1972, 1978), Edwards (1980a, 1980b), Herskovits (1937, 1943), Peter Kloss (1985), Juliene Lipson (1980), Mischel (1957), Simpson (1980), and others. Many of these studies have focused on the eclectic Afro-American cultures, since these settings provide an excellent "laboratory" for the study of syncretism and related cultural processes.

In defining syncretism, various scholars emphasize different aspects of the borrowing and blending process. Herskovits (1948, 553–54; 1955, 492) viewed syncretism as the process whereby old and new meanings and forms are combined in contact situations. According to Edwards (1980b, 292), "It is a process which involves the creation of entirely new culture patterns out of the fragmented pieces of histor- ically separate systems." Lipson (1980, 102) writes that "the term is more recently being used to describe any combination of elements from diverse sources." Edmonson (1960, 192) notes that the process is a selective and integrative one. A reasonable summary definition, then, might be as follows: Syncretism is the integrating or blending of se- lected meanings (ideology) and/or forms (material culture) from di- verse sociocultural traditions, resulting in the creation of entirely new meanings (ideology) and/or forms (material culture).

180

Herskovits was the first to point out the multilayered nature of syncretism. Going beyond the particularism of Franz Boas to a more implicit and general conception of culture, he viewed particular or explicit phenomena as manifestations of a deeper level of mental or psychological patterns. He stressed the importance of looking through form to get at meaning. Because of his emphasis on the multilayered aspect of sociocultural phenomena, Herskovits (1948, 553–58; 1955, 493–95) believed that syncretism involved wholesale reinterpretation, since a blending of values, meanings, and the like occurred in association with the blending of overt elements. Edwards (1980b, 293) writes that syncretism "operates simultaneously at different levels of abstraction and generality."

At the most basic level, then, there are two distinct types of syncretism. *Simple* syncretism involves the combination of "the visible forms of two previously distinct traditions" (Edwards 1980b, 12). *Complex* syncretism involves the blending of meanings, attitudes, and so on from two distinct cultural traditions.

While Herskovits saw syncretism and reinterpretation as concomitant processes, Edwards goes further to posit an actual association between the two:

My own view is that synthesis and reinterpretation are more intimately related. I can hardly conceive of a blending of previously separate cultural elements without a corresponding reinterpretation of their roles and meanings. Simply the fact that the parental forms are supported by unlike values requires that a readjustment of these values must accompany the uniting of the forms. (Edwards 1980b, 313, 316)

Certainly synthesis and reinterpretation are concomitant processes, but they do not appear to be necessarily simultaneous; in many cases an initial period of synthesis seems to be followed by reinterpretation and elaboration. For example, in colonial Mexico, when a syncretism of religious elements occurred as a result of the contact between Spanish Catholicism and indigenous (primarily Aztec) religions, the indigenous groups, at least initially, incorporated the forms rather than the meanings of Catholicism (Brenner 1970, 144; and Serna 1892, 326–27; cited in Madsen 1960, 29). Simple syncretism (form synthesis) was the rule during the early period of contact, and complex syncretism (reinterpretation and elaboration), if it occurred at all, followed much later.

Although there is little documentation on the origins of *orisha* worship in Trinidad, my research supports the contention that the initial syncretism between Catholicism and the Yoruba-derived African religion occurred on the level of form only. As one of my contacts explained, his ancestors in earlier times in Trinidad would simply use a statue or some other representation of a Catholic saint to stand in the place of an African god so as not to draw attention to their African religious activities. As far as the Africans were concerned, the shrine was devoted to, say, Ogun and not Saint Michael. In time, however, the initial synthesis of form gave way to elaboration on a broader scale involving the fusion of ideology and meaning, and many *orisha* worshipers now view the two figures as aspects of the same deity.

Acculturation in both colonial Mexico and Trinidad involved "directed culture change" (Linton 1940, 501–2), at least initially. Perhaps an alteration or change in ideology is more likely to occur in situations of passive contact. In the context of nondirected or unforced contact, the potential recipient has the opportunity to pick and choose from the various elements of the donor culture and to make reasoned adjustments in his or her own ideology; such a scenario allows the extraneous elements to be integrated effectively.

We can explain the Catholic component of the Orisha religion in light of these comments. As we saw earlier, the Kabbalah and Spiritual Baptist components served to supplement the existing religious system and to broaden the purview of the original open system; by this means, redundancy in constructing and developing the religious system was avoided. Likewise, worshipers have been reluctant to incorporate the Hindu component fully because of its perceived similarity to *orisha* worship; therefore, for the most part, only simple borrowing has occurred. The existence of a full-blown syncretism involving a component — in this instance, Catholic — that was perceived to be virtually equivalent to the African component calls into question the assumption that redundancy is generally avoided. The Catholic case, however, seems to be an exception brought about by a forced and directed intrusion of Catholic elements into African ones. The simple syncretism that occurred during the early period of the development of the Orisha religion set the stage for the complex syncretism that we see today.

This argument assumes that if the contact between Europeans and transplanted Africans had been passive and nondirected, syncretism involving Catholic and African religious elements would not have occurred. We cannot, of course, reconstruct the original situation. But it seems possible that the recent tendency toward the Africanization of *orisha* worship in Trinidad is an indication of the worshipers' reluctance to synthesize similar elements in passive contact contexts.

The process of syncretism in the Orisha and other Afro-American religions involving Catholic saints and African gods has been largely haphazard and inconsistent, another indication that the initial blending was done under duress. The Catholic counterparts of the *orisha* noted in Chapter Ten are shown in Table 9. Many worshipers associate Peter with Ebeje; some pair him with Agare. For Shakpana, worshipers recognize two associations, although Saint Jerome is more common than the prophet Ezekiel.

Most adherents recognize no Catholic counterpart for five of the sixteen most prominent *orisha*, but the absence of syncretism in these cases can be easily explained.

As noted earlier, there is some confusion regarding the nature of Elefa; his offering is considered dangerous, and many prefer not to deal with him or the offering. Since he lacks well-defined and popularly recognized personality characteristics, drawing an association between Elefa and a Catholic saint is problematic, as it is also for Eshu. In the past, some worshipers associated Eshu with Satan or the devil, but this can be attributed to the erroneous assumption on the part of the Church, early writers, and some worshipers that Eshu is purely evil, whereas in fact Yoruba mythology considers him a trickster. Very few if any worshipers now equate Eshu with Satan.

Gurum, whom worshipers describe as being a mineral or a cave man, and Mama Lata, whose name is a derivation of the original French patois *Maman de la Terre*, Mother of the Earth, may be Trini *orisha*; since I could find no mention of them in the literature on Yoruba religion, it seemed that the lack of syncretism might be due to the fact that worshipers had not yet recognized Gurum and Mama Lata during the early period of Catholic incorporation into *orisha* worship. Leader Scott, however, argued that Gurum (whom he equated with the African Olokbo) and Mama Lata *are* African-derived:

As a matter of fact, Nigeria has lost many of its songs, prayers, ceremonies, practices, and traditions with the migration of slaves in the diaspora. . . . Researchers and anthropologists within the last twenty years are finding out that some of the practices of the Orisha religion in the New World are those traditions which were lost through the passage of migration.

To say that Mama Lata is a local *orisha* in truth and in fact is to say that

Mama Lata is a local interpretation of a specific [African-derived] *orisha* with certain characteristics. The passage of time has changed the words and meanings.

The absence of a written theology in the Yoruba language and the oppression of the Orisha religion has forced the drawing of similarities with other influences and the changing of words to which people can more easily relate. . . . As a matter of fact, it has been those not necessarily affiliated with the religion who have conveniently changed the pronunciation of words in Orisha songs and prayers. (Personal correspondence, March 16, 1991)

If both Gurum and Mama Lata are in fact African-derived, then the absence of African-Catholic syncretism in their cases cannot be attributed to their not being present in the Orisha religion during the time when early worshipers were incorporating Catholic traits into their belief system. Perhaps early adherents could not find a thematically appropriate association between these two *orisha* and particular Catholic saints.

Finally, Obatala — like Olodumare, Odudua, and Olorun — is one of a handful of *orisha* whose exalted position in the pantheon generally precludes their manifesting themselves in the form of possessed worshipers; Obatala possessions do occur but are extremely rare. These four *orisha* are all derived from Yoruba mythology, and since most worshipers do not acknowledge particular personality traits for them, they cannot easily be associated with particular Catholic saints. Some worshipers do, however, see a parallel between the Christian God and Olodumare and consider Obatala, Olorun, and Odudua to be part of the godhead, associating one or more of them with Jesus or the Holy Ghost.

The other *orisha* listed in Table 9 have Catholic counterparts that are known to practically everyone, and these associations have apparently been part of *orisha* worship lore in Trinidad since the beginning. The two basic theories regarding the motives for syncretization of the *orisha* and the saints are (1) that the Africans used a Catholic facade to camouflage their religious practice and thus avoid persecution by the colonial authorities, and (2) that worshipers voluntarily paired the *orisha* and the saints according to analogous characteristics (see Chapter Five). It seems likely that the original syncretism, since it occurred in a directed contact situation, would tend to support the first theory. We can test this hypothesis by looking at some specific associations between saints and *orisha*. Some of these associations seem reasonable and

TABLE 9
Orisha *and Their Catholic Counterparts*

Orisha	Saints (or Prophets)
Dada	Anthony
Ebeje (and Agare)	Peter
Elefa	(none recognized)
Emanje	Anne
Erele	Jonah
Eshu	(none recognized)
Gurum (Olokbo?)	(none recognized)
Mama Lata	(none recognized)
Obatala	(none recognized)
Ogun	Michael
Osain	Francis
Oshun	Philomena
Oya	Catherine
Shakpana	Jerome (and Ezekiel)
Shango	John

based on analogy; others seem arbitrary, as if reflecting the forced and intrusive character of early contact — though, of course, one can only guess at what might have been the early *orisha* worshipers' ideas and notions concerning these *orisha* and saints, or what their sources were.

Shango, the god of thunder, lightning, and fire, was a physically powerful man and a great warrior when he walked the earth.[1] Orisha adherents associate him with Saint John the Baptist, the baptizer of Jesus Christ and a hermit who lived in the desert preaching an aggressive gospel concerning the coming messiah.[2] Although the folklore and legends of the two figures turn up few similarities, John the Baptist does sometimes appear iconographically as a bearded old man dressed in animal skins (*Encyclopedia of World Art* 1966, 664), an image that worshipers may have associated with Shango.

It is important to remember, however, that in Trinidad Shango is also a general name used to denote more than one spirit. Leader Scott explained that worshipers use seven different terms for this group of spirits: Saint John the divine, Saint John the Revelator, and Saint John the Baptizer identify one spirit; Saint John the Shepherd and Saint John of the Cross refer to another; Saint John of Lightning and

Thunder and Saint John and the Harbinger identify one spirit each —
resulting in a total of four distinct spirits. I found only three of the
seven names in the literature: Saint John the Divine, Saint John the
Baptizer, and Saint John of the Cross — in Christian belief, three different people — but since more than two hundred Johns have been
canonized or beatified, the other designations could easily have been
drawn from them. The folklore and legends associated with John the
Divine (one of the twelve apostles) and John of the Cross (a sixteenth-
century Spanish mystic), like those for John the Baptist, share little
similarity with the tales of Shango.

.Osain is an herbalist who lives in the bush, a powerful medicine
man. Worshipers explain that he too is one spirit with many aspects.
Indeed, up to seven different manifestations of Osain may be present at
one time; I myself have seen as many as five. A few contacts identified
three "brothers" or aspects of Osain as Elesije, Ere Osa, and Kiripiti,
but these are not known to many worshipers. Adherents syncretize
Osain with "Saint Francis." Of some fifty-five persons named Francis
who have been canonized or beatified by the Catholic Church, *orisha*
worshipers often associate Osain with Francis Xavier (a sixteenth-
century Jesuit missionary) and Francis of Assisi (founder of the Fran-
ciscan order). The latter lived in a cave, healed and cared for the sick
(primarily lepers), and loved the creatures of the forest; he is often
depicted as preaching in the forest surrounded by animals — characteristics that resemble those of Osain. In many shrines, however, worshipers surround Osain's stool with Hindu paraphernalia and may even
plant a Hindu-style flag to mark it. Some explain that Osain is derived
from or is similar to a Native American deity recognized in Brazil and
that Osain has been associated with Hinduism because of a confusion
between the two uses of the word "Indian." On the other hand, identification as an "Indian man" can perhaps be attributed to Francis
Xavier's work in the Orient; he traveled extensively in India, Japan, Sri
Lanka, and other areas of the Far East, and his missionary work in
those areas is well known.

It appears that the tendency to perceive of Shango and Osain as
having different "brothers" or aspects is strictly Trinidadian, for they
are not so represented in Yoruba lore. It may be that *orisha* worshipers
have used the various character traits of each *orisha* as the basis for
postulating distinct spirits or aspects. Or perhaps the conception of
Shango and Osain as multi-aspectual is simply a strategy to aid in

identifying possessing agencies that manifest themselves in a variety of behavior patterns.

Orisha worshipers syncretize Ogun, the Yoruba god of iron, steel, and war, with Saint Michael the Archangel, who is God's warrior against Satan and the anti-Christ and is usually depicted brandishing a sword and standing atop a slain dragon or a demonlike figure. A few worshipers, generally the older and ostensibly more knowledgeable ones, say that Ogun too has many aspects or sides, which these individuals sometimes associate with Saint George and with the archangels Raphael and Gabriel.[3]

Oya is Shango's wife and, as such, is associated with the wind, lightning bolts, and thunderstorms. Worshipers equate her with Saint Catherine, although which of the eight saints that go by this name is not clear. Much the same can be said for the syncretism of Oshun (a goddess of water and beauty) and Saint Philomena, and of Emanje (a water goddess) and Saint Anne. Erele is a hunter and a water god, and his association with Jonah (an Old Testament prophet rather than a saint) seems reasonable, given Jonah's adventures in the sea.

Orisha is only one of the Afro-American religions that have made such associations. When the African-derived religions of the New World are viewed as a whole, however, we find that African god–Catholic saint pairings vary considerably. Table 10 provides a list of some associations made by adherents of various religions practiced in Brazil, Cuba, Grenada, and Haiti, with Trinidadian Orisha noted first for comparison. If we assume that the legends and lore of the Catholic saints and African gods were at least similar in the slave-based plantation societies of the colonial period, variation from place to place would surely not be so extreme had worshipers based their *orisha*-saint associations on reasoned analogy. Perhaps the high degree of variation may be at least partly attributed to the fact that Africans in these areas were all on the receiving end of directed and intrusive contact.

If the apparently haphazard and variegated nature of the African god–Catholic saint pairings reflects at least a passive or subconscious response to colonial domination, Africanization may be an aggressive and volitional reaction to the vestiges of colonialism. The recent trend toward the Africanization of worship in Trinidad is one of the few mechanisms that serves to counter traditional eclecticism and the various system-expanding processes at work in the Orisha religion.

The Orisha religion in Trinidad is currently enjoying an unprece-

TABLE 10
Orisha–*Saint Syncretisms in Brazil and the Caribbean*

Religion	Ogun	Shango	Oshun	Oya	Emanje
Orisha	Michael	John	Philomena	Catherine	Ann
Umbanda	George	Jerome	Barbara	—	Our Lady of Glory, Conception
Vodoun	Santiago	Barbara	—	Teresa	—
Santería	Michael, Peter	Barbara	Our Lady of Charity	Our Lady of Candles	The Virgin of Regla
Candomblé	Anthony	Jerome, Peter, John, Barbara	(local spirit)	—	Our Lady of Conception

Sources: Brown 1986, 97–103; Deive 1979, 240–41; Efunde 1978, 85; Simpson 1978, 185–86.

dented degree of freedom and self-determination. Legal persecution came to an end in the 1950s, and the Black Power Movement of the early 1970s ushered in a new African consciousness. As a result of "Black Power militancy" in the Caribbean in the 1970s, *orisha* worship became more African-oriented, and there was "less emphasis on the Catholic praying and chanting" (Henry 1983, 64). The Orisha religion has apparently flourished since that time. On her return trip to Trinidad in 1979, Henry also found that there had been "an astonishing resurgence" of the Orisha religion and that "both the membership and the number of ceremonial establishments had increased" (1983, 63). Of thirty-four shrines I sampled, twenty-five had been built within the past twenty years.

Clearly, the resurgence of *orisha* worship has been accompanied by an increased emphasis on the African aspect of the religion at the expense of the Catholic. Most of what I refer to as "African" is what worshipers perceive as African. Implicit in their behavior and attitudes is the notion that if they were to eliminate Catholic, Spiritual Baptist, Hindu, and Kabbalistic elements from the Orisha religious system, the remaining beliefs and practices would be purely African. This notion is largely a valid one, given the extensive use of the Yoruba language and the existence of West African religious elements in *orisha* worship (discussed in Chapter Four).

The Africanization of the Orisha religion is now only a grassroots movement, but there are indications that it is increasing in popularity. The two primary ethnographers of the Orisha religion in Trinidad, Mischel (1958) and Simpson (1965), who conducted their research in the 1950s and early 1960s, make no mention of this Africanizing tendency; in fact, they seem to emphasize the Catholic component. During her fieldwork in 1979, Henry (1983) appears to have been the first to observe the Africanization of the Orisha religion. My older contacts confirm that "old time" or "long time" *orisha* worship was highly Catholicized. In my sample of shrine ages, the only five I found that were older than thirty years were all significantly Catholic; for example, the shrine heads prominently displayed pictures and statues of Catholic figures and, more often than not, used Catholic terminology to refer to the deities. My sample is small, of course, but it does support the contention that the Orisha religion was once more Catholic than it is now.

Leader Scott agreed that there had been a gradual trend toward Africanization of the Orisha religion:

> If there is a change to mention, it is that the Orisha religion is trying to move away from [Catholicism, Hinduism, and so on]. . . . There is now a better understanding of their [the worshipers'] existence, and more consciousness of their [African] roots, and they are trying to be more original like using more of the Yoruba language, more now than before. As a matter of fact, the Yoruba language used to be used. . . . But there was a period of time [when English was more popular] . . . because of the presence of English culture and that sort of thing, and there was that type of input into the religion. Now at this stage and time, with this sort of new consciousness, it [the Orisha religion] is trying to get back to its roots. . . . It's becoming more African. (Interview, Basta Hall Village, December 1, 1988)

An excellent example of this "new consciousness" striving "to get back to its roots" is the Orisa Youths Cultural Organization founded in 1985 by young *orisha* worshipers. This group of mostly young men makes annual Orisha pilgrimages to the sea and disseminates literature containing Yoruba prayers (see the examples in Chapter Eleven) and information about African history and culture.

The trend toward Africanization appears to be only incipient at present, but there are signs that it is on the increase. Traditionally, for example, worshipers recited much of the liturgy in languages other than Yoruba, such as French patois and English. Today, however, many worshipers are emphasizing Yoruba and consider it the proper language of *orisha* worship. Whereas in the past it was only the *mongba* or *iya* who could conduct worship in Yoruba, the goal of some individuals is to popularize a Yoruba liturgy that all worshipers can follow and recite. Perhaps the person who has been most involved in this effort is Elder Biddeau. Drawing on his knowledge of the language, he wrote an exclusively Yoruba liturgy for *orisha* worship and personally typed and distributed copies for others to use. Edmond David has distributed copies of Orisha songs and prayers written in Yoruba, as well, and his efforts have been especially influential among young worshipers.

It is not uncommon to hear Orisha adherents complain of the Catholic prayers that are said during an *ebo*, and some *mongba* and *iya* do their best to limit such prayers. As noted in Chapter Eleven, not all feast nights begin with Christian prayers and singing; three *ebo* that I attended began with drumming and singing for the *orisha*, and at others the Christian session could be described as perfunctory at best. Of the *ebo* that I attended at thirty different shrines, eighteen displayed one or more of the following omissions: the ceremony did not begin with a session of Christian prayers and singing; no Christian prayers were cited once the African part began; no Catholic images and iconography were used to mark shrines or stools in the *chapelle* or elsewhere; neither a Bible nor a rosary was present in the *chapelle* or the *palais*; the names of saints were not invoked or cited during the ceremony. And at twenty-five of the thirty shrines there was no Spiritual Baptist church in the compound. Insofar as a religion can be known from the behavior of its adherents, these facts are at least suggestive of a tendency toward Africanization.

FOURTEEN

The Transmission of Religious Knowledge in the Orisha Religion

The *structure of the Orisha religion*, as we have seen, facilitates and even encourages variation. Its loose organizational structure, its oral liturgy, its multiethnic membership, and its open system make the religion a complex and dynamic system of beliefs and practices that is highly susceptible to change. Not surprisingly, then, the enculturation of Orisha religious knowledge is characterized by mechanisms that permit a fairly high degree of change from one generation to the next.

Cultural inheritance and evolution, though somewhat analogous to genetic inheritance and Darwinian evolution, are guided by different processes and motivations. Cultural inheritance and the transmission of cultural information are not standardized or methodical, do not necessarily produce traits that are biologically functional, and generally confer no Darwinian fitness advantage on their carriers, since their ability to survive or to produce offspring is not necessarily linked to the culture they embrace (Cavalli-Sforza and Feldman 1981, 15; Richerson and Boyd 1989, 120). Cultural change may result from innovation or independent creation, from copying mistakes that take place during enculturation, or from contact and subsequent hybridization between two formerly distinct (cultural) populations. Recipients may acquire cultural information throughout their lives, from sources other than their biological parents; their ability to receive and process this information depends on their genetically acquired capacities, but within those limits individuals are free to select, alter, and pass on cultural information in any way they choose, as their circumstances permit (Boyd and Richerson 1985, 7–8).

There are a number of ways of viewing cultural transmission. One involves looking at the direction of transmission and whether it

191

takes place within the family. Thus, using the terms developed by L. L. Cavalli-Sforza and M. W. Feldman (1981), we may say that vertical transmission is information exchange that passes from parent to (biological) child; horizontal transmission takes place between members of the same generation, inside or outside the family; and oblique transmission occurs between a member of one generation and a member of a later generation who is not the first person's biological child but may be of the same family. Another set of terms, adapted from Barry Hewlett and Cavalli-Sforza (1986), differentiates the number or extent of sources and recipients: many individuals may transmit cultural information to many others (many-to-many) or to a single individual (many-to-one), or one individual may transmit information to another individual (one-to-one) or to recipients as a group (one-to-many). Finally, donors may transmit information directly, as a conscious task, or indirectly, through the effect of their activities. Thus, if the elders of a society are entrusted with the task of passing on secret, traditional information to a young ruler when he assumes the throne, they can be said to be engaging in oblique, many-to-one, direct transmission.

These concepts can be usefully applied to the transmission of knowledge in the Orisha religion. The most influential individuals are the *mongba* and *iya*. This relatively small group of individuals (thirty-five or so at present) exerts more influence on the religion than any other group, both directly and indirectly. *Mongba* and *iya* directly influence the information exchange process chiefly in two ways. For one thing, they will transfer selected bits of their religious knowledge to particular individuals, especially biological and spiritual sons and daughters. As rank-and-file worshipers and *mongba* and *iya* themselves confirm, however, they generally do not pass on their religious knowledge in toto to anyone. Their reluctance to share such knowledge except in piecemeal form can apparently be attributed to the intense competition among *mongba* and *iya* for status — which, as we have seen, is based heavily on the worshipers' perception of their knowledge — and to the fear that the student might use this knowledge against the teacher (even close acquaintances have been known to engage in spiritual warfare against one another). The other way in which *mongba* and *iya* directly transmit information is by assisting neophytes who have been "instructed" (through mourning, visions, or dreams) to carry on an *ebo*. The one who supervises the *ebo*, however, can fashion the proceedings to his or her liking; consequently, the resulting worship pattern is a highly personalized one, based on the dictates of one individual. By virtue of the fact that these priests and priestesses guide and direct annual *ebo* that may be attended by two hundred or more worshipers, they also play a role in the indirect transfer of religious information. Information transfer at feasts, however, is more properly a case of many-to-many transmission, discussed below.

The influence of the relatively small group made up of shrine heads, elders, *mongba*, and *iya* should not be underestimated. Given the natural imbalance of social status, intellect, speaking skills, and opportunity among individuals, one-to-many information exchange is an important type in all societies:

> Just as it is obvious that all individuals do not adopt an innovation at the same time, so it is obvious also that all persons do not exert an equal amount of influence on the adoption decisions of others. Those individuals who have a greater share of influence are called "opinion leaders" because they take the lead in influencing the opinions of others. Opinion leaders are defined as those individuals from whom others seek advice and information. (Rogers 1962, 208)

As Everett Rogers (1962, 237–47) goes on to note, opinion leaders are typically more cosmopolitan and innovative than others in their group, have a higher social status, and are more socially active. The *mongba* and *iya* whom my contacts ranked most highly can all be characterized in these terms; most have traveled extensively, are well read, are quite active on the feast circuit, and have a standard of living above the norm.

In any case of one-to-many cultural transmission, there is always the potential for certain individuals who are initially admired for one (or several) particular trait(s) to become influential in a general way:

> We say that indirect bias occurs when individuals choose whom to imitate, based on some cultural trait like prestige, and then imitate that person's other traits without further decision making. We are all familiar with the role that especially attractive, popular, and successful people play in the spread of fads and fashion. This is a simple example of indirectly biased transmission. (Richerson and Boyd 1989, 121)

According to Robert Boyd and Peter Richerson (1985, 243), three types of traits need to be recognized in an analysis of indirect bias. "Indicator traits" are those characteristics of an opinion leader that are admired by the group as a whole; it is these traits that initially draw attention to the opinion leader. "Preference traits" are generally held values that serve as a reference for evaluating indicator traits. Finally, "indirectly biased traits" are those characteristics of an opinion leader that assume their importance and popularity strictly by virtue of their association with indicator traits.

The criterion cited most frequently by respondents asked to assess the prestige or ability of *mongba* and *iya* was "knowledge of the rituals and beliefs." It was obvious, however, that there were other criteria at work as well. Nine of the top eleven *mongba* and *iya* chosen by the respondents had symbolically complex shrines; Kabbalah paraphernalia were prominently displayed at six of these and Hindu paraphernalia at seven. The significant positive correlation between these two variables, knowledge and shrine complexity, may have been dependent and causal, even though respondents were aware of only one. (Just one questionnaire respondent selected the criterion "presence of Hindu elements," and just one chose "presence of Kabbalah elements.") We may tentatively conclude that one of these traits is an indicator trait and the other an indirectly biased trait. The more general, implicit preference trait may be linked to the respect Trinidadians have for education, especially higher education. Many Trinidadians travel abroad for university training, and Oxford or Cambridge graduates are highly respected. These sentiments may be reflected in the group's choice of "knowledge" as the most important criterion in assessing the value of a particular *mongba* or *iya*. "Knowledge," then, may be an indicator trait that initially draws attention to the *mongba* or *iya*, and "shrine complexity" an indirectly biased trait.

It seems surprising that seven of the eleven top priests and priestesses chosen by the questionnaire respondents practice the Kabbalah, given the generally negative attitude many worshipers have toward this form of worship. This association may be an example of what Boyd and Richerson (1985, 267) call a "runaway process."[1] Here, knowledge of the Kabbalah happens to be associated with other traits that are more overtly recognized. In other words, we can attribute the popularity of the Kabbalah to indirect bias. As long as the indicator trait "knowledge" is selected, the Kabbalah is unwittingly selected as well.

Although the one-to-many mechanism is obviously crucial for information transfer in the Orisha religion, other mechanisms are at work too. For example, just by attending an *ebo* one can learn which implements, sacrificial foods, Yoruba prayers, drum rhythms, and songs are appropriate for particular *orisha*. Similarly, one can learn proper ritual behavior from the actions of the participants. I was able to take an active role — including playing the drums, putting out Eshu's food, and interacting with the *orisha* — about six months after I began attending feasts, although certainly I was attending a very large number of feasts in a relatively short period of time.

One also acquires cultural knowledge through mourning. As it is practiced in Trinidad, mourning is primarily associated with the Spiritual Baptist religion, but because of the close relationship between the two religions, many Orisha adherents have undergone Spiritual Baptist mourning. Half of the forty-two *orisha* worshipers sampled by the questionnaire said that they had mourned, in most cases more than once. One shrine head explained that she received instructions for her feast the third time she mourned, having observed religious rites from Africa, India, Syria, and China during her spiritual travels. A popular shrine head in west-central Trinidad who has mourned twelve times described his experiences:

In my case, none of my family was in it [*orisha* worship]. . . . It [religious knowledge] was given to me by mourning. . . . You see I have my own [Spiritual Baptist] church. I went to mourn and I was given this church to build. I was given the *chapelle* and *palais* to build during my travels.

And I was given the name of my church, and I was given the animals to mind. They told me that at a certain time, I would know what the animals were for. As time went on and I continue mourning . . . it was told to me that I was supposed to give feasts. . . .

During my mourning they [Kabbalah entities] visit me. I did not know about the Kabbalah. But when I was on my throne and traveling, they visit me. They give me certain things to do on the Kabbalistic side. (Interview, north of Chaguanas, January 3, 1989)

Some practitioners, however, explained that regardless of the worshiper's experiences, the decision to accept or reject certain instructions received while mourning is one's own: an individual may or may not choose to follow a "negative" (Kabbalistic) path even if instructed spiritually to do so. I was never told, however, that Spiritual Baptist- or Orisha-oriented instructions could be ignored.

Leader Scott said that he too learned of the *orisha* by following an essentially Spiritual Baptist track but explained that one learns by active participation in the Orisha religion as well as by mourning:

I did go to feasts when I was young, but I knew much more of the Spiritual Baptist faith. It was later when I was more mature in my Spiritual Baptist faith that I got more involved with the *orisha*.

As a matter of fact, my first real contact with *orisha* was when I was on the mourning ground, during spiritual travel. It was during that experience that I first understood the meaning of flags, how to put them down, and so on. Although I had seen them before, I did not quite understand them. . . . It was during my spiritual travels and being instructed by the spirit [that I learned these things].

There are one or two things that you get spiritually, and the rest you get by being involved. To put this in a better perspective, I am not much of a song leader or a drum beater. [In my spiritual travels I] learned what a song means [and] what it is sung for. (Interview, Basta Hall Village, December 1, 1988)

Leon London, a prominent drummer and *mongba*, stated that mourning is the source of all the "mixing" (the borrowing of elements, with or without subsequent syncretism) that one sees today in the Orisha religion, the medium through which Spiritual Baptist, Hindu, and even Kabbalistic elements have entered *orisha* worship. He explained that mourning has only recently become an important part of the Orisha religion:

You see long time [ago] it was only Yoruba people, Kongo people, and the Baptist people in Trinidad. The Baptist people used to have to hide in the forest to mourn. It was only the Spiritual Baptist people that was mourning. Orisha people never mourned. It start mixing from my mother's days. (Interview, Fyzabad, February 19, 1989)

As pointed out in Chapter Six, however, one hypothesis regarding the origins and growth of the Spiritual Baptist religion holds that the Orisha and Spiritual Baptist religions share a similar developmental history. This would suggest that mourning has always been practiced in both.

Whatever the case, mourning is obviously an important source of religious knowledge for *orisha* worshipers. Equally significant, however, is the fact that the mystical and existential nature of the mourning ritual allows the worshiper to interject knowledge gained during his or her own personal experiences into the general body of religious knowledge. It is thus an important source of change and variation. If this process were to continue unabated, of course, the beliefs and rituals of the religion would become so diffused as to render it nonviable. Perhaps it is in response to this possibility that worshipers have developed a policing or tempering mechanism: as we have seen, the leader, mother, or other "officers" of the church can discern the truth or falsity of mourners' statements and evaluate the legitimacy of their experiences. Mourning, then, is not totally subjective and personal, but it is nevertheless an important source of knowledge and change.

In summary, the transmission of religious knowledge in the Orisha religion is primarily the result of three processes. First, the transmission from the *mongba/iya* to rank-and-file worshipers is an example of one-to-many oblique transmission when the *mongba* or *iya* is from an older generation than the worshiper, and of one-to-many horizontal transmission when both parties are of the same generation. In a few cases, when there is a biological relationship between the two parties, one-to-many or one-to-one vertical transmission occurs.

Second, transmission to rank-and-file worshipers through the feast context is an example of many-to-many horizontal and oblique transmission forms, since anyone may be considered a transmitter or a transmittee. Of course, vertical transmission may occur as well in this context.

Third, information from the mystical/psychological/metaphysical realm (those terms are drawn from worshipers' own descriptions) is transmitted to the individual through mourning. The complex, secretive, and mysterious character of the mourning ritual can make it virtually ineffable. In such cases, in the absence of contradicting data, the worshipers' explanation (the "cognized model": Rappaport 1967, 238) is as valid as or more valid than others because it is obviously an important determinant of behavior. We could call it one-to-one (intra-) horizontal transmission, or, since the mourning process apparently draws on the beliefs and lore of the religion as a whole, we could also designate it many-to-one.

The eclectic nature of *orisha* worship and the high degree of variability that exists on the level of shrines and on the level of the individual can now be explained, at least in part, as a result of the manner in which religious knowledge is exchanged. One-to-many transmission, perhaps the most important mechanism here, potentially produces the most rapid cultural change of all the various transmission types (Hewlett and Cavalli-Sforza 1986, 923), since one individual directly affects a number of individuals. The somewhat existential and personal nature of the mourning ritual potentially brings about change and variation on the individual level and, subsequently, on the group level. When the two processes combine — one-to-many transmission where the transmitter mourns regularly — the potential for change and variation is even greater than is the case when only one of these processes is at work.

FIFTEEN

The Transformation of the
Orisha Religious System

The development of the Orisha religion, or at least that complex of religious activities of which it is the focus, has involved the incorporation of selected elements from four additional sources over the course of roughly 150 years. Therefore, any model of such a process needs to consider not only the components being borrowed but also the way in which these components were incorporated into the existing religious system, plus an examination of those factors — ethnicity, historical context, the nature of the borrowed traits, and so on — that influence the borrowing and incorporation process. Let us begin by reviewing what has been established thus far.

The Catholic Church has a long history in Trinidad and was, in fact, in place on the island when Africans began arriving in large numbers toward the end of the eighteenth century. The movement of Africans to the New World at that time no doubt involved the concomitant transfer of at least bits and pieces of one or more African religions, but it appears that the Yoruba-based Orisha religion became a significant form of worship only after the arrival of large numbers of Yoruba beginning in the 1830s.

Although complete emancipation occurred in 1838, the Europeans continued to dominate and oppress the Africans long after that, as the anti-drumming ordinance of 1883 and the Shouters Prohibition Ordinance of 1917 indicate. Thus, the initial fusion of elements of Catholicism and the transplanted Orisha religion occurred during a period of forced and directed contact, from the perspective of the Africans. This fact lends some credence to the camouflage theory, the notion that Catholic-Orisha syncretism was the result of Africans' efforts to hide their religion behind a facade of Catholicism. Yet we cannot ignore a basic similarity of the two religious systems in regard to their respective

199

pantheons of anthropomorphized deities on the one hand and saints on the other. The forced and directed nature of the contact between Africans and Europeans is certainly significant here, but this parallel no doubt facilitated the process.

The Orisha religion was well established by the time the Spiritual Baptists first appeared in the early part of the twentieth century. We do not know exactly when Spiritual Baptist elements became a part of *orisha* worship, but given the fact that the practitioners of both religions were members of the same ethnic and socioeconomic class, the relationship is not surprising. I am avoiding the term "syncretism" in this case because there is no indication that worshipers have fused traits from the two religions to create an entirely new trait. As we have seen throughout this book, however, the Spiritual Baptist religion is very much a part of the Orisha religion's complex of activities.

Hinduism has been present on the island since approximately 1850. This religion has coexisted with the Orisha religion in a pluralistic fashion until recently, when shrine heads began placing posters of Hindu deities and other Hindu religious materials in their compounds. As was the case with the Spiritual Baptist religion, most of what has occurred here is the borrowing and subsequent superimposition of Hindu elements onto those of the Orisha religion. Still although I observed it in only a handful of cases, an inchoate syncretism involving the pantheons of the two religions has occurred.

The members of the two religions, Orisha and Hindu, come from dissimilar ethnic backgrounds and have often viewed one another with suspicion and contempt, although they have displayed a willingness to work together when facing the common enemy of colonialism. Nevertheless, it seems clear that we must look at more than history and ethnicity to explain the interrelationship between the two religions. One factor that we must consider is the ease with which worshipers have made associations between Hindu deities and *orisha*. Again, as with Catholicism, the spirits in both religions are highly anthropomorphized, thus facilitating syncretic association, yet because of the "redundancy factor" discussed earlier, Orisha-Hindu syncretism is rare on the island.

Finally, the Kabbalah has apparently been present in Trinidad since early colonial times, but it appears—although the details are admittedly sketchy—that the Kabbalah has only recently become popular among large numbers of *orisha* worshipers. In seeking causes for an association between the two religions, we should not overlook the fact that the primary practitioners of the Kabbalah are drawn from the same ethnic and socioeconomic class as those of the Orisha religion. Worshipers have not syncretized Kabbalistic and Orisha traits, but, given the widespread perception of the former as diabolical and theurgical and the latter as positive and largely nonmanipulable, many have combined them to form a more comprehensive religious system than either of the two original ones.

Table 11 lists these various factors for each religious component vis-à-vis the Orisha religion, with the addition of Islam for purposes of comparison. Breaking down the various factors this way allows us to conclude (tentatively) that, in regard to the tendency to syncretize the religious elements of different systems, the fact that religions are perceived to be similar seems to counteract historical, ethnic, and socioeconomic factors not conducive to such a process. Another factor however, may override or at least counter the tendency to syncretize: Africanization. This antisyncretic process would seem to be at least partly a response to redundancy; it is the feeling of some worshipers that the inclusion of Catholic saints unnecessarily complicates the Orisha religion, since the respective spirits of both religions are perceived to be similar, if not the same, in many respects.

As we saw earlier, a religion with a history of fragmentation and consequent reconstruction, such as the Orisha religion, can be thought of as an open system involved in a teleological process that is slowly driving it toward ideological closure; during this process, worshipers generally avoid redundancy and contradiction in both the borrowing and integration of extraneous elements. The early incorporation of apparently redundant Catholic traits into the Orisha religion is not a refutation of this notion, because the process occurred during a period when the recipient culture was under extreme cultural duress from an oppressive donor culture. In addition, given the patchwork nature of the Orisha religion in its early stages, the Catholic elements might very well have allowed for a theological extension of the original system. Since these factors seem no longer to be significant, and since the incorporation of Catholic elements seems no longer to serve a useful purpose, some worshipers are now rejecting them.

Orisha-Hindu syncretism is currently incipient at best, and given that the two religions resisted interpenetration for well over a century, it seems unlikely that there will be further development in this regard.

TABLE 11

Relationship Between the Orisha Religion and Other Religious Traditions

Religion	Syncretism	Historical Contact	Ethnicity, Socioeconomic Class of Adherents	Belief Systems
Catholicism	yes	forced	dissimilar	somewhat similar
Spiritual Baptist	no	somewhat forced	same	dissimilar
Hinduism	incipient	unforced	ethnically dissimilar; socioeconomically similar	somewhat similar
Kabbalah	no	unforced	same	dissimilar
Islam	no	unforced	somewhat similar	dissimilar

In fact, it seems possible that just the opposite will occur, since Hindu elements are also being subjected to the reformation of Africanization. This process may be receiving impetus from the demographic intrusion of non-Africans that has accompanied the borrowing of Hindu elements. Although, as noted in Chapter Nine, approximately 10 percent of those present at a typical Orisha *ebo* are Indian, traditional *orisha* worshipers seem to view the influx of Indians as a threat to African hegemony in the daily affairs of the religion and perhaps, more generally, as a threat to Afro-Trinidadian identity (Houk 1993a). Africanization, at least in regard to this particular religious component, can be interpreted as a response to these threats.

We can attribute the presence and influence of both the Spiritual Baptist and Kabbalistic components primarily to two factors. First, both belief systems are sufficiently dissimilar from Orisha and each other as to constitute a novel contribution to that complex of activities centered on the Orisha religion. Second, because Orisha, Spiritual Baptist, and Kabbalah practitioners are all drawn from the same ethnic and socioeconomic classes, some sort of contact was probably inevitable.

I have included Islam for comparison. This religion has also been present on the island for well over one hundred years, but there has been virtually no borrowing or syncretism involving Islamic and Orisha traits.[1] This is not surprising, since not only are Trinidadian Muslims predominantly Indian, but there was no historical reason for such a process to occur. Orisha adherents regard the Islamic system as strictly monotheistic and somewhat limited theologically, and consequently as having little to offer their culturally rich, polytheistic religious system. The Orisha religion, with its various forms of worship, is much more than a collection of assorted beliefs and practices, however; it is the result of the manipulation of these components by its practitioners at every level, from the rank-and-file worshipers (by means of knowledge gained during mourning, for example) up to the *mongba* and *iya* who direct the annual feasts. The lack of island-wide organization and the highly integrative and change-oriented mechanisms of knowledge transmission combine to produce a religious system that is complex and multifarious at any one point in time and dynamic when viewed diachronically. Only time will tell whether or not the anti-assimilative Africanization sentiment, now evident at only a handful of shrines but growing in popularity, will eventually garner enough support to arrest the transformative processes that have historically been integral components of the religion.

The present form and structure of the Orisha religion, then, is a result of the interplay of counterbalancing forces. On the one hand, certain structurally inherent mechanisms have facilitated and continue to facilitate the further expansion of the system. These include the initial open-system form of the Orisha religion; its decentralized organizational structure; the highly personal and subjective nature of mourning; the prevalence of the one-to-many type in the transmission of religious knowledge; and the direct relationship between the prestige of shrine heads, *mongba*, and *iya* and their willingness and ability to integrate components of a number of religious traditions into their worship complex. Given the highly complex and sometimes confusing forms of *orisha* worship on the island and the many varieties of shrine layouts and of personal religious sentiment, it is obvious that these centrifugal forces have acted virtually unchecked for some time.

On the other hand, it is true that worshipers from different areas and shrines come together weekly during the feast season, and pilgrimage of this sort has perhaps worked to delimit the boundaries of the system, although I would guess that this mechanism has served only to slow down expansion. Other centripetal forces, however, such as the Africanization movement and the consolidation efforts of the Opa Orisha (Shango), may effectively counter the inertia of system expansion.

One might hypothesize that a continually expanding religious system will at some point begin to tax the patience and enthusiasm of its adherents. Perhaps there is a critical limit, so to speak, beyond which dynamic and eclectic religious systems begin to break down, resulting in an effective reduction of the range of acceptable beliefs and practices or, possibly, schism and the formation of several different groups. Certainly, by any standard of measurement and evaluation, the complex, confusing, multicultural, and multicomponential Orisha religious system has reached or is rapidly approaching this limit. Perhaps the recent trend toward Africanization could be cited as evidence to that effect.

The Orisha religion differs from the so-called great or world religions in that its adherents acknowledge and tolerate an unusually large range of worship patterns. As we have seen, however, *orisha* worship is not simply a hodgepodge of elements taken arbitrarily from this or that source but, rather, a religious system that worshipers have crafted from selected components drawn from five traditions. Nevertheless, its dynamic and complex nature make it confusing to the casual observer. Even many worshipers have trouble explaining, for example, the relationship between Catholic saints and Yoruba *orisha*, the role of Hinduism, and the inclusion of the Kabbalah in their worship repertoire. But however perplexing the Orisha religion sometimes is to the worshipers themselves, it still has meaning for them.

The individual struggle to come to terms with a particular culture-specific ideology — in this case, religion — is merely part of a more general effort to create or construct a world view that is meaningful. This struggle, in which ideology is individualized to conform to the dictates of individual subjectivity, has long been a focus of concern in the humanities and social sciences and has been addressed in particular by phenomenological sociologists and existentialists.

The development of self is a long and often laborious process of interaction between the individual and the society or the collective of which he or she is part (Mead 1934, 135). Interaction, of course, implies and requires communication. In turn, communication, at least of the sort we are discussing here, is symbolic. Eventually, through the process of symbolic interaction, the individual is able to synthesize the seemingly disparate and chaotic bits of experiential data into a (somewhat) coherent whole, George Mead's "generalized other."

This self-building process is a highly dynamic one and, when taken to its logical conclusion, becomes a matter of personal survival; the apparently constructive relationship between the individual and society eventually becomes destructive:

> The world that people create in the process of social exchange is, following Durkheim, a "reality *sui generis.*" It possesses a thing-like quality—the quality of objective facticity. But again the reality of this world is not an intrinsic quality, nor is it given once and for all. Culture must be constructed and reconstructed as a continuous process. It remains real, in the sense of subjective plausibility, only as it is confirmed and reconfirmed by oneself in relation with social others. [Peter] Berger acknowledges with Marx that the process whereby man's world becomes an objective reality can reach an extreme in the process of "reification." What is in fact a human product is perceived as having a reality in and of itself, as an alien reality no longer recognizable as a product. In this situation man is alienated (in a strictly technical sense of the word, not in its popular, pejorative meaning). (Wuthnow et al. 1984, 24–25)

Humans as *Homo faber* have constructed their own reality, but unfortunately, somewhere along the line they have forgotten that they have done so (Berger and Pullberg 1965, 200).

This issue is of primary concern to existentialists, particularly theologians and philosophers. Many theologians view the struggle for meaning optimistically, arguing that doubt and uncertainty are ameliorated or assuaged by embracing the Absolute. Existential philosophers generally consider the struggle to be a curse that cannot be resolved but can be transformed into something positive if we focus on our humanity.

Søren Kierkegaard, the eminent Danish theologian, argued that an understanding of the Absolute cannot be gained inductively because induction is an "approximation process" that can only bring us closer and closer to the truth (1941, 177–78). He contends that truth is subjectivity and that we can come to terms with doubt and uncertainty only if we realize the ultimate transcendency of the Absolute.

Jean-Paul Sartre, on the other hand, resigns himself to the fact that man "himself will have made what he will be," that "man is nothing else but what he makes of himself," and that "we are alone, with no excuses"; without the assumption of an Absolute, "man is condemned to be free" (1965, 36, 41). He further asserts that it is only through our awareness of our dilemma that we can ever realize the essential reality of our existence, of what it means to be human.

The phenomenological sociologists and the existentialists, then, describe the human enterprise as a struggle between humans' desire to be, to show that they count, and a sometimes overpowering and always overwhelming world that stands ready to defeat them at every turn. Individuals will use any and every stratagem at their disposal to facilitate their quest for an existence that they find meaningful. The philosophical aspects of this issue become immediately anthropological when we focus on these stratagems of world building. Such stratagems will, of course, be those that are available to the individual; that is, they will be cultural. (The creative genius is an anomalous occurrence, and I am bracketing that case here.) Because of the group-specific, arbitrary, and generally alogical nature of cultural knowledge and the high degree of redundancy required to disseminate it, countless versions exist on a global scale. It is at this point that cultural relativism becomes pertinent: the stratagems that the individual "chooses" (I am assuming that this process is not always a conscious one) will be those that are familiar and, consequently, those that she or he feels will be the most successful.

The *orisha* worshipers in Trinidad have a variety of stratagems at their disposal; ideologically, they may "wander" long distances and in many different directions before bumping into heresy. The *orisha* worshiper in Trinidad is "condemned to be free," in Sartrean terms, not because he or she is working upon the assumption that God does not exist but rather because God has so many faces.

The Orisha religious system is a product of the interaction between specific sociohistorical factors and the human capacity to adapt and persevere in a meaningful way. Worshipers have incorporated the rituals, beliefs, and paraphernalia of four other religious traditions into *orisha* worship, but each case is unique. I have argued that the general process of borrowing, incorporation, and (if it goes that far) syncretism is characterized by the lack or avoidance of redundancy and contradiction. The incorporation of the Kabbalah and of Spiritual Baptist components served to broaden or extend the existing religious system without being either redundant or contradictory. Worshipers perceive Hinduism, with its anthropomorphized gods and goddesses, to be similar to the Orisha religion in this regard; however, though certain Hindu elements are found at Orisha shrines, for the most part only simple borrowing, not syncretism, has occurred. Furthermore, it is my contention that in the absence of forced, directed, and intrusive contact factors, we would not expect such syncretism to occur. Finally, though there has been extensive syncretism of Catholic and Orisha elements and though their perceived similarities make for a redundant belief system, this syncretism occurred as a result of contact between the two religions during the period of European colonization in Trinidad, a classical situation of forced contact.

Characteristic of the Orisha religion are the processes and structural mechanisms that make it amenable to change and predisposed to variation. Important among these is the one-to-many type of cultural transmission — involving *mongba/iya* and rank-and-file worshipers — which can serve as a medium for rapid cultural change. Another noteworthy source of cultural transmission is the mourning ritual; the individualistic and existential nature of mourning also permits rapid change, although there are counteracting mechanisms that serve to control variation from this source. Worshipers' association of the success of a *mongba* or *iya* with his or her ability to manipulate a variety of beliefs and practices also tends to engender variability. Other mechanisms facilitate change and variation as well. Countering these dissipative processes, however, is the structure of the feast circuit, which regularly brings together worshipers from different parts of Trinidad; the recent development of the Opa Orisha (Shango) and its attempt to consolidate the various shrines around the island; and, most significantly, the recent movement toward Africanization. The present form of the religion can be viewed as the result of the interplay of these opposing forces.

The Orisha religion, then, is a highly eclectic religious system characterized by mechanisms that serve both to engender variability and to oppose it. Within this system *orisha* worshipers have fashioned religious practices that meet the reality-constructing needs of a variety of individual sentiments.

The prognosis for further growth in the Orisha religion is good. The number of active shrines, estimated at only a dozen or so in the early 1960s (Henry 1983, 63), has risen to over 150, many of these newly established. The recent influx of Indians and the success of several *mongba* and *iya* in achieving that status without having hereditary ties to the religion are facts indicating that Orisha can meet the religious needs of an increasingly diverse group drawn from a variety of ethnic and socioeconomic backgrounds. If the Africanization movement becomes a major force in the religion, however, its restrictive and anti-assimilative nature will eventually give rise to a religious system that, in comparison with the existing one, is highly specialized and narrowly focused. Such a scenario would likely be accompanied by the defection of members who are now being served by the eclecticism of the present system, and a lack of interest on the part of some who might otherwise be considered potential members. Yet perhaps there is reason to regard the Africanization movement more optimistically. It is certainly conceivable that like all nativisitic movements, it could encourage group unity as it focuses attention on cultural roots. Perhaps homogenization of the religion would foster long-term growth and stability, with shrine heads, *mongba*, and *iya* cooperating under a common banner rather than competing against one another as they do now.

In the final analysis, the Africanization movement will probably effectively temper further system expansion without, however, seriously compromising the inherent flexibility that has made the Orisha religious system so highly adaptive to the needs and sentiments of many individuals living in the complex, dynamic, and multicultural society of Trinidad. If so, a balance will be established between two contrary forces: on the one hand, retaining the variability and flexibility of a religious system that attracts and serves the needs of worshipers from diverse backgrounds; on the other hand, meeting the need to arrest or at least decelerate expansion of the system before the already precarious coherence of the group is further threatened. Given such a balance, the interplay of diverse sentiments, needs, and desires will usher this ancient religion into the twenty-first century and beyond.

Appendixes,
Notes, Glossary,
References,
and Index

Appendix A

A Demographic Estimate of
Spiritual Baptists

There are approximately 250 towns and villages in Trinidad, about half of which are located in areas dominated demographically by Indians; these, not surprisingly, contain few if any Spiritual Baptist churches. A small village in areas of high African concentration, however, may contain as many as three or four churches; therefore, we can estimate the average number of Spiritual Baptist churches per town or village as two, for a total of 500. There are three major urban areas (*Annual Statistical Digest* 1988, 12). If we estimate 30 Spiritual Baptist churches for Port of Spain (pop. 55,800), 15 for San Fernando (pop. 33,395) in largely Indian west-central Trinidad, and 5 for Arima (pop. 24,112), we can add another 50, for a total of 550 Spiritual Baptist churches on the island. Although Glazier (1983, 87) notes that some Spiritual Baptist congregations may number well over 200 members, the average for all churches is certainly much lower; some rural churches can have congregations as small as 10. On the basis of my work at 25 or so churches around the island, I estimate the average membership to be approximately 20. Using that figure, we can calculate the total number of Spiritual Baptists as about 11,000. This is close to the estimate of 10,000 that Glazier cites as the figure quoted to him most often by his informants (1983, 7).

Appendix B

A Demographic Estimate of
Orisha Worshipers

To estimate the number of Spiritual Baptists in Trinidad, one can simply multiply the average congregation size by the total number of their churches. Estimating the total number of *orisha* worshipers, however, is considerably more difficult. As noted in Chapter Nine, virtually the only time worshipers come together is at the annual *ebo*. We could simply multiply the average attendance during a feast night by the total number of shrines, but there are problems with such an approach. Because many people attend more than one feast per year, counts taken at several different feasts would be inflated by the number of people counted more than once. Further, not all of the approximately 156 shrines on the island hold a feast every year; since ten or so do not, the annual total of feasts must be revised to 146. If we account for these factors, however, we can then make a reasonably accurate estimate of the total number of worshipers.

I made head counts at 30 different shrines during one night of the annual *ebo* and found an average attendance of 83.43 people per night. (Since attendance varies from Tuesday to Friday night, I attempted to distribute the counts equally, although Friday counts were somewhat underrepresented.) Multiplying this average by the number of feasts given during the year produces a total of $(83.43)(146) = 12,180.78$. But because of the movement between feasts by the same individuals, the first factor must be adjusted.

In a survey of *orisha* worshipers ($N = 42$) I found that the average number of feasts attended by each individual per year was 14.6, so the same individual would be counted on the average 14.6 different times in a survey of 146 shrines. My survey, however, included 30 shrines or about 20.55 percent of the total, so the same individual would have been counted $0.2055 \times 14.6 = 3.00$ times. In other words, during my survey of 30 feast nights, the same individual would have been counted about three times on the average.

The average attendance figure can now be adjusted accordingly. The total count over the 30 shrines was 2,503. Reducing this figure to reflect the fact that some worshipers were counted more than once can be done by first deducting

83.43 per every 10 feasts or $(83.43)(3) = 250.29$ from the initial total of 2,503 to obtain an adjusted total, and then dividing that figure by 30 (the total number of feast nights surveyed): $(2,503 - 250.29)/30 = 75.09$. Since it accounts for redundancy, this adjusted average can now be multiplied by the total number of feasts to obtain a figure for the total number of *orisha* worshipers: $(75.09)(146) = 10,963$ (rounded off to the nearest whole number).

It is quite likely however, that the figure of 75.09 is still too large because my survey of feasts included the 5 that worshipers chose in a questionnaire as being the most popular. Further, the sample of 30 was biased in that I, not unlike most worshipers, attended only those feasts that were relatively accessible, resulting in counts that were probably inflated in comparison with average feast attendance at all shrines.

I corrected the average feast night attendance figure by using information obtained from a student's *t*-test of the mean of the average attendance sample. (This test will tell us—with some degree of certainty—that the mean attendance figure of all feasts will fall within a certain range.) A 95 percent confidence interval resulted in a lower-end value of 65.25. Adjusting this figure for redundancy in the same manner as above results in a revised total of 58.73 per feast night. Thus, the final revised figure for the total number of worshipers is $(58.73)(146) = 8,575$ (rounded off to the nearest whole number).

Other adjustments that could be made here would result in a different value. For example, as I noted, the number of feasts attended per year per individual was found to be 14.6. Because the range (3–50) and the standard deviation (11.99) were both quite large, however, the actual figure could be significantly smaller, which would result in an increase in the total number of worshipers, or larger, which would result in a decrease.

Notes

PREFACE

1. The Kabbalah in Trinidad has been subject to a unique pattern of development and, consequently, differs somewhat from "Kabbalah" understood in a general sense. Thus, it is only the Trinidadian version of this belief system that I describe here as "diabolical."

CHAPTER ONE

1. The word *orisha* functions as both singular and plural. The same is true of *ebo*, *mongba*, and *iya*.

2. Technically, a *mongba* is a priest of the Yoruba god Shango, but the term is commonly used to refer to males who maintain Orisha shrines and conduct various rituals in the religion. The female counterpart to *mongba* is *iya*. Other titles used include *baba olorisha* and *iya olorisha*, the ranking male and female heads of the religion; *baba*, a term of respect generally reserved for the most knowledgeable and experienced *mongba*; and "elder," a title used somewhat interchangeably with *baba*.

3. A "leader" is a ranking male head of a Spiritual Baptist church. A ranking female head is referred to as "mother."

CHAPTER FOUR

1. Brandon (1989–90, 207) notes the similar influx of Yoruba into Cuba in the 1840s.

2. In this discussion, for the Yoruba data I rely on Awolalu 1979; Bascom 1969; Delano 1978; Ellis 1894; Forde 1951; and Simpson 1962. The Trinidad data are mainly from my own research but also from Mischel 1957; Mischel and Mischel 1958; and Simpson 1962, 1964, 1965.

215

3. A similar correspondence was found by Desmangles (1977:13–14), who noted the appearance of several important Dahomean religious terms in Haitian Vodoun.

CHAPTER FIVE

1. Trotman (1976) uses similar resources to compare *orisha* worship in Trinidad and Guyana during the nineteenth century.

CHAPTER SIX

1. The term "Rada," according to Warner (1971, 45), refers to people from Allada, a seventeenth-century Dahomean city.

CHAPTER TEN

1. The following statistical results were obtained from my sample: mean, 14.85 years; minimum value, 1 year; maximum value, 75 years; standard deviation, 15.21 years. (The standard deviation is larger than the mean because of the inclusion of one particularly large value, 75 years; if it is disregarded, we get a standard deviation of about 11 years.) Assuming that we are working with a simple random sample and that the shrine age values of the population are normally distributed (assumptions that are reasonable in this case), application of the student's *t* confidence interval statistic results in a range of 9.54–20.16 years. (This statistic tells us that there is a 95 percent probability that the mean of the population — the average age of all shrines on the island — falls somewhere within this range.) Thus, the mean value I obtained from the sample is reasonably accurate.

2. When these factors are considered, it appears likely that the mean of 14.85 years is a conservative estimate and that the actual value could be near the upper end of the confidence interval: i.e., 20.16 years.

CHAPTER THIRTEEN

1. Orisha lore and legends are drawn from Awolalu 1979; Bascom 1969; Delano 1978; Ellis 1894; Forde 1951; Lucas 1948; and Parrinder 1953.

2. Catholic lore and legends are drawn from Benedictine Monks 1966; Bittle 1958; Delaney 1980; and Farmer 1978.

3. The perception of Ogun as multi-aspectual is popular in Haiti (Hurbon 1978, 106–7; Marcelin 1949, 2:38–78) and Brazil (Bastos 1979, 40, 77; Valente 1955, 100, 102–3) as well.

CHAPTER FOURTEEN

1. This process is the cultural analogue to Fisher's notion (1958; cited in Boyd and Richerson 1985, 259) of runaway sexual selection of particular traits.

CHAPTER FIFTEEN

1. I did observe one Islamic symbol, a crescent moon with a star inside, at a handful of strongly Baptist Orisha compounds (Spiritual Baptists sometimes speak of encountering Islam or its symbolism during mourning), and I know of one shrine head north of Port of Spain who plants a flag for Muhammad but uses him "on the Kab side." Crowley (1957, 822) suggested a syncretism between Osain and the Muslim saint Hossein, but I found no worshipers who were aware of this association.

Glossary

ashogun: A priest of sacrifice, the individual who slays the animals at the annual *ebo.*

baba: A title of respect accorded the more knowledgeable and experienced elders in the Orisha religion.

baba olorisha: The ranking male in the Orisha religion.

banquet: A Kabbalah ceremony involving the conjuration and manifestation of entities.

bemba: One of the three drums beaten at Orisha ceremonies, the lead or middle-range drum.

chapelle: A small sanctuary at an Orisha shrine which houses stools and various implements of the *orisha.*

congo: One of the three drums beaten at Orisha ceremonies, the low-range drum.

conjuror: The individual who invokes a Kabbalah entity at a banquet.

desieni: That part of an Orisha initiation involving the washing of the head.

ebo (sing. and pl.): The feast(s) of offering and celebration in the Orisha religion.

elder: A term of respect used somewhat interchangeably with *baba.*

entity: A Kabbalistic spirit.

horse: A term designating an individual who serves as a medium for an *orisha* possession.

hounsis: An individual who has been ritualistically prepared for possession by a particular *orisha.*

iya (sing. and pl.): A female who directs an *ebo*, a priestess of the Orisha religion.

iya olorisha: Technically, the ranking female in the Orisha religion; in practice, the ranking female in either of the two Orisha religious organizations in Trinidad.

leader: Title given to the highest ranking male in the membership hierarchy of a particular Spiritual Baptist church.

219

mo juba: A standard phrase in many Yoruba prayers; it may be roughly translated "I honor, praise, salute [you]."

mongba (sing. and pl.): A male who directs an *ebo*, a priest of the Orisha religion.

mother: Title given to the highest ranking female in the membership hierarchy of a particular Spiritual Baptist church.

mourning: An extended period of fasting, isolation, and trance in which the "pilgrim" undergoes a series of spiritual experiences; generally associated with the Spiritual Baptist religion.

Opa Orisha (Shango): A primary organization of the Orisha religion in Trinidad, currently the most visible and powerful group.

operator: The individual who conducts a Kabbalah banquet and controls the manifesting entities.

orisha (sing. and pl.): The African-derived gods and spirits of the Yoruba.

Orisha Movement: An Orisha religious organization, currently second in scope and visibility to the Opa Orisha (Shango).

oumalay: One of the three drums beaten at *orisha* ceremonies, the high-range drum.

palais: A covered, open-sided structure at an Orisha shrine inside which drumming and singing for the *orisha* occur.

perogun: A three-sided, roofless structure at an Orisha shrine containing the stools and flags for the *orisha*.

pundit: A Hindu priest.

Shango: The Yoruba god of thunder, lightning, and fire. The name is sometimes used synonymously with "Orisha religion," an indication of the traditional popularity of this *Orisha* in Trinidad.

singbare: That part of an Orisha initiation involving the incising of the head.

stool: A small shrine for an *orisha*, saint, Baptist power, Hindu deity, or Kabbalah entity, generally consisting of various materials and paraphernalia (some of which may be buried) and a flag.

thanksgiving: A Spiritual Baptist ceremony involving praying, singing, and the feeding of children.

References

Annual Statistical Digest. 1988. No. 34. Port of Spain, Trinidad: Office of the Prime Minister, Central Statistical Office.

Anstey, Roger. 1975. "The Volume and Profitability of the British Slave Trade, 1761–1807." In *Race and Slavery in the Western Hemisphere: Quantitative Studies*, ed., Stanley L. Engerman and Eugene D. Genovese, pp. 3–31. Princeton, N.J.: Princeton University Press.

Argyle, W. J. 1966. *The Fon of Dahomey: A History and Ethnography of the Old Kingdom.* Oxford: Clarendon.

Awolalu, J. O. 1979. *Yoruba Beliefs and Sacrificial Rites.* London: Longman.

Bascom, William. 1969. *The Yoruba of Southwestern Nigeria.* New York: Holt, Rinehart & Winston.

Bastide, Roger. 1972. *African Civilizations in the New World.* Trans. Peter Green. New York: Harper & Row.

———. 1978. *The African Religions of Brazil: Toward a Sociology of the Interpenetration of Civilizations.* Trans. Helen Sebba. Baltimore, Md.: Johns Hopkins University Press.

Bastos, Abguar. 1979. *Os Cultos Magico-Religiosos no Brasil.* São Paulo, Brazil: Editora Hucitec.

Benedictine Monks of St. Augustine's Abbey, Ramsgate. 1966. *The Book of Saints: A Dictionary of Persons Canonized or Beatified by the Catholic Church.* 5th ed. New York: Thomas Y. Crowell.

Berger, Peter, and Stanley Pullberg. 1965. "Reification and the Sociological Critique of Consciousness." *History and Theory* 4 (2): 196–211.

Bittle, Berchmans. 1958. *A Saint a Day: According to the Liturgical Calendar of the Church.* Milwaukee: Bruce.

Black, Jan K., Howard I. Blutstein, Kathryn T. Johnston, and David S. McMorris. 1976. *Area Handbook for Trinidad and Tobago.* Washington, D.C.: U.S. Government Printing Office.

Boddy, Janice. 1988. "Spirits and Selves in Northern Sudan: The Cultural Therapeutics of Possession and Trance." *American Ethnologist* 15 (1): 4–27.

Bourguignon, Erica. 1970. "Ritual Dissociation and Possession Belief in Caribbean Negro Religion." In *Afro-American Anthropology: Contemporary Perspectives*, ed. Norman E. Whitten Jr. and John F. Szwed, pp. 87–101. New York: Free Press.

———. 1973. "Introduction: A Framework for the Comparative Study of Altered States of Consciousness." In *Religion, Altered States of Consciousness, and Social Change*, ed. Erica Bourguignon, pp. 3–35. Columbus: Ohio State University Press.

———. 1979. *Psychological Anthropology: An Introduction to Human Nature and Cultural Differences.* New York: Holt, Rinehart & Winston.

Boyd, Robert, and Peter J. Richerson. 1985. *Culture and the Evolutionary Process.* Chicago: University of Chicago Press.

Brandon, George. 1989–90. "African Religious Influences in Cuba, Puerto Rico, and Hispaniola." *Journal of Caribbean Studies* 7 (2–3): 201–31.

———. 1990. "Sacrificial Practices in Santeria, an African-Cuban Religion in the United States." In *Africanisms in American Culture*, ed. Joseph E. Holloway, pp. 119–47. Bloomington: Indiana University Press.

Brenner, Anita. 1970. *Idols behind Altars: The Story of the Mexican Spirit.* Boston: Beacon Press.

Brereton, Bridget. 1981. *A History of Modern Trinidad, 1783–1962.* Kingston, Jamaica: Heinemann Educational Books.

Brown, Diana DeG. 1986. *Umbanda: Religion and Politics in Urban Brazil.* Ann Arbor, Mich.: UMI Research Press.

Buckley, Roger N. 1979. *Slaves in Red Coats: The British West India Regiments, 1795–1815.* New Haven, Conn.: Yale University Press.

Cannon, Walter B. 1942. "Voodoo Death." *American Anthropologist* 44 (2): 169–81.

Carmichael, Gertrude. 1961. *The History of the West Indian Islands of Trinidad and Tobago, 1498–1900.* London: Alvin Redman.

Carr, Andrew T. 1953. "A Rada Community in Trinidad." *Caribbean Quarterly* 3 (1): 35–54.

Cavalli-Sforza, L. L., and M. W. Feldman. 1981. *Cultural Transmission and Evolution: A Quantitative Approach.* Princeton, N.J.: Princeton University Press.

Clifford, James, and George E. Marcus, eds. 1986. *Writing Culture: The Poetics and Politics of Ethnography.* Berkeley: University of California Press.

Cohn, Raymond L. 1985. "Deaths of Slaves in the Middle Passage." *Journal of Economic History* 45 (3): 685–92.

Crapanzano, Vincent. 1987. "Spirit Possession." In *The Encyclopedia of Religion*, ed. Mircea Eliade et al., 14:12–19. New York: Macmillan.

Craton, Michael. 1982. *Testing the Chains: Resistance to Slavery in the British West Indies*. Ithaca, N.Y.: Cornell University Press.

Crowley, Daniel J. 1957. "Plural and Differential Acculturation in Trinidad." *American Anthropologist* 59 (5): 817–24.

Curtin, Philip D. 1969. *The Atlantic Slave Trade: A Census*. Madison: University of Wisconsin Press.

———. 1975. "Measuring the Atlantic Slave Trade." In *Race and Slavery in the Western Hemisphere: Quantitative Studies*, ed. Stanley L. Engerman and Eugene D. Genovese, pp. 107–28. Princeton, N.J.: Princeton University Press.

Dan, Joseph, ed. 1986. *The Early Kabbalah*. Trans. Ronald C. Kiener. New York: Paulist Press.

Day, Charles William. 1852. *Five Years' Residence in the West Indies*. 2 vols. London: Whittaker, Treacher.

Deerr, Noel. 1949–50. *The History of Sugar*. 2 vols. London: Chapman & Hall.

Deive, Carlos Esteban. 1979. *Vodú y magia en Santo Domingo*. Santo Domingo: Museo del Hombre Dominicano.

Delaney, John J. 1980. *Dictionary of Saints*. Garden City, N.Y.: Doubleday.

Delano, Isaac O. 1978. *The Soul of Nigeria*. New York: AMS Press.

Deren, Maya. 1991. *Divine Horsemen: The Living Gods of Haiti*. 1953. Auth'd. ed. Kingston, N.Y.: McPherson.

Desmangles, Leslie G. 1977. "African Interpretations of the Christian Cross in Vodun." *Sociological Analysis* 38 (1): 13–24.

Devereux, George. 1967. *From Anxiety to Method in the Behavioral Sciences*. New York: Humanities Press.

Eastwell, Harry D. 1982. "Voodoo Death and the Mechanism for Dispatch of the Dying in East Arnhem, Australia." *American Anthropologist* 84 (1): 5–17.

Edmonson, Munro S. 1960. "Nativism, Syncretism, and Anthropological Science." In *Nativism and Syncretism*, ed. Margaret Harrison and Robert Wauchope, pp. 182–203. Middle American Research Institute Publication 19. New Orleans, La.: Tulane University.

Edwards, Jay D. 1980a. "Cultural Syncretism in the Louisiana Creole Cottage." *Louisiana Folklore Miscellany* 3:9–26.

———. 1980b. "The Evolution of Vernacular Architecture in the Western Caribbean." In *Cultural Traditions and Caribbean Identity: The Question of Patrimony*, ed. S.J.K. Wilkerson, pp. 291–339. Gainesville: University of Florida, Center for Latin American Studies.

Efunde, Agun. 1978. *Los Secretos de la Santería*. Miami, Fla.: Ediciones Cubamerica.

Elder, Jacob D. 1988. *African Survivals in Trinidad and Tobago.* London: Karia Press.

Ellis, A. B. 1894. *The Yoruba-Speaking Peoples of the Slave Coast of West Africa.* London: Chapman & Hall.

Encyclopedia of World Art. 1966. S.v. Saints, Iconography of. New York: McGraw-Hill.

Farmer, David Hugh. 1978. *The Oxford Dictionary of Saints.* Oxford: Clarendon Press.

Fisher, R. A. 1958. *The Genetical Theory of Natural Selection.* Rev. ed. New York: Dover.

Forde, Daryll. 1951. *The Yoruba-Speaking Peoples of Southwestern Nigeria.* London: SWI.

Francis, E. K. 1976. *Interethnic Relations: An Essay in Sociological Theory.* New York: Elsevier.

Franco, Jose L. 1979. "The Slave Trade in the Caribbean and Latin America." In *The General History of Africa: Studies and Documents,* vol. 2, *The African Slave Trade from the Fifteenth to the Nineteenth Century,* pp. 88–100. Paris: UNESCO.

Gellner, Ernest. 1992. *Postmodernism, Reason, and Religion.* London: Routledge.

Glazier, Stephen D. 1979. "Caribbean Religions as 'Peripheral' Cults: A Reevaluation." Paper presented at the Conference of the Caribbean Studies Association, Martinique.

———. 1981. "Leadership Roles, Church Organization, and Ritual Change among the Spiritual Baptists of Trinidad." Ph.D. diss., University of Connecticut.

———. 1983. *Marchin' the Pilgrims Home: Leadership and Decision-Making in an Afro-Caribbean Faith.* Westport, Conn.: Greenwood Press.

González-Wippler, Migene. 1985. *Tales of the Orishas.* New York: Original Publications.

Gopaul-Whittington, Viola. 1983. *History and Writings of the Spiritual Baptists.* Port of Spain, Trinidad: Printing Plus.

Gordon, Jacob U. 1979. "Yoruba Cosmology and Culture in Brazil: A Study of African Survivals in the New World." *Journal of Black Studies* 10 (2): 231–44.

Greenbaum, Lenora. 1973. "Societal Correlates of Possession Trance in Sub-Saharan Africa." In *Religion, Altered States of Consciousness, and Social Change,* ed. Erika Bourguignon, pp. 39–57. Columbus: Ohio State University Press.

Griffith, Ezra E. H., Thelouizs English, and Violet Mayfield. 1980. "Possession, Prayer, and Testimony: Therapeutic Aspects of the Wednesday Night Meeting in a Black Church." *Psychiatry* 43 (2): 120–28.

Gussler, Judith. 1973. "Social Change, Ecology, and Spirit Possession among the South African Nguni." In *Religion, Altered States of Consciousness, and*

Social Change, ed. Erika Bourguignon, pp. 88–126. Columbus: Ohio State University Press.

Harricharan, Thomas. 1981. *The Catholic Church in Trinidad, 1498–1852.* Vol. 1. Port of Spain, Trinidad: Inprint Caribbean.

Haskins, Jim. 1978. *Voodoo and Hoodoo: Their Traditions and Craft as Revealed by Actual Practitioners.* New York: Stein & Day.

Henney, Jeanette. 1974. "Spirit-Possession Belief and Trance Behavior in Two Fundamentalist Groups in St. Vincent." In *Trance, Healing and Hallucination*, ed. Irving I. Zaretsky, pp. 1–111. New York: Wiley.

Henry, Frances. 1983. "Religion and Ideology in Trinidad: The Resurgence of the Shango Religion." *Caribbean Quarterly* 29 (3–4): 63–69.

Herskovits, Melville J. 1937. "African Gods and Catholic Saints in New World Negro Belief." *American Anthropologist* 39 (4): 635–43.

———. 1941. *The Myth of the Negro Past.* New York: Harper.

———. 1943. "The Southernmost Outposts of New World Africanisms." *American Anthropologist* 45 (4): 495–510.

——— 1948. *Man and His Works: The Science of Cultural Anthropology.* New York: Knopf.

———. 1955. *Cultural Anthropology.* New York: Knopf.

———. 1966. *The New World Negro: Selected Papers in Afroamerican Studies.* Ed. Frances S. Herskovits. Bloomington: Indiana University Press.

Herskovits, Melville J., and Frances S. Herskovits. 1947. *Trinidad Village.* New York: Knopf.

———. 1964. *Trinidad Village.* New York: Octagon Books.

Hewlett, Barry S., and L. L. Cavalli-Sforza. 1986. "Cultural Transmission among Aka Pygmies." *American Anthropologist* 88 (4): 922–34.

Higman, B. W. 1979. "African and Creole Slave Family Patterns in Trinidad." In *Africa and the Caribbean: The Legacies of a Link*, ed. Margaret E. Crahan and Franklin W. Knight, pp. 41–64. Baltimore, Md.: Johns Hopkins University Press.

———. 1984. *Slave Populations of the British Caribbean, 1807–1834.* Baltimore, Md.: Johns Hopkins University Press.

Hoetink, Harry. 1979. "The Cultural Links." In *Africa and the Caribbean: The Legacies of a Link*, ed. Margaret E. Crahan and Franklin W. Knight, pp. 20–40. Baltimore, Md.: Johns Hopkins University Press.

Houk, James. 1986. "Patterns of Spirit Possession in Two Afro-American Religious Groups in Trinidad: The Spiritual Baptists and the *Shango* Cult." M.A. thesis, Louisiana State University.

———. 1992. "The *Orisha* Religion in Trinidad: A Study of Culture Process and Transformation." Ph.D. diss., Tulane University.

———. 1993a. "Afro-Trinidadian Identity and the Africanization of the *Orisha* Religion." In *Trinidad Ethnicity*, ed. Kevin A. Yelvington, pp. 161–79. London: Macmillan.

———. 1993b. "The Terminological Shift from 'Afro-American' to 'African-American': Is the Field of Afro-American Anthropology Being Redefined?" *Human Organization* 52 (3): 325–28.

Huggins, A. B. 1978. *The Saga of the Companies.* Princes Town, Trinidad: Twinluck.

Hunt, Chester L., and Lewis Walker. 1974. *Ethnic Dynamics: Patterns of Intergroup Relations in Various Societies.* Homewood, Ill.: Dorsey Press.

Hurbon, Laennec. 1978. *Dios en el Vudú haitiano.* Buenos Aires: Ediciones Castenada.

Idel, Moshe. 1988. *Kabbalah: New Perspectives.* New Haven, Conn.: Yale University Press.

John, A. M. 1988. *The Plantation Slaves of Trinidad, 1783–1816: A Mathematical and Demographic Enquiry.* Cambridge: Cambridge University Press.

Kehoe, Alice B., and Dody H. Giletti. 1981. "Women's Proponderance in Possession Cults: The Calcium-Deficiency Hypothesis Extended." *American Anthropologist* 83 (3): 549–61.

Kierkegaard, Søren. 1941. *Concluding Unscientific Postscript to the Philosophical Fragments.* Trans. David F. Swenson and Walter Lowrie. Princeton, N.J.: Princeton University Press.

Kiev, Ari. 1961. "Spirit Possession in Haiti." *American Journal of Psychiatry* 118 (2): 133–38.

Kingsley, Charles. 1871. *At Last: A Christmas in the West Indies.* New York: Macmillan.

Klass, Morton. 1961. *East Indians in Trinidad: A Study of Cultural Persistence.* New York: Columbia University Press.

Kloss, Peter. 1985. "Syncretic Features of Contemporary Maroni River Carib Religious Belief." *Anthropologica* 63–64:197–206.

Knight, Franklin W. 1983. "The Caribbean Sugar Industry and Slavery." *Latin American Research Review* 18 (2): 219–30.

Knutsson, Karl E. 1975. "Possession and Extra-institutional Behavior: An Essay on Anthropological Micro-analysis." *Ethnos* 40 (1–4): 244–72.

Laguerre, Michel S. 1989. *Voodoo and Politics in Haiti.* New York: St. Martin's Press.

Lambek, Michael. 1988. "Spirit Possession/Spirit Succession: Aspects of Social Continuity among Malagasy Speakers in Mayotte." *American Ethnologist* 15 (4): 710–31.

Langness, Lewis. 1976. "Hysterical Psychoses and Possessions." In *Culture-Bound Syndromes, Ethnopsychiatry, and Alternate Therapies,* ed. William P. Lebra, 4:56–67. Honolulu: University Press of Hawaii.

Lara, Oruno D. 1979. "Negro Resistance to Slavery and the Atlantic Slave Trade from Africa to Black America." In *The General History of Africa: Studies and Documents,* vol. 2, *The African Slave Trade from the Fifteenth to the Nineteenth Century,* pp. 101–14. Paris: UNESCO.

Leacock, Seth, and Ruth Leacock. 1972. *Spirits of the Deep: A Study of an Afro-Brazilian Cult.* Garden City, N.Y.: Doubleday Natural History Press.

Leahy, Vincent. 1980. *Catholic Church in Trinidad, 1797–1820.* Arima, Trinidad: St. Dominic Press.

Leonard, Anne P. 1973. "Spirit Mediums in Palau: Transformations in a Traditional System." In *Religion, Altered States of Consciousness, and Social Change,* ed. Erica Bourguignon, pp. 129–78. Columbus: Ohio State University Press.

Lewis, I. M. 1966. "Spirit Possession and Deprivation Cults." *Man,* n.s. 1 (3): 307–29.

———. 1971. *Ecstatic Religion: An Anthropological Study of Spirit Possession and Shamanism.* New York: Penguin Books.

———. 1983. "Spirit Possession and Biological Reductionism: A Rejoinder to Kehoe and Giletti." *American Anthropologist* 85 (2): 412–13.

———. 1986. *Religion in Context: Cults and Charisma.* Cambridge: Cambridge University Press.

Lex, Barbara W. 1974. "Voodoo Death: New Thoughts on an Old Explanation." *American Anthropologist* 76 (4): 818–23.

Lieber, Michael. 1981. *Street Scenes: Afro-American Culture in Urban Trinidad.* Cambridge, Mass.: Schenkman.

Linton, Ralph. 1940. *Acculturation in Seven American Tribes.* Ed. Ralph Linton. New York: Appleton-Century.

Lipson, Juliene G. 1980. "Jews for Jesus: An Illustration of Syncretism." *Anthropological Quarterly* 53 (2): 101–10.

Lovejoy, Paul E. 1983. *Transformations in Slavery: A History of Slavery in Africa.* Cambridge: Cambridge University Press.

Lowenthal, Ira P. 1978. "Ritual Performance and Religious Experience: A Service for the Gods in Southern Haiti." *Journal of Anthropological Research* 34 (3): 392–414.

Lucas, J. O. 1948. *The Religion of the Yorubas.* London: C.M.S. Bookshop.

Madsen, William. 1960. *The Virgin's Children: Life in an Aztec Village Today.* Austin: University of Texas Press.

Mahabir, Noorkumar, and Ashram Maharaj. 1989. "Hindu Elements in the Shango/Orisha Cult of Trinidad." In *Indenture and Exile: The Indo-Caribbean Experience,* ed. Frank Birbalsingh. Toronto: TSAR.

Marcelin, Milo. 1949. *Mythologie Vodou (rite Arada).* 4 vols. Port-au-Prince, Haiti: Ediciones Castenada.

Marcus, George E., and Michael M. Fischer. 1986. *Anthropology as Cultural Critique: An Experimental Moment in the Human Sciences.* Chicago: University of Chicago Press.

McLeod, Malcolm D. 1981. *The Asante.* London: British Museum Publications.

Mead, George H. 1934. *Mind, Self, and Society from the Standpoint of a Social Behaviorist.* Chicago: University of Chicago Press.

Metraux, Alfred. 1972. *Voodoo in Haiti.* Trans. Hugo Charteris. New York: Schocken Books.

Mintz, Sidney. 1974. Foreword. In *The Caribbean Sugar Industries: Constraints and Opportunities,* ed. G. B. Hagelberg, pp. vii–xiii. New Haven, Conn.: Yale University Press.

Mischel, Frances O. 1957. "African 'Powers' in Trinidad: The Shango Cult." *Anthropological Quarterly* 30 (2): 45–59.

———. 1958. "A Shango Religious Group and the Problem of Prestige in Trinidadian Society." Ph.D. diss., Ohio State University.

Mischel, Walter, and Frances Mischel. 1958. "Psychological Aspects of Spirit Possession." *American Anthropologist* 60 (2): 249–60.

Mulira, Jessie G. 1990. "The Case of Voodoo in New Orleans." In *Africanisms in American Culture,* ed. Joseph E. Holloway, pp. 34–68. Bloomington: Indiana University Press.

Muñoz, Agosto de. 1974. *El fenómeno de la posesión en la religión Vudú: Un estudio sobre la posesión por los espíritus y su relación con el ritual en el Vudú.* Río Piedras: Universidad de Puerto Rico.

Nasr, Seyyed Hossein. 1981. *Knowledge and the Sacred: The Gifford Lectures, 1981.* New York: Crossroad.

Needham, Rodney. 1967. "Percussion and Transition." *Man,* n.s. 2 (4): 606–14.

Neher, Andrew. 1962. "A Physiological Explanation of Unusual Behavior in Ceremonies Involving Drums." *Human Biology* 34 (2): 151–60.

Newson, Linda A. 1976. *Aboriginal and Spanish Colonial Trinidad: A Study in Culture Contact.* London: Academic Press.

Niehoff, Arthur, and Juanita Niehoff. 1960. *East Indians in the West Indies.* Milwaukee, Wis.: Milwaukee Public Museum Publications in Anthropology.

O'Connell, M. C. 1982. "Spirit Possession and Role Stress among the Xesibe of Eastern Transkei." *Ethnology* 21 (1): 21–37.

Oesterreich, T. K. 1966. *Possession, Demoniacal and Other, among Primitive Races, in Antiquity, the Middle Ages, and Modern Times.* Trans. D. Ibberson. New Hyde Park, N.Y.: University Books.

Ong, Aihwa. 1988. "The Production of Possession: Spirits and the Multinational Corporation in Malaysia." *American Ethnologist* 15 (1): 28–42.

Oosten, Jarich. 1985. "Cultural Anthropological Approaches." In *Contemporary Approaches to the Study of Religion,* ed. Frank Whaling, 2:231–64. New York: Mouton.

Ottley, C. R. 1974. *Slavery Days in Trinidad: A Social History of the Island from 1797–1838.* Trinidad: Ottley.

Oxaal, Ivar. 1982. *Black Intellectuals and the Dilemmas of Race and Class in Trinidad.* Cambridge, Mass.: Schenkman.

Parks, Alfrieta V. 1981. "The Conceptualization of Kinship among the Spiritual Baptists of Trinidad." Ph.D. diss., Princeton University.

Parrinder, Geoffrey. 1953. *Religion in an African City.* London: Oxford University Press.

———. 1970. *West African Religion: A Study of the Belief of Akan, Ewe, Yoruba, Ibo, and Kindred Peoples.* New York: Barnes & Noble.

Pressel, Esther. 1973. "Umbanda in São Paulo: Religious Innovation in a Developing Society." In *Religion, Altered States of Consciousness, and Social Change,* ed. Erica Bourguignon, pp. 264–318. Columbus: Ohio State University Press.

———. 1974. "Umbanda Trance and Possession in São Paulo, Brazil." In *Trance, Healing, and Hallucination: Three Field Studies in Religious Experience,* ed. Irving I. Zaretsky, pp. 113–225. New York: Wiley.

Price, Richard. 1973. "Introduction: Maroons and Their Communities." In *Maroon Societies: Rebel Slave Communities in the Americas,* ed. Richard Price, pp. 1–30. Garden City, N.Y.: Anchor/Doubleday.

Rappaport, Roy A. 1967. *Pigs for the Ancestors: Ritual in the Ecology of a New Guinea People.* New Haven, Conn.: Yale University Press.

———. 1989. "Law and Meaning, Discovery and Construction." Paper presented at the eighty-eighth annual meeting of the American Anthropological Association, Washington, D.C.

Richerson, Peter J., and Robert Boyd. 1989. "A Darwinian Theory for the Evolution of Symbolic Cultural Traits." In *The Relevance of Culture,* ed. Morris Freilich, pp. 120–42. New York: Bergin & Garvey.

Rogers, Everett M. 1962. *Diffusion of Innovations.* New York: Free Press.

Rouget, Gilbert. 1985. *Music and Trance: A Theory of the Relations between Music and Possession.* Chicago: University of Chicago Press.

Rubin, Vera. 1962. "Culture, Politics, and Race Relations." *Social and Economic Studies* 11 (4): 433–55.

Ryan, Selwyn D. 1972. *Race and Nationalism in Trinidad and Tobago: A Study of Decolonization in a Multiracial Society.* Toronto: University of Toronto Press.

Sangren, Steven. 1988. "Rhetoric and the Authority of Ethnography: 'Postmodernism' and the Social Reproduction of Texts." *Current Anthropology* 29 (3): 405–35.

Sartre, Jean-Paul. 1965. *Essays in Existentialism.* Ed. Wade Baskin. Secaucas, N.J.: Citadel Press.

Schaya, Leo. 1971. *The Universal Meaning of the Kabbalah.* Trans. Nancy Pearson. London: Allen & Unwin.

Schubert, Kurt. 1967. "Cabala." In *New Catholic Encyclopedia,* 2:1031–35. New York: McGraw-Hill.

Serna, Jacinto de la. 1892. "Manual de ministros de Indios." *Anales del Museo Nacional* (Mexico City) 6:261–479.

Sheinkin, David. 1986. *Path of the Kabbalah.* New York: Paragon House.

Simpson, George E. 1945. "The Belief System of Haitian *Vodun*." *American Anthropologist* 47 (1): 35–59.

———. 1955. "Political Cultism in West Kingston." *Social and Economic Studies* 4 (2): 133–49.

———. 1962. "The Shango Cult in Nigeria and Trinidad." *American Anthropologist* 64 (6): 1204–19.

———. 1964. "The Acculturative Process in Trinidadian Shango." *Anthropological Quarterly* 37 (1): 16–27.

———. 1965. *The Shango Cult in Trinidad.* Rio Piedras: University of Puerto Rico, Institute of Caribbean Studies.

———. 1966. "Baptismal 'Mourning' and 'Building' Ceremonies of the Shouters in Trinidad." *Journal of American Folklore* 79 (314): 537–50.

———. 1976. "Religions of the Caribbean." In *The African Diaspora: Interpretive Essays*, ed. Martin L. Kilson and Robert I. Rotberg, pp. 280–311. Cambridge, Mass.: Harvard University Press.

———. 1978. *Black Religions in the New World.* New York: Columbia University Press.

———. 1980. *Religious Cults of the Caribbean: Trinidad, Jamaica, and Haiti.* 3d ed. Caribbean Monograph Series, no. 15. Rio Piedras: University of Puerto Rico, Institute of Caribbean Studies.

Souza, Gérson Ignez de, and Tancredo da Silva Pinto. 1976. *Negro e branco na cultura religiosa afro-brasileira, os egbás: Umbanda, Kabala e Magia.* Rio de Janeiro: Gráfica Editora Aurora.

Steckel, Richard N., and Richard A. Jensen. 1986. "New Evidence on the Causes of Slave and Crew Mortality in the Atlantic Slave Trade." *Journal of Economic History* 46 (1): 57–77.

Thomas, Eudora. 1987. *A History of the Shouter Baptists in Trinidad and Tobago.* Tacarigua, Trinidad: Calaloux Publications.

Thompson, Robert F. 1983. *Flash of the Spirit: African and Afro-American Art and Philosophy.* New York: Random House.

Tippet, A. R. 1976. "Spirit Possession as It Relates to Culture and Religion: A Survey of Anthropological Literature." In *Demon Possession: A Medical, Historical, Anthropological, and Theological Symposium*, ed. John W. Montgomery, pp. 143–74. Minneapolis, Minn.: Bethany Fellowship.

Trotman, David V. 1976. "The *Yoruba* and *Orisha* Worship in Trinidad and British Guinea: 1838–1870." *African Studies Review* 19 (2): 1–17.

Turner, Victor. 1969. *The Ritual Process: Structure and Anti-Structure.* Ithaca, N.Y.: Cornell University Press.

Tylor, Edward B. 1896. *Anthropology: An Introduction to the Study of Man and Civilization.* New York: Appleton.

Valente, Waldemar. 1955. *Sincretismo religioso afro-brasileiro*. São Paulo: Biblioteca Pedagógica Brasileira.

Waite, Arthur E. 1970. *The Book of Ceremonial Magic*. Rev. ed. Secaucus, N.J.: Carol.

———. 1972. *The Book of Black Magic and of Pacts*. 1898. York Beach, Maine: Weiser.

Wallace, A.F.C. 1959. "Cultural Determinants of Response to Hallucinatory Experience." *Archives of General Psychiatry* 1 (1): 58–69.

Wallman, Joseph. 1958. *The Kabbalah: From Its Inception to Its Evanescence*. Brooklyn, N.Y.: Theological Research.

Ward, Colleen A. 1980. "Spirit Possession and Mental Health: A Psycho-Anthropological Perspective." *Human Relations* 33 (3): 149–63.

Ward, Colleen A., and Michael H. Beaubrun. 1979. "The Psychodynamics of Demon Possession." University of the West Indies Collections, Trinidad.

Warner, Maureen. 1971. "African Feasts in Trinidad." *African Studies Association of the West Indies Bulletin*, no. 4 (December).

Warner, W. Lloyd. 1958. *A Black Civilization: A Social Study of an Australian Tribe*. New York: Harper & Row.

Warner-Lewis, Maureen. 1991. *Guinea's Other Suns: The African Dynamic in Trinidad Culture*. Dover, Mass.: Majority Press.

Werblowsky, R. J. 1983. "Cabala." In *Man, Myth, and Magic: The Illustrated Encyclopedia of Mythology, Religion, and the Unknown*, pp. 381–87. New York: Marshall Cavendish.

Wigoder, Geoffrey. 1989. "Mysticism, Jewish." In *The Encyclopedia of Judaism*, ed. Geoffrey Wigoder et al., pp. 512–15. New York: Macmillan.

Williams, Eric E. 1964. *History of the People of Trinidad and Tobago*. London: Andre Deutsch.

Williams, Mervyn R. 1985. "Song from Valley to Mountain: Music and Ritual among the Spiritual Baptists ('Shouters') of Trinidad." M.A. thesis, Indiana University.

Wood, Donald. 1968. *Trinidad in Transition: The Years after Slavery*. London: Oxford University Press.

World Factbook 1990. 1990. Washington, D.C.: Central Intelligence Agency.

Wünsche, August. 1908. "Cabala." In *The New Schaff-Herzog Encyclopedia of Religious Knowledge*, pp. 326–31. New York: Funk & Wagnalls.

Wuthnow, Robert, James D. Hunter, Albert Bergesen, and Edith Kurzweil. 1984. *Cultural Analysis: The Work of Peter L. Berger, Mary Douglas, Michel Foucault, and Jürgen Habermas*. London: Routledge & Kegan Paul.

Zaretsky, Irving I., and Cynthia Shambaugh. 1978. Introduction to *Spirit Possession and Spirit Mediumship in Africa and Afro-America: An Annotated Bibliography*, ed. Irving I. Zaretsky and Cynthia Shambaugh, pp. ix–xxiii. New York: Garland.

Index